Lecture Notes in Computer Science 9152

Commenced Publication in 1973
Founding and Former Series Editors:
Gerhard Goos, Juris Hartmanis, and Jan van Leeuwen

Dimitris Kolovos · Manuel Wimmer (Eds.)

Theory and Practice of Model Transformations

8th International Conference, ICMT 2015
Held as Part of STAF 2015
L'Aquila, Italy, July 20–21, 2015
Proceedings

Springer

Editors
Dimitris Kolovos
University of York
York
UK

Manuel Wimmer
Vienna University of Technology
Vienna
Austria

ISSN 0302-9743   ISSN 1611-3349 (electronic)
Lecture Notes in Computer Science
ISBN 978-3-319-21154-1   ISBN 978-3-319-21155-8 (eBook)
DOI 10.1007/978-3-319-21155-8

Library of Congress Control Number: 2015943041

LNCS Sublibrary: SL2 – Programming and Software Engineering

Printed on acid-free paper

Springer International Publishing AG Switzerland is part of Springer Science+Business Media
(www.springer.com)

Foreword

Software Technologies: Applications and Foundations (STAF) is a federation of a number of leading conferences on software technologies. It provides a loose umbrella organization for practical software technologies conferences, supported by a Steering Committee that provides continuity. The STAF federated event runs annually; the conferences that participate can vary from year to year, but all focus on practical and foundational advances in software technology. The conferences address all aspects of software technology, from object-oriented design, testing, mathematical approaches to modeling and verification, model transformation, graph transformation, model-driven engineering, aspect-oriented development, and tools.

STAF 2015 was held at the University of L'Aquila, Italy, during July 20–24, 2015, and hosted four conferences (ICMT 2015, ECMFA 2015, ICGT 2015 and TAP 2015), a long-running transformation tools contest (TTC 2015), seven workshops affiliated with the conferences, a doctoral symposium, and a project showcase (for the first time). The event featured six internationally renowned keynote speakers, a tutorial, and welcomed participants from around the globe.

This was the first scientific event in computer science after the earthquake that occurred in 2009 and affected L'Aquila. It is a small, and yet big step toward the grand achievement of restoring some form of normality in this place and its people.

The STAF Organizing Committee thanks all participants for submitting and attending, the program chairs and Steering Committee members for the individual conferences, the keynote speakers for their thoughtful, insightful, and engaging talks, the University of L'Aquila, Comune dell'Aquila, the local Department of Human Science, and CEA LIST for their support: *Grazie a tutti!*

July 2015   Alfonso Pierantonio

Preface

This volume contains the papers presented at ICMT 2015: the 8th International Conference on Model Transformation held during July 20–21, 2015, in L'Aquila as part of the STAF 2015 (Software Technologies: Applications and Foundations) conference series. ICMT is the premier forum for researchers and practitioners from all areas of model transformation.

Model transformation encompasses a variety of technical spaces, including modelware, grammarware, dataware, and ontoware, a variety of model representations, e.g., based on different types of graphs, and a range of transformation paradigms including rule-based transformations, term rewriting, and manipulations of objects in general-purpose programming languages.

The study of model transformation includes transformation languages, tools, and techniques, as well as properties (such as modularity, composability, and parameterization) of transformations. An important goal of the field is the development of dedicated model transformation languages, which can enable the specification of complex transformations in a rigorous manner and at an appropriate level of abstraction.

The efficient execution of model queries and transformations by scalable transformation engines on top of large graph data structures is also a key challenge for an increasing number of application scenarios. Novel algorithms as well as innovative (e.g., distributed) execution strategies and domain-specific optimizations are sought in this respect. To achieve impact on software engineering in general, methodologies and tools are required to integrate model transformation into existing development environments and processes.

This year, ICMT received 34 submissions. Each submission was reviewed by at least three Program Committee members. After an online discussion period, the Program Committee accepted 16 papers as part of the conference program. These papers included regular research, application, tool demonstration, and exploratory papers presented in the context of five sessions on foundations, applications, new paradigms, change and reuse, and validation and verification of transformations.

Many people contributed to the success of ICMT 2015. We are grateful to the Program Committee members and reviewers for the timely delivery of reviews and constructive discussions under a very tight review schedule. We would also like to thank Javier Troya (Vienna University of Technology) for serving as the Web chair of ICMT 2015. Last but not least, we would like to thank the authors who constitute the heart of the model transformation community for their enthusiasm and hard work.

May 2015

Dimitris Kolovos
Manuel Wimmer

Organization

General Chair

Alfonso Pierantonio   Università degli Studi dell'Aquila, Italy

Program Chairs

Dimitris Kolovos   University of York, UK
Manuel Wimmer   Vienna University of Technology, Austria

Publication Chairs

Louis Rose   University of York, UK
Javier Troya   Vienna University of Technology, Austria

Publicity Chair

James R. Williams   University of York, UK

Web Chair

Javier Troya   Vienna University of Technology, Austria

Steering Committee

Jordi Cabot   Inria-École des Mines de Nantes, France
Juan de Lara   Universidad Autónoma de Madrid, Spain
Davide Di Ruscio   Università degli Studi dell'Aquila, Italy
Keith Duddy   Queensland University of Technology, Australia
Martin Gogolla   University of Bremen, Germany
Jeff Gray   University of Alabama, USA
Zhenjiang Hu   National Institute of Informatics Tokyo, Japan
Gerti Kappel   Vienna University of Technology, Austria
Richard Paige   University of York, UK
Alfonso Pierantonio Università degli Studi dell'Aquila, Italy
  (Chair)
Laurence Tratt   King's College London, UK
Antonio Vallecillo   Universidad de Málaga, Spain
Daniel Varro   Budapest University of Technology and Economics, Hungary
Eelco Visser   Delft University of Technology, The Netherlands

Program Committee

Achim D. Brucker	SAP AG, Germany
Rubby Casallas	University of los Andes, Colombia
Antonio Cicchetti	Mälardalen University, Sweden
Tony Clark	Middlesex University, UK
Benoit Combemale	IRISA, Université de Rennes 1, France
Krzysztof Czarnecki	University of Waterloo, Canada
Alexander Egyed	Johannes Kepler University, Austria
Gregor Engels	University of Paderborn, Germany
Claudia Ermel	Technische Universität Berlin, Germany
Jesus Garcia-Molina	Universidad de Murcia, Spain
Holger Giese	Hasso Plattner Institute at the University of Potsdam, Germany
Esther Guerra	Universidad Autónoma de Madrid, Spain
Reiko Heckel	University of Leicester, UK
Ludovico Iovino	Università degli Studi dell'Aquila, Italy
Frédéric Jouault	TRAME Team, ESEO, France
Marouane Kessentini	University of Michigan, USA
Jens Knoop	Vienna University of Technology, Austria
Thomas Kuehne	Victoria University of Wellington, New Zealand
Jochen Kuester	IBM Research Zurich, Switzerland
Philip Langer	EclipseSource, Austria
Tihamer Levendovszky	Vanderbilt University, USA
Ralf Lämmel	Universität Koblenz-Landau, Germany
Fernando Orejas	Universitat Politècnica de Catalunya, Spain
Marc Pantel	IRIT/INPT, Université de Toulouse, France
Dorina Petriu	Carleton University, Canada
Istvan Rath	Budapest University of Technology and Economics, Hungary
Bernhard Rumpe	RWTH Aachen University, Germany
Houari Sahraoui	Université De Montréal, Canada
Andy Schürr	Technische Universität Darmstadt, Germany
Jim Steel	University of Queensland, Australia
Perdita Stevens	University of Edinburgh, UK
Eugene Syriani	University of Montreal, Canada
Jesús Sánchez Cuadrado	Universidad Autónoma de Madrid, Spain
Gabriele Taentzer	Philipps-Universität Marburg, Germany
Massimo Tisi	Inria-École des Mines de Nantes, France
Mark Van Den Brand	Eindhoven University of Technology, The Netherlands
Tijs Van Der Storm	Centrum Wiskunde & Informatica, The Netherlands
Pieter Van Gorp	Eindhoven University of Technology, The Netherlands
Hans Vangheluwe	University of Antwerp, Belgium and McGill University, Canada
Gergely Varro	Technische Universität Darmstadt, Germany

Janis Voigtländer   University of Bonn, Germany
Dennis Wagelaar   HealthConnect, Belgium
Edward Willink   Willink Transformations Ltd., UK
Haiyan Zhao   Peking University, China
Albert Zuendorf   Kassel University, Germany

Additional Reviewers

Anjorin, Anthony
Berardinelli, Luca
Beyhl, Thomas
Blouin, Dominique
Debreceni, Csaba
Demuth, Andreas
Dávid, István
Eickhoff, Christoph
George, Tobias
Gholizadeh, Hamid
Grieger, Marvin

Groves, Lindsay
Hölldobler, Katrin
Kessentini, Wael
Kuiper, Ruurd
Leblebici, Erhan
Matragkas, Nicholas
Mengerink, Josh
Meyers, Bart
Raco, Deni
Troya, Javier

Contents

Transformation Validation and Verification

Foundations of Model Transformation

Change Management

Change Propagation in an Internal Model Transformation Language

Georg Hinkel[✉]

Forschungszentrum Informatik (FZI), Haid-und-Neu-Straße 10-14,
Karlsruhe, Germany
hinkel@fzi.de

Abstract. Despite good results, Model-Driven Engineering (MDE) has not been widely adopted in industry. According to studies by Staron and Mohaghegi [1,2], the lack of tool support is one of the major reasons for this. Although MDE has existed for more than a decade now, tool support is still insufficient. An approach to overcome this limitation for model transformations, which are a key part of MDE, is the usage of internal languages that reuse tool support for existing host languages. On the other hand, these internal languages typically do not provide key features like change propagation or bidirectional transformation. In this paper, we present an approach to use a single internal model transformation language to create unidirectional and bidirectional model transformations with optional change propagation. In total, we currently provide 18 operation modes based on a single specification. At the same time, the language may reuse tool support for C#. We validate the applicability of our language using a synthetic example with a transformation from finite state machines to Petri nets where we achieved speedups of up to 48 compared to classical batch transformations.

1 Introduction

Model-driven engineering (MDE) is an approach to raise the level of abstraction of systems in order to be able to cope with increasing system complexity. However, while MDE is widely adopted in academia, it is not as popular in industry, primarily because of the lack of stable tool support [1,2]. In addition, Meyerovich et al. [3] have shown that most developers only change their primary language when either there is a hard technical project limitation or there is a significant amount of code that can be reused. In MDE, the 'heart and soul' are model transformations [4], but as general-purpose languages are not suitable for this task [4], there is a plethora of specialized model transformation languages. This may hamper the adoption of MDE in industry as well as developers may not want to use model transformation languages for the reasons found by Meyerovich.

To solve both of these issues, a promising approach is to integrate the abstractions from model transformation languages into general-purpose languages in the form of internal languages. This way, tool support for the host language can be inherited and developers may stick to the languages that they are used to.

© Springer International Publishing Switzerland 2015
D. Kolovos and M. Wimmer (Eds.): ICMT 2015, LNCS 9152, pp. 3–17, 2015.
DOI: 10.1007/978-3-319-21155-8_1

Therefore, several languages exist that follow this approach. However, we observed that they only operate in a rather imperative way. In this context, rather imperative means that these languages contain less control flow abstractions than declarative model transformation languages such as QVT-R [5]. In particular, only few approaches support bidirectional transformation and to the best of our knowledge none of these languages supports change propagation, a feature that is mostly provided by declarative languages like Triple Graph Grammars (TGGs) that have an implementation supporting change propagation [6–8].

In this paper, we show that this is not a general restriction of internal languages. For this, we implement an internal language in C# supporting multi-directional model transformation as well as multiple change propagation patterns. This language has a few limitations that we discuss in Sect. 7, which we believe are only technical restrictions.

We have validated our approach on an example transformation of Finite State Machines to Petri Nets. With our prototype language, we only have a single specification and are able to obtain 18 different model transformations.

The rest of this paper is structured as follows: Sect. 2 explains our running example with the synchronization of Finite State Machines and Petri Nets. Section 3 introduces some foundations. In particular, Sect. 3.1 explains the internal model transformation language (MTL) that the approach is based on for the model transformation part while Sect. 3.2 explains self-adjusting computations that the change propagation mechanism is based on. Section 4 explains in short how we extended this approach for reversable expressions. Section 5 describes our prototype language and the various operation modes. Section 6 validates our language on a synthetic example. Section 7 then shows the limitations of our approach. Finally, Sect. 8 lists related work and Sect. 9 concludes the paper.

2   Finite State Machines to Petri Nets

Throughout the paper, both to explain our approach and for validation, we use the running example of the transformation of Finite State Machines to Petri Nets, two well known formalisms in theoretical computer science. Both of them are well suited to describe behaviors but each of them has its advantages which is why both of them are widely used. Finite state machines can be easily transformed to Petri nets.

However, for model synchronization the example of Finite State Machines and Petri Nets is a rather synthetic one as usually only one of these formalisms is used. We use it as our running example though as the involved metamodels are rather simple and structurally similar but yet different. Real application scenarios would rather center on the synchronization of artifacts like the source code, architecture information in UML diagrams and potentially performance engineering models such as the Palladio Component Model (PCM) [9].

The metamodel that we use for finite state machines is depicted in Fig. 1. Finite state machines consist of states and transitions where transitions hold a reference to the incoming and outgoing states and states hold a reference to the incoming and outgoing transitions. States can be start or end states.

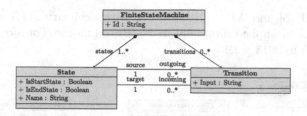

Fig. 1. The metamodel for finite state machines

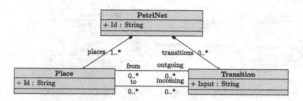

Fig. 2. The metamodel for Petri Nets

The metamodel of Petri Nets is depicted in Fig. 2. Petri Nets consist of places and transitions. Unlike state machines where states are modeled explicitly, the state of a Petri Net is the allocation of tokens in the network.

The transformation from finite state machines to Petri Nets now transforms each state to a place. Transitions in the finite state machine are transformed to Petri Net transitions with the source and target places set accordingly. End states are transformed to a place with an outgoing transition that has no target place and therefore 'swallows' tokens.

The backward transformation from Petri Nets to Finite state charts is not always well defined since Petri Net transitions may have multiple source or target places. However, if the Petri Net is an image of a finite state machine under the above transformation, then the backward transformation is useful to have.

3 Foundations

Our approach is a bridge between technologies that already exist. We combine and adapt a model transformation framework with a framework for self-adjusting computation. Thus, we briefly introduce both of them in this section.

3.1 NMF Transformations

NMF stands for .NET Modeling Framework[1] and is an open-source project to support MDE on the .NET platform. NMF Transformations [10] is a sub-project of NMF that supports model transformation. It consists of a model transformation framework and internal DSL for C# on top of it (NMF Transformations Language, NTL). Both framework and DSL are inspired by the transformation

---

[1] http://nmf.codeplex.com/.

languages QVT [5] and ATL [11] but work with arbitrary .NET objects. The language has been applied internally in NMF and at the Transformation Tool Contest (TTC) in 2013 [12,13].

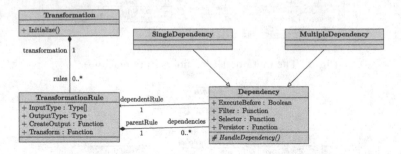

Fig. 3. Abstract syntax of NMF TRANSFORMATIONS

Figure 3 shows an excerpt of NMF Transformations' abstract syntax. Model transformations consist of transformation rules that are in NTL represented as public nested classes of a model transformation class. The transformation rules create computations that represent a transformation of a particular model element. Transformation rules can have dependencies specifying what other transformation rules should be called if a computation is executed. These dependencies may contain selectors, filters and persistors which are called to register the dependent model elements on the target. These dependencies are specified using special method calls where function typed attributes of the dependencies like selectors, filters or persistors are specified as lambda expressions.

Because NTL operates independently of containment hierarchies, the structure of the model transformation is entirely encoded in the transformation dependencies. The idea is that the transformation rules specify locally what other elements should be transformed and whether they should be transformed before the current transformation rule. The transformation engine then resolves these dependencies and executes all computations when their dependencies are met. The rules themselves are imperative with an access to the trace, i.e. to all correspondences that have been found so far. In NTL, the rule body is specified as an overridden method that takes the input and output model element of the transformation rule as well as a transformation context which can be used to query the trace.

3.2 Self-Adjusting Computation

Self-adjusting or incremental computation refers to the idea to adjust a computation using dependency tracking rather than recomputing the whole computation when the input data changes. This is done by modifiable references represented by a monad [14] and a system that creates a dynamic dependency graph based on these [15]. Further research has shown that such self-adjusting programs can be implicitly inferred from a batch specification [16]. That means, from an expression $x + y$ where x and y are modifiable references, a dynamic dependency graph is built where x and y are nodes. Each node holds its current value. In this situation, the system builds a new node for $x + y$ holding a reference to both x and y so that the sum changes as soon as either x or y change. Creating a self-adjusting program from a traditional (batch) specification is possible for purely functional programs [16] since they do not contain side effects. However, approaches for imperative languages exist as well [17,18] but are not working implicitly.

In this paper, we use an implementation of these ideas within the NMF project, NMF Expressions[2]. This approach is suitable for our needs as it contains dedicated collection support and is likewise implemented as an internal DSL for C# and therefore suitable to combine it with NMF Transformations. Furthermore, unlike [16] it does not operate on the source code and therefore can be used in a compiling environment. NMF Expressions operates on CLR objects that implement the .NET platform default notification interfaces, similar to the EMF Notification API. A model representation code that implements these interfaces can be generated from a metamodel using NMF code generators.

4   Reversability of Expressions

The essence of modifiable references from self-adjusting computation is that they inform clients whenever their value has changed. For change propagation, it is also necessary to be able to change it if possible. Therefore, we have refined the monads used in NMF Expressions (INotifyValue and INotifyEnumerable) to account for a categorial interpretation of lenses [19]. In this interpretation, a lense l between types A and B consists of a partial function $l \nearrow: A \rightarrow B$ called the get function and $l \searrow: A \times B \rightarrow A$ called the put function. In category theory, A and B are objects of the category of types.

For example, consider the expression $x + c$ for some modifiable references x and c. Through the modifiable monad, we know that whenever x changes its value, also the value of the sum may change. For the lense, the expression resembles the get function. The lense now allows us to assign a value, say 42 to the sum given that the reference c is constant. This is applied by setting $x = 42 - c$, the put function of the respective lense. The lense is represented by its get function which we expect to be decorated with a put function reference.

For memory efficiency reasons, the analysis whether a given expression is constant is only performed at runtime. Thus, we use a twofold mechanism. We let the classes implementing the dynamic dependency graph nodes optionally implement the refined lense monad interface and added a property to this interface to question whether an expression really is invertible, much like the IsReadonly property used in .NET collections.

Thus, at initialization time we know that the expression $x + c$ might be a lense, depending on whether at least one of either x or c is constant. On the other

---

[2] http://nmfexpressions.codeplex.com/.

hand, other operators like the value equality cannot be reverted in general. It is unclear how to set an expression $x == c$ to `false`, in particular, what value to assign to x. This can be solved by additional parameters that are only taken into account when reversing the operation, such as a method EqualsOrDefault providing the missing information with a third parameter.

An example of an operation beyond arithmetics is FirstOrDefault that returns the first item of a collection or the default value of a type (null for a reference type and zero for numeric types) if the collection is empty. If we were to assign $x.FirstOrDefault() = y$, we can distinguish the following cases:

1. The collection x contains y and y is the first element. In this case, we do not have to change x since the assignment is already satisfied.
2. The collection x contains y but not as the first element. In this case, we have multiple options. We could either move y to be the first element (matching the semantics of getting the literally first element) or leave the collection unchanged (with the semantics of getting any element e.g. in an unordered collection). This is because a single functional implementation can implement multiple semantics that need different reversability behaviors.
3. The collection x does not contain y. In this case, we add y to the collection x. We can either add it as first element if x is an ordered collection or add it to x at all, if x is unordered.
4. The element y is the element type default value. In this case we again have multiple options. In our implementation we clear the collection x.

The main learning point from this example is that the same operational implementation of an operator can match multiple lense semantics. In the example of FirstOrDefault, we have two versions realizing the two options in case 2. On the other hand, this limits the possibility for implicitly inferring a reversibility semantics from existing code since there we don't know how a particular operator has been used. Thus, we decorate each operator with its reversability behavior explicitly.

5   Multimode Model Transformations with an Internal DSL

This section will first demonstrate NMF applied to the running example of Petri nets and finite state machines and afterwards explain how multimode model synchronization is achieved using this syntax.

5.1   Synchronization of Finite State Machines and Petri Nets

Like a model transformation in NMF Transformations that consists of multiple transformation rules represented by public nested classes inheriting from a TransformationRule base class, model synchronizations of NMF Synchronizations consist of synchronization rules. These synchronization rules implicitly define two transformation rules for NMF Transformations, one for each direction. A minimal example for a model synchronization is therefore depicted in Listing 1.

```
1   public class PSM2PN : ReflectiveSynchronization
2   {
3     public class AutomataToNet : SynchronizationRule<FiniteStateMachine, PetriNet> {...}
4   }
```

Listing 1. A model synchronization in NMF SYNCHRONIZATIONS

Similar to TGGs, we distinguish the sources and targets of a model transformation as Left Hand Side (LHS) and Right Hand Side (RHS) although these sides are not represented as graphs. Synchronization rules in NMF Synchronizations define the LHS and RHS model elements they operate on through the generic type arguments of the SynchronizationRule base class they need to inherit from and have multiple methods they can override.

The most important method to override is the method to determine when an element of the LHS should match an element of the RHS. For the AutomataToNet-rule, we simply return true since both RHS and LHS model elements are the root elements of their respective models and should be unique.

The second most important method to override is the DeclareSynchronization method. Here, we define what actions should be taken if the synchronization rule is executed for two corresponding model elements. The DeclareSynchronization method of *AutomataToNet* looks as depicted in Listing 2.

```
1   public override void DeclareSynchronization()
2   {
3     SynchronizeMany(SyncRule<StateToPlace>(),
4       fsm => fsm.States, pn => pn.Places);
5     SynchronizeMany(SyncRule<TransitionToTransition>(),
6       fsm => fsm.Transitions, pn => pn.Transitions.Where(t => t.To.Count >0));
7     SynchronizeMany(SyncRule<EndStateToTransition>(),
8       fsm => fsm.States.Where(state => state.IsEndState),
9       pn => pn.Transitions.Where(t => t.To.Count == 0));
10    Synchronize(fsm => fsm.Id, pn => pn.Id);
11  }
```

Listing 2. The DeclareSynchronization method of AutomataToNet

The meaning of the statements in Listing 2 is as follows: When handling the synchronization of a finite state machine with a Petri Net, the synchronization engine should establish correspondencies between the states and the places using the StateToPlace rule, synchronizing the states of the finite state machine with the places of a Petri Net. This synchronization rule is straight forward, matches states and places based on their names and synchronizes them afterwards. For a given state of a state machine, the synchronization engine only looks for corresponding places in the Places reference of the corresponding Petri Net.

Similarly, the transitions of the finite state machine should be matched with the transitions of the Petri Net, but only with those that have at least one target place. This means that if a new transition is added to the Petri Net transitions or an existing transition is assigned a first target place, then the synchronization engine will try to match this transition to an existing finite state machine transition. If conversely, a transition is added to the finite state machine, the synchronization engine will add the corresponding transition to the Petri Net, hoping that it satisfies the condition that the count is greather than zero. To find the corresponding transition on the respective other side, the ShouldCorrespond method depicted in Listing 3 is used.

```
1  public override bool ShouldCorrespond(FSM.Transition left, PN.Transition right,
       ISynchronizationContext context)
2  {
3      var stateToPlace = SyncRule<StateToPlace>().LeftToRight;
4      return left.Input == right.Input
5          && right.From.Contains(context.Trace.ResolveIn(stateToPlace, left.StartState))
6          && right.To.Contains(context.Trace.ResolveIn(stateToPlace, left.EndState));
7  }
```

Listing 3. Matching transitions

This method uses the trace abilities of NMF Transformations that is still accessible in NMF Synchronizations, i.e. it accesses the corresponding place for a given state in the transformation rule from LHS to RHS and uses it to decide whether the transitions should match. This trace entry exists regardless of the synchronization direction, i.e. the synchronization always creates two trace entries.

Lines 7–9 of Listing 2 indicate that the remaining transitions should be synchronized with the end states of the state machine. The symmetric correspondence check fails in this case because the synchronization engine will look for a suitable state in the end states of the machine. If the state is not yet marked as an end state, the synchronization engine will not find it. Thus, we have to override this behavior and particularly look for the state which is corresponding to the transitions origin.

```
1  public override void DeclareSynchronization()
2  {
3      SynchronizeLeftToRightOnly(SyncRule<StateToPlace>(),
4          state => state.IsEndState ? state : null,
5          transition => transition.From.FirstOrDefault());
6  }
```

Listing 4. One way synchronizations

Next, it is necessary to connect or disconnect the Petri Net transition to the correct place. This only has to be done in the LHS to RHS direction since this information is already encoded in the IsEndState attribute in the finite state machine state. We have to limit the scope of this synchronization job because the synchronization initialization otherwise raises an exception since the conditional expression of the LHS is not reversible. This is depicted in Listing 4.

Line 10 in Listing 2 tells that the Identifiers of both finite state machine and Petri Net should be synchronized. In this case, it is not necessary to provide a synchronization rule since both identifiers are strings and the string will just be copied.

5.2   Multimode Synchronization

To support multiple modes of transformations, especially to support optional change propagation, it is crucial to step into the compilation process of the language. If some model element is used in a change propagation, it is necessary to create dynamic dependency graphs for these expressions in order to receive updates when these expressions change their value.

Gladly, C# has an option to retrieve lambda expressions as an abstract syntax tree (called expression tree) instead of compiled code. This is the one and only syntax feature that we use from C# that makes our language impossible to implement in other languages (apart from Visual Basic). However, we believe that other languages like Java or in particular Xtend will soon adapt this feature as well, making our approach applicable to other languages.

We support six different synchronization modes that can be combined with three different change propagation modes. The synchronization modes are as follows:

- **LeftToRight:** the transformation ensures that all model elements on the LHS have some corresponding model elements on the RHS. However, the RHS may contain model elements that have no correspondence on the LHS.
- **LeftToRightForced:** the transformation ensures that all model elements on the LHS have some corresponding model elements in the RHS. All elements in the RHS that have no corresponding elements in the LHS are deleted.
- **LeftWins:** the transformation ensures that all model elements on the LHS have some corresponding model elements in the RHS and vice versa. Synchronization conflicts are resolved by taking the version at the LHS.
- **RightToLeft, RightToLeftForced, RightWins:** same as the above but with interchanged roles of RHS and LHS

The change propagation modes are the following:

- **None:** no change propagation is performed. In this case, also no dynamic dependency graphs for any expressions are created as they are not necessary.
- **OneWay:** change propagation is only performed in the main synchronization direction, i.e. LHS to RHS for the first three synchronization modes and RHS to LHS otherwise.
- **TwoWay:** change propagation is performed in both directions, i.e. any changes on either side will result in appropriate changes in the other side.

We support all synchronization modes and all change propagation modes for all synchronizations. In particular, the synchronization is initialized for all possible modes and the applicable mode is specific to a synchronization run and is provided together with the input arguments, i.e. LHS and RHS initial models. At this initialization, we generate code to minimize the performance impact when no change propagation should be performed, i.e. the synchronization should run with a performance comparable to a transformation without change propagation as e.g. pure NMF Transformations. However, we provide overloads of the

Synchronize and SynchronizeMany methods that only act on a particular synchronization direction. This is required as some synchronizations need to assign some expressions that are not reversible and would thus otherwise raise an exception at synchronization initialization.

6   Validation

We tested the correctness and evaluated the performance of NMF Synchronizations by applying it to the Finite States to Petri Nets example that we already used to explain the approach. In typical applications of a model synchronization, the LHS side is edited in subsequent edit operations either performed by a user through an editor or programatically. Then, the appropriate RHS model is required for analysis purposes or as an alternate view on the modeled reality. For such subsequent model changes, it is important to minimize the response time from changing the LHS model to having the RHS model updated accordingly (or vice versa). Often it is also important to get a change notification to be able to understand what changes in the RHS model were caused by the changes to the LHS model but although such change notifications can be supplied by NMF Synchronizations with change propagation enabled we do not take this feature into account for the evaluation.

To analyze the response time from elementary changes in the finite state machine to the updated Petri Net, we designed a benchmark where we generate a sequence of 100 elementary model changes to the finite state machine. After each model change, we ensure that the Petri Net is changed accordingly, either by performing change propagation or by regenerating the net fresh from scratch. To take the different sizes of finite state machines into account, we performed our experiment for different sizes (10, 20, 50, 100, 200, 500 and 1000 states). The genereated workload on these finite state machines shall reflect edit operations as done by a user. In particular, we generate the following elementary changes (percentage on the overall change workload in brackets):

- Add a state to the finite state machine (30 %)
- Add a transition to the finite state machine with random start and end state (30 %)
- Remove a random state and all of its incoming and outgoing transitions (10 %)
- Remove a random transition from the finite state machine (10 %)
- Toggle end state of a random state (5 %)
- Change the target state of a randomly selected transition to a random other state (5 %)
- Rename a state (9 %)
- Rename the finite state machine (1 %)

The validation works as follows: For every run of our benchmark, we generate a finite state machine of a given size n representing the number of states. We then generate a sequence of 100 elementary model changes acting on randomly selected model elements of the finite state machine. For each of these actions, the action itself must be performed and the Petri Net must be updated or newly created appropriately.

We compare three implementations of this task. The first option is the solution using NMF Synchronizations running in batch mode, i.e. the synchronization is run as a transformation from its left side to its right side with change propagation switched off. Next, we use the same synchronization code without any modification and use it in incremental mode, i.e. from left to right with change propagation mode switched on to OneWay. Finally, we use an implementation for this transformation task in NTL, basically taken from previous work [10]. This solution works pretty similar to the batch mode version, but lacks some of the overhead implied by the NMF Synchronizations implementation. NMF Transformations used with NTL showed good performance results compared with other (batch mode) model transformation languages at the TTC 2013 [12,13] so we think it is a fair comparison.

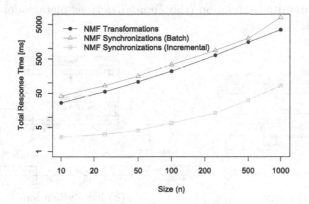

Fig. 4. Performance results

We did two runs of the experiment. In the first run, we check the generated Petri Net after each workload item in order to test the correctness of NMF Synchronizations. Here, we basically assume the implementation in NMF Transformations correct. In a second run of the experiment, we evaluated the execution time to apply all the elementary model changes in sequence and updating the Petri Net accordingly after each change (either by rerunning the transformation or by propagating changes). The application of 100 elementary model changes and updating the Petri Net is still a matter of milliseconds, but this way the precision gets in a reasonable scale.

Figure 4 shows the performance results achieved on an AMD Athlon X4 630 processor clocked at 2.81 Ghz in a system with 4 GB RAM. However, the code for our used benchmark is available as open source on Codeplex[3] so that the interested reader can obtain results for any other machines as well.

The results indicate that even for very small models such as a finite state machine with just 10 states, it is already beneficial to use the change propagation

---

[3] http://nmfsynchronizationsbenchmark.codeplex.com/.

built into NMF Synchronizations. For the larger models, the speedup gets larger until it stabilizes at about 48 so that the curves appear parallel. Without change propagation, NMF Synchronizations is only slower than NMF Transformations by a constant factor, indicating that the transformation runs efficiently when change propagation is disabled. This may be useful in environments with limited memory or when no change propagation is needed.

7   Limitations of the Language

Currently, we assume in our implementation that a correspondence between model elements once established will not change during the lifecycle of both objects. This is a strong assumption and there are simple counter-examples. Consider for instance two metamodels of family relations where the gender is realized as IsFemale attribute (the *Persons* metamodel on the left hand of Fig. 5) and using an inheritance relation (the *FamilyRelations* metamodel on the right hand of Fig. 5).

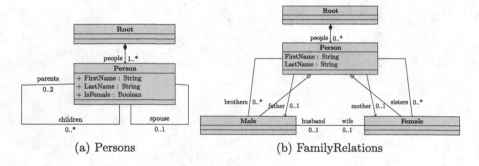

(a) Persons   (b) FamilyRelations

Fig. 5. Metamodels of the counter-example

An instance of the Person class of the Persons metamodel with gender male clearly corresponds to an instance of the Male class on the FamilyRelations metamodel. However, if the gender is changed to female for some reason, then the corresponding model element should then be a Female instance and all references should be updated accordingly. Thus, the identity of one of the model elements of a correspondence relation changes. This is currently not supported by our language although there is no technical limitation.

8   Related Work

Model Transformation Languages as Internal Languages. Some experiences exist with creating model transformation languages as internal languages like RubyTL [20], ScalaMTL [21], FunnyQT [22] or SDMLib[4]. The goals to use an

---
[4] http://sdmlib.org/.

existing language as host language are diverse and range from an easier implementation [23], reuse of the static type system [21], inherited tool support [10], reusing the expression evaluation, easier integration into the host language up to less learning points for developers. The degree in which these goals can be met depends very much on the selected host language, as e.g. tool support can only be inherited if some tool support exists but a concise syntax can usually only be achieved with host languages having a rather flexible syntax. To the best of our knowledge, current internal transformation languages cannot cope with change propagation. We do also believe that this implementation is only possible if the internal language can see the abstract syntax tree of the host language expressions, which is far away from being common in typical host languages. The only alternative is to use a fluent style internal language that limits the reuse of expressions and tool support.

Model Transformation Languages with Change Propagation. Some external model transformations languages support incremental change propagation. Triple Graph Grammars, for example, have been implemented in an incremental manner [6–8] and with support for concurrent model changes and semi-automatic conflict resolution [24]. Lauder *et al.* [25] provided an incremental synchronization algorithm that statically analyzes rules to determine the influence range while retaining formal properties. The runtime complexity of this algorithm depends on the change not on the model. An overview of incremental TGG tools was provided by Leblebici *et al.* [26].

Self-Adjusting Computation. Self-adjusting or incremental computation refers to the idea that systems use a dynamic dependency graph to track how to change their outputs when the input changes rather than recomputing the whole program output. This is usually achieved either by adding explicit new language primitives for self-adjusting computation [15,27]. However, Chen et al. [16] presented an approach to infer these newly added primitives from type annotations so that effectively self-adjusting programs may be written in StandardML, which is close to our approach. However, the approach of Chen is based on a general-purpose language that is not suitable for the specification of model transformations or synchronizations. Since the language primitives in NMF Synchronizations are fitted to the concepts of model transformation, we have more insights on how to execute the transformations incrementally.

9   Conclusion

In this paper, we have presented NMF Synchronizations, an internal DSL for bidirectional model transformation and synchronization with optional change propagation. Despite it is only a proof of concept and therefore has some limitations, the approach encourages the development of model transformation languages as internal DSLs as it shows that one of the key challenges, supporting declarative model transformations, can be overcome. In particular, NMF

Synchronizations support in total 18 different operation modes from a single specification. For a synthetic example, the optional change propagation has shown speedups of up to 48, whereas the classic batch mode execution is still available with low overhead.

References

1. Staron, M.: Adopting model driven software development in industry – a case study at two companies. In: Wang, J., Whittle, J., Harel, D., Reggio, G. (eds.) MoDELS 2006. LNCS, vol. 4199, pp. 57–72. Springer, Heidelberg (2006)
2. Mohagheghi, P., Gilani, W., Stefanescu, A., Fernandez, M.A.: An empirical study of the state of the practice and acceptance of model-driven engineering in four industrial cases. Empirical Softw. Eng. **18**(1), 89–116 (2013)
3. Meyerovich, L.A., Rabkin, A.S.: Empirical analysis of programming language adoption. In: Proceedings of the 2013 ACM SIGPLAN International Conference on Object Oriented Programming Systems Languages & Spplications, pp. 1–18. ACM (2013)
4. Sendall, S., Kozaczynski, W.: Model transformation the heart and soul of model-driven software development. Technical report (2003)
5. Object Management Group, Meta Object Facility (MOF) 2.0 Query/View/Transformation Specification (2011). http://www.omg.org/spec/QVT/1.1/PDF/
6. Giese, H., Wagner, R.: Incremental model synchronization with triple graph grammars. In: Wang, J., Whittle, J., Harel, D., Reggio, G. (eds.) MoDELS 2006. LNCS, vol. 4199, pp. 543–557. Springer, Heidelberg (2006)
7. Giese, H., Hildebrandt, S.: Efficient model synchronization of large-scale models, 28. Universitätsverlag Potsdam (2009)
8. Giese, H., Wagner, R.: From model transformation to incremental bidirectional model synchronization. Softw. Syst. Model. **8**(1), 21–43 (2009)
9. Becker, S., Koziolek, H., Reussner, R.: The Palladio component model for model-driven performance prediction. J. Syst. Softw. **82**, 3–22 (2009)
10. Hinkel, G.: An approach to maintainable model transformations using internal DSLs, Master thesis (2013)
11. Jouault, F., Kurtev, I.: Transforming models with ATL. In: Bruel, J.-M. (ed.) MoDELS 2005. LNCS, vol. 3844, pp. 128–138. Springer, Heidelberg (2006)
12. Hinkel, G., Goldschmidt, T., Happe, L.: An NMF Solution for the Flowgraphs case study at the TTC 2013. In: Sixth Transformation Tool Contest (TTC 2013), ser. EPTCS (2013)
13. Hinkel, G., Goldschmidt, T., Happe, L.: A NMF solution for the Petri Nets to State Charts case study at the TTC 2013. In: Sixth Transformation Tool Contest (TTC 2013), ser. EPTCS (2013)
14. Carlsson, M.: Monads for incremental computing. ACM SIGPLAN Not. **37**(9), 26–35 (2002)
15. Acar, U.A.: Self-adjusting computation. Ph.D. thesis, Citeseer (2005)
16. Chen, Y., Dunfield, J., Hammer, M.A., Acar, U.A.: Implicit self-adjusting computation for purely functional programs. J. Funct. Program. **24**(01), 56–112 (2014)
17. Acar, U.A., Ahmed, A., Blume, M.: Imperative self-adjusting computation. ACM SIGPLAN Not. **43**, 309–322 (2008). ACM
18. Hammer, M.A., Acar, U.A., Chen, Y.: Ceal: a c-based language for self-adjusting computation. ACM Sigplan Not. **44**, 25–37 (2009). ACM

19. Foster, J.N., Greenwald, M.B., Moore, J.T., Pierce, B.C., Schmitt, A.: Combinators for bi-directional tree transformations: a linguistic approach to the view update problem. SIGPLAN Not. **40**(1), 233–246 (2005)

20. Cuadrado, J.S., Molina, J.G., Tortosa, M.M.: RubyTL: a practical, extensible transformation language. In: Rensink, A., Warmer, J. (eds.) ECMDA-FA 2006. LNCS, vol. 4066, pp. 158–172. Springer, Heidelberg (2006)

21. George, L., Wider, A., Scheidgen, M.: Type-safe model transformation languages as internal DSLs in scala. In: Hu, Z., de Lara, J. (eds.) ICMT 2012. LNCS, vol. 7307, pp. 160–175. Springer, Heidelberg (2012)

22. Horn, T.: Model querying with FunnyQT. In: Duddy, K., Kappel, G. (eds.) ICMB 2013. LNCS, vol. 7909, pp. 56–57. Springer, Heidelberg (2013)

23. Barringer, H., Havelund, K.: TRACECONTRACT: a scala DSL for trace analysis. In: Butler, M., Schulte, W. (eds.) FM 2011. LNCS, vol. 6664, pp. 57–72. Springer, Heidelberg (2011)

24. Hermann, F., Ehrig, H., Ermel, C., Orejas, F.: Concurrent model synchronization with conflict resolution based on triple graph grammars. In: de Lara, J., Zisman, A. (eds.) Fundamental Approaches to Software Engineering. LNCS, vol. 7212, pp. 178–193. Springer, Heidelberg (2012)

25. Lauder, M., Anjorin, A., Varró, G., Schürr, A.: Efficient model synchronization with precedence triple graph grammars. In: Ehrig, H., Engels, G., Kreowski, H.-J., Rozenberg, G. (eds.) ICGT 2012. LNCS, vol. 7562, pp. 401–415. Springer, Heidelberg (2012)

26. Leblebici, E., Anjorin, A., Schürr, A., Hildebrandt, S., Rieke, J., Greenyer, J.: A comparison of incremental triple graph grammar tools. Electronic Communications of the EASST **67**, (2014). http://journal.ub.tuberlin.de/eceasst/article/view/939/928

27. Burckhardt, S., Leijen, D., Sadowski, C., Yi, J., Ball, T.: Two for the price of one: a model for parallel and incremental computation. ACM SIGPLAN Notices **46**, 427–444 (2011). ACM

Origin Tracking + Text Differencing = Textual Model Differencing

Riemer van Rozen[1]([✉]) and Tijs van der Storm[2,3]

[1] Amsterdam University of Applied Sciences, Amsterdam, The Netherlands
rozen@cwi.nl
[2] Centrum Wiskunde and Informatica, Amsterdam, The Netherlands
[3] Universiteit van Amsterdam, Amsterdam, The Netherlands

Abstract. In textual modeling, models are created through an intermediate parsing step which maps textual representations to abstract model structures. Therefore, the identify of elements is not stable across different versions of the same model. Existing model differencing algorithms, therefore, cannot be applied directly because they need to identify model elements across versions. In this paper we present Textual Model Diff (TMDIFF), a technique to support model differencing for textual languages. TMDIFF requires origin tracking during text-to-model mapping to trace model elements back to the symbolic names that define them in the textual representation. Based on textual alignment of those names, TMDIFF can then determine which elements are the same across revisions, and which are added or removed. As a result, TMDIFF brings the benefits of model differencing to textual languages.

1 Introduction

Model differencing algorithms (e.g., [1]) determine which elements are added, removed or changed between revisions of a model. A crucial aspect of such algorithms that model elements need to be identified across versions. This allows the algorithm to determine which elements are still the same in both versions. In textual modeling [6], models are represented as textual source code, similar to Domain-Specific Languages (DSLs) and programming languages. The actual model structure is not first-class, but is derived from the text by a text-to-model mapping, which, apart from parsing the text into a containment hierarchy also provides for reference resolution. After every change to the text, the corresponding structure needs to be derived again. As a result, the identities assigned to the model elements during text-to-model mapping are not preserved across versions, and model differencing cannot be applied directly.

Existing approaches to textual model differencing are based on mapping textual syntax to a standard model representation (e.g., languages built with Xtext are mapped to EMF [5]) and then using standard model comparison tools (e.g., EMFCompare [2,3]). As a result, model elements in both versions are matched using name-based identities stored in the model elements themselves. One approach is to interpret such names as globally unique identifiers: match model

© Springer International Publishing Switzerland 2015
D. Kolovos and M. Wimmer (Eds.): ICMT 2015, LNCS 9152, pp. 18–33, 2015.
DOI: 10.1007/978-3-319-21155-8_2

elements of the same class, irrespective of their location in the containment hierarchy of the model. Another approach is to only match elements in collections at the same position in the containment hierarchy.

Unfortunately, both approaches have their limitations. In the case of global names, the language cannot have scoping rules: it is impossible to have different model elements of the same class with the same name. On the other hand, matching names relative to the containment hierarchy entails that scoping rules must obey the containment hierarchy, which limits flexibility.

In this paper we present TMDIFF, a language-parametric technique for model differencing of textual languages which does support languages with complex scoping rules, but at the same time is agnostic of the model containment hierarchy. As a result, different elements with the same name, but in different scopes can still be identified. TMDIFF is based on two key techniques:

- **Origin Tracking.** In order to map model element identities back to the source, we assume that the text-to-model mapping applies origin tracking [7,19]. Origin tracking induces an *origin relation* which relates source locations of definitions to (opaque) model identities. Each semantic model element can be traced back to its defining name in the textual source, and each defining name can be traced forward to its corresponding model element.
- **Text Differencing.** TMDIFF identifies model elements by textually aligning definition names between two versions of a model using traditional text differencing techniques (e.g., [11]). When two names in the textual representations of two models are aligned, they are assumed to represent the "same" model element in both models. In combination with the origin relation this allows TMDIFF to identify the corresponding model elements as well.

The resulting identification of model elements can be passed to standard model differencing algorithms, such as the one by Alanen and Porres [1].

TMDIFF enjoys the important benefit that it is fully language parametric. TMDIFF works irrespective of the specific binding semantics and scoping rules of a textual modeling language. In other words, how the textual representation is mapped to model structure is irrelevant. The only requirement is that semantic model elements are introduced using symbolic names, and that the text-to-model mapping performs origin tracking.

The contributions of this paper are summarized as follows:

- We explore how textual differencing can be used to match model elements based on origin tracking information.
- We provide a detailed description of TMDIFF, including a prototype implementation.
- The feasibility of the approach is illustrated by applying TMDIFF in the context of a realistic, independently developed DSL.

2   Overview

Here we introduce textual model differencing using a simple motivating example that is used as a running example throughout the paper. Figure 1 shows a state

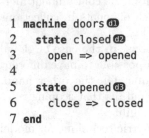

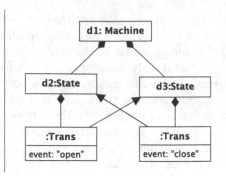

```
1  machine doors d1
2     state closed d2
3        open => opened
4
5     state opened d3
6        close => closed
7  end
```

Fig. 1. $Doors_1$: a simple textual representation of a state machine and its model.

machine model for controlling doors. It is both represented as text (left) and as object diagram (right). A state machine has a name and contains a number of state declarations. Each state declaration contains zero or more transitions. A transition fires on an event, and then transfers control to a new state.

The symbolic names that *define* entities are annotated with unique labels d_n. These labels capture *source locations* of names. That is, a name occurrence is identified with its line and column number and/or character offset[1]. Since identifiers can never overlap, labels are guaranteed to be unique, and the actual name corresponding to label can be easily retrieved from the source text itself. For instance, the machine itself is labeled d_1, and both states closed and opened are labeled d_2 and d_3 respectively.

The labels are typically the result of *name analysis* (or reference resolution), which distinguishes definition occurrences of names from use occurrences of names according to the specific scoping rules of the language. For the purpose of this paper it is immaterial how this name analysis is implemented, or what kind of scoping rules are applied. The important aspect is to know which name occurrences represent definitions of elements in the model.

By propagating the source locations (d_i) to the fully resolved model, symbolic names can be linked to model elements and vice versa. On the right of Fig. 1, we have used the labels themselves as object identities in the object model. Note that the anonymous Transition objects lack such labels. In this case, the objects do not have an identity, and the difference algorithm will perform structural differencing (e.g., [20]), instead of semantic, model-based differencing [1].

Figure 2 shows two additional versions of the state machine of Fig. 1. First the machine is extended with a locked state in $Doors_2$ (Fig. 2a). Second, $Doors_3$ (Fig. 2c), shows a grouping feature of the language: the locked state is part of the locking group. The grouping construct acts as a scope: it allows different states with the same name to coexist in the same state machine model.

Looking at the labels in Figs. 1 and 2, however, one may observe that the labels used in each version are disjoint. For instance, even though the defining

---

[1] For the sake of presentation, we use the abstract labels d_i for the rest of the paper, but keep in mind that they represent source locations.

```
1  machine doors d4
2    state closed d5
3      open => opened
4      lock => locked
5
6    state opened d6
7      close => closed
8
9    state locked d7
10     unlock => closed
11
12 end
```

(a) *Doors*$_2$

```
1  machine doors d8
2    state closed d9
3      open => opened
4      lock => locking.locked
5
6    state opened d10
7      close => closed
8
9    locking d11  {
10     state locked d12
11       unlock => closed
12   }
13 end
```

(b) *Doors*$_3$

Fig. 2. Two new versions of the simple state machine model *Doors*$_1$.

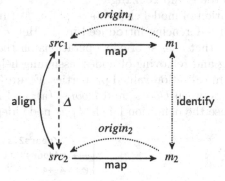

Fig. 3. Identifying model elements in m_1 and m_2 through origin tracking and alignment of textual names.

name occurrences of the machine **doors** and state **closed** occur at the exact same location in *Doors*$_2$ and *Doors*$_3$, this is an accidental artifact of how the source code is formatted. Case in point is the name **locked**, which now has moved down because of the addition of the group construct.

The source locations, therefore, cannot be used as (stable) identities to used during model differencing. The approach taken by TMDIFF involves determining added and removed definitions by aligning the textual occurrences of defining names (i.e. labels d_i). Based on the origin tracking between the textual source and the actual model it then becomes possible to identify which model elements have survived changing the source text.

This high-level approach is visualized in Fig. 3. src_1 and src_2 represent the source code of two revisions of a model. Each of these textual representations is mapped to a proper model, m_1 and m_2 respectively. Mapping text to a model induces origin relations, $origin_1$ and $origin_2$, mapping model elements back to the source locations of their defining names in src_1 and src_2 respectively.

By then aligning these names between src_1 and src_2, the elements themselves can be identified via the respective origin relations.

TMDIFF aligns textual names by interpreting the output of a textual `diff` algorithm on the model source code. The diffs between $Doors_1$ and $Doors_2$, and $Doors_2$ and $Doors_3$ is shown in Fig. 4. As can be seen, the diffs show for each line whether it was added ("+") or removed ("-"). By looking at the line number of the definition labels d_i it becomes possible to determine whether the associated model element was added or removed.

For instance, the new `locked` state was introduced in $Doors_2$. This can be observed from the fact that the diff on the left of Fig. 4 shows that the name "locked" is on a line marked as added. Since the names `doors`, `closed` and `opened` occur on unchanged lines, TMDIFF will identify the corresponding model elements (the machine, and the 2 states) in $Doors_1$ and $Doors_2$. Similarly, the diff between $Doors_2$ and $Doors_3$ shows that only the group `locking` was introduced. All other entities have remained the same, even the `locked` state, which has moved into the group `locking`.

With the identification of model elements in place, TMDIFF applies a variant of the standard model differencing introduced in [1]. Hence, TMDIFF deltas are imperative edit scripts that consist of edit operations on the model. Edit operations include creating and removing of nodes, assigning fields, and inserting or removing elements from collection-valued properties. Figure 5 shows the TMDIFF edit scripts computed between $Doors_1$ and $Doors_2$ (a), and $Doors_2$ and $Doors_3$ (b). The edit scripts use the definition labels d_n as node identities.

```
--- a/doors1.sl
+++ b/doors2.sl
@@ -3,0 +4
+    lock => locked
@@ -6,0 +8,3
+
+    state locked
+       unlock => closed
```

```
--- a/doors2.sl
+++ b/doors3.sl
@@ -4 +4
-       lock => locked
+       lock => locking.locked
@@ -8,0 +9
+    locking {
@@ -10,0 +12
+    }
```

Fig. 4. Textual diff between $Doors_1$ and $Doors_2$, and $Doors_2$ and $Doors_3$. (The diffs are computed by the `diff` tool included with the `git` version control system. We used the following invocation: `git diff --no-index --patience --ignore-space-change --ignore-blank-lines --ignore-space-at-eol -U0 <old> <new>`.)

```
create State d7
d7 = State("locked",[Trans("unlock",d2)])
d2.out[1] = Trans("lock", d7)
d1.states[2] = d7
```

```
create Group d11
d11 = Group("locking",[d7])
remove d4.states[2]
d4.states[2] = d11
```

(a) `tmdiff` $Doors_1$ $Doors_2$ (b) `tmdiff` $Doors_2$ $Doors_3$

Fig. 5. TMDIFF differences between $Doors_i$ and $Doors_{i+1}$ ($i \in 1, .., 2$)

The edit script shown in Fig. 5a captures the difference between source version $Doors_1$ and target version $Doors_2$. It begins with the creation of a new state d_7. On the following line d_7 is initialized with its name (`locked`) and a fresh collection of transitions. The transitions are *contained* by the state, so they are created anonymously (without identity). Note that the created transition contains a (cross-)reference to state d_2. The next step is to add a new transition to the out field of state d_2 (which is preserved from $Doors_1$). The target state of this transition is the new state d_7. Finally, state d_7 is inserted at index 2 of the collection of states of the machine d_1 in $Doors_1$.

The edit script introducing the grouping construct `locking` between $Doors_2$ and $Doors_3$ is shown in Fig. 5b. The first step is the creation of a new group d_{11}. It is initialized with the name `"locking"`. The set of nested states is initialized to contain state d_7 which already existed in $Doors_2$. Finally, the state with index 2 is removed from the machine d_4 in $Doors_3$, and then replaced by the new group d_{11}.

In this section we have introduced the basic approach of TMDIFF using the state machine example. The next section presents TMDIFF in more detail.

3   TMDIFF in More Detail

3.1   Top-Level Algorithm

Figure 6 shows the TMDIFF algorithm in high-level pseudo code. Input to the algorithm are the source texts of the models (src_1, src_2), and the models themselves (m_1, m_2). The first step is identifying model elements of m_1 to elements in m_2 using the matching technique introduced above. The match function is further described in the next sub section (Sect. 3.2).

```
list[Operation] tmDiff(str src₁, str src₂, obj m₁, obj m₂) {
  <A, D, M> = match(src₁, src₂, m₁, m₂)
  Δ = [ new Create(dₐ, dₐ.class) | dₐ ←A ]
  M' = M + { <dₐ, dₐ> | dₐ ←A }
  Δ += [ new SetTree(dₐ, build(dₐ, M')) | dₐ ←A ]
  for (<d₁, d₂> ←M)
    Δ += diffNodes(d₁, d₁, d₂, [], M')
  Δ += [ new Delete(d_d) | d_d ←D ]
  return Δ
}
```

Fig. 6. TMDIFF

Based on the matching returned by match, TMDIFF first generates global Create operations for nodes that are in the A set. After these operations are created, the matching M is "completed" into M', by mapping every added object to itself. This ensures that reverse lookups in M' for elements in m_2 will always be defined. Each entity just created is initialized by generating SetTree operations which reconstruct the containment hierarchy for each element d_a using the build function. The function diffNodes then computes the difference between each pair of nodes originally identified in M. The edit operations will be anchored at object d_1 (first argument). As a result, diffNodes produces edits on "old" entities, if possible. Finally, the nodes that have been deleted from m_1 result in global Delete actions.

3.2 Matching

The match function uses the output computed by standard diff tools. In particular, we employ a diff variant called *Patience Diff*[2] which is known to often provide better results than the standard, LCS-based, algorithm [12].

```
Matching match(str src₁, str src₂, obj m₁, obj m₂) {
    P₁ = project(m₁)
    P₂ = project(m₂)
    <L_add, L_del> = split(diff(src₁, src₂))

    i = 0, j = 0; A = {}, D = {}; M = {}
    while (i < |P₁| ∨ j < |P₂|) {
        if (i < |P₁| ∧ P₁[i].line ∈ L_del)
            D += {P₁[i].object}; i += 1; continue
        if (j < |P₂| ∧ P₂[j].line ∈ L_add)
            A += {P₂[j].object}; j += 1; continue
        if (P₁[i].object.class = P₂[j].object.class)
            M += {<P₁[i].object, P₂[j].object>}
        else
            D += {P₁[i].object}; A += {P₂[j].object}
        i += 1; j += 1
    }
    return <A, D, M>;
}
```

Fig. 7. Matching model elements based on source text diffs.

The matching algorithm is shown in Fig. 7. The function match takes the textual source of both models (src_1, src_2) and the actual models as input (m_1, m_2). It first projects out the origin and class information for each model. The resulting projections P_1 and P_2 are sequences of tuples $\langle x, c, l, d \rangle$, where x is the symbolic name of the entity, c its class (e.g. State, Machine, etc.), l the textual line it occurs on and d the object itself.

As an example, the projections for $Doors_1$ and $Doors_2$ are as follows:

$$P_1 = \begin{array}{ll} [\ \langle \text{doors,} & Machine, 1, d_1 \rangle, \\ \langle \text{closed,} & State, \quad 2, d_2 \rangle, \\ \langle \text{opened,} & State, \quad 5, d_3 \rangle\ ] \end{array}$$

$$P_2 = \begin{array}{ll} [\ \langle \text{doors,} & Machine, 1, d_4 \rangle, \\ \langle \text{closed,} & State, \quad 2, d_5 \rangle, \\ \langle \text{opened,} & State, \quad 6, d_6 \rangle, \\ \langle \text{locked,} & State, \quad 9, d_7 \rangle\ ] \end{array}$$

---

[2] See: http://bramcohen.livejournal.com/73318.html.

The algorithm then partitions the textual `diff` in two sets L_{add} and L_{del} of added lines (relative to src_2) and deleted lines (relative to src_1). The main **while**-loop then iterates over the projections P_1 and P_2 in parallel, distributing definition labels over the A, D and M sets that will make up the matching. If a name occurs unchanged in both src_1 and src_2, an additional type check prevents that entities in different categories are matched.

The result of matching is a triple $M = \langle A, D, I \rangle$, where $A \subseteq L_Y$ contains new elements in Y, $D \subseteq L_X$ contains elements removed from X, and $I \subseteq L_X \times L_Y$ represents identified entities.

For instance the matchings between $Doors_1$, $Doors_2$, and between $Doors_2$ and $Doors_3$ are:

$$M_{1,2} = \langle \{d_7\}, \{\}, \{\langle d_1, d_4 \rangle, \langle d_2, d_5 \rangle, \langle d_3, d_6 \rangle\} \rangle$$
$$M_{2,3} = \langle \{d_{11}\}, \{\}, \{\langle d_4, d_8 \rangle, \langle d_5, d_9 \rangle, \langle d_6, d_{10} \rangle, \langle d_7, d_{12} \rangle\} \rangle$$

3.3   Differencing

The heavy lifting of TMDIFF is realized by the diffNodes function. It is shown in Fig. 8. It receives the current context (ctx), the two elements to be compared (t_1 and t_2), a Path p which is a list recursively built up out of names and indexes and the matching relation to provide reference equality between elements in t_1 and t_2. diffNodes assumes that both t_1 and t_2 are of the same class. The algorithm then loops over all fields that need to be differenced. Fields can be of four

```
list[Operation] diffNodes(obj ctx, obj t₁, obj t₂, Path p, Matching M) {
    assert t₁.class = t₂.class;
    Δ = []
    for (f ←m₁.class.fields) {
        if (f.isPrimitive && t₁[f] ≠ t₂[f])
            Δ += [new SetPrim(ctx, p+[f], t₂[f])];
        else if (f.isContainment)
            if (m₁[f].class = m₂[f].class)
                Δ += diffNodes(ctx, t₁[f], t₂[f], p+[f], M)
            else
                Δ += [new SetTree(ctx, p+[f], build(m₂[f], M))]
        else if (f.isReference && M⁻¹[t₂[f]] ≠ t₁[f] )
            Δ += [new SetRef(ctx, p+[f], M⁻¹[t₂[f]] )]
        else if (f.isList)
            Δ += diffLists(ctx, t₁[f], t₂[f], p+[f], M)
    }
    return Δ
}
```

Fig. 8. Differencing nodes.

kinds: primitive, containment, reference or list. For each case the appropriate edit operations are generated, and in most cases the semantics is straightforward and standard. For instance, if the field is list-valued, we delegate differencing to an auxiliary function diffLists (not shown) which performs Longest Common Subsequence (LCS) differencing using reference equality. The interesting bit happens when differencing reference fields. References are compared via the matching M. Figure 8 highlights the relevant parts.

In order to know whether two references are "equal", diffNodes performs a reverse lookup in M on the reference in t_2. If the result of that lookup is different from the reference in t_1 the field needs to be updated. Recall that M was augmented to M' (cf. Fig. 6) to contain entries for all newly created model elements. As a result, the reverse lookup is always well-defined. Either we find an already existing element of t_1, or we find a element created as part of t_2.

4   Case Study: Derric

4.1   Implementation in RASCAL

We have implemented TMDIFF in RASCAL, a functional programming language for meta programming and a language workbench for developing textual Domain-Specific Languages (DSLs) [8]. The code for the algorithm, and the application to the example state machine language and the case study can be found on GitHub[3].

Since RASCAL is a textual language workbench [4] all models are represented as text, and then parsed into an abstract syntax tree (AST). Except for primitive values (string, boolean, integer etc.), all nodes in the AST are automatically annotated with source locations to provide basic origin tracking.

Source locations are a built-in data type in RASCAL (**loc**), and are used to relate sub-trees of a parse tree or AST back to their corresponding textual source fragment. A source location consists of a resource URI, an offset, a length, and begin/end and line/column information. For instance, the name of the closed state in Fig. 2 is labeled:

|project://textual-model-diff/input/doors1.sl|(22,6,<2,8>,<2,14>)

Because RASCAL is a functional programming language, all data is immutable. As a result graph-like structure cannot be directly represented. Instead we represent the containment hierarchy of a model as an AST, and represent cross-references by explicit relations **rel[loc** from, **loc** to], once again using source locations to represent object identities.

4.2   Differencing Derric File Format Descriptions

To evaluate TMDIFF on a real-life DSL and see if it computes reasonable deltas, we have applied it to the version history of *file format specifications*. These file

---

[3] https://github.com/cwi-swat/textual-model-diff.

format specifications are written in Derric, a DSL for digital forensics analysis [16]. Derric is a grammar-like DSL: it contains a top-level regular expression, specifying the binary layout of file formats. Symbols in the regular expression refer to *structures* which define the building blocks of a file format. Each structure, in turn has a number of field declarations, with constraints on length or contents of the field.

There are 3 kinds of semantic entities in Derric: the file format, structures, and fields. Inside the regular expression, symbolic names refer to structures. Structures themselves refer to other structures to express inheritance. Finally, field constraints may refer to fields defined in other structures or defined locally in the enclosing structure.

In an earlier study, the authors of [17] investigated whether Derric could accommodate practical evolution scenarios on Derric programs. This has resulted in a public Github repository, containing the detailed history of three file format descriptions, for GIF, PNG and JPEG[4].

For each description, we have applied TMDIFF on subsequent revisions, and compared the resulting edit scripts to the ordinary textual diffs produce by the Git version control system[5]. The results are shown in Table 1. The first three columns identify the file and the two consecutive revisions (Git hashes) that have been compared. Column 4, 5 indicate the number of lines added and removed, as computed by the standard diff tool used by Git. To approximate the relative size of the changes, column 6 shows the number of line additions and removals per line of code in the source revision. The following eight columns then show how often each of the edit operations occurred in the delta computed by TMDIFF. The results are summarized in the next three columns, showing the total number of operations, the percentage indicating the number of operations per original AST node, and the number of nodes literally built by the delta. The last column contains the log message to provide an intuition of the intent of the revision.

Table 1 shows that some operations actually were never computed by TMDIFF. For instance, there are no Delete operations. This can be explained from the fact that, indeed, all revisions involve adding elements to the file descriptions; nothing is actually ever deleted.

The operations SetPrim and SetRef did not occur either. The reason is that there are no revisions at that level of granularity. Most changes are additions of structures and/or fields, or changes to the sequence constraints of a file format. In both cases, references and primitives end up as part of InsertTree operations. An example is shown in Fig. 9. The left and right columns show fragments of two versions of the GIF file format. The only change is and additional optional element at the end of the **sequence** section. The delta computed by TMDIFF is shown at the bottom of the figure. It consists of a single InsertTree operation. Within the inserted tree, one finds actual references to the structures CommentExtension and DataBlock.

---

[4] https://github.com/jvdb/derric-eval.
[5] The actual command: `git diff --patience --ignore-blank-lines --ignore-all-space` R_1 R_2 *path*.

Table 1. Applying TMDIFF to revisions of derric fileformat specifications.

File	R_1	R_2	+lines	−lines	(+,−)/LOC (%)	#Create	#Delete	#InsertTree	#InsertRef	#Remove	#SetPrim	#SetRef	#SetTree	Total	#edits/#nodes (%)	#nodes ∈ Δ	Log message
gif.derric	fc43456	2c28d2a	2	2	2.8	1	0	0	1	2	0	0	1	5	1.2	8	Removed required value range on GraphicControlExtension.DisposalMethod.
	2c28d2a	a3cb744	2	2	2.8	0	0	1	0	1	0	0	0	2	0.5	12	Added optional GraphicControlExtension to initial CommentExtension subsequence.
	a3cb744	7cd6500	5	4	6.4	0	0	2	0	1	0	0	0	3	0.7	10	GraphicControlExtension is now optional in the main sequence.
	7cd6500	cd76b13	1	4	3.5	0	0	1	0	7	0	0	0	8	1.9	8	Removed last three fields from ApplicationExtension.
	cd76b13	46379ec	2	2	2.9	0	0	1	0	1	0	0	0	2	0.5	13	Added optional GraphicControlExtension to final CommentExtension subsequence.
	46379ec	d09ac40	2	2	2.9	0	0	1	0	1	0	0	0	2	0.5	1	Trailer is now optional.
	d09ac40	9b3f919	2	2	2.9	0	0	1	0	1	0	0	0	2	0.5	1	ZeroBlock is now optional in the main sequence.
	9b3f919	872cd67	2	1	2.2	0	0	1	0	0	0	0	0	1	0.2	2	Added optional CommentExtension subsequence with a single DataBlock and no ZeroBlock to main sequence.
png.derric	d71a7c4	3922516	22	2	17.1	10	0	0	1	5	1	0	10	27	7.8	32	Added private Macromedia (Adobe) Fireworks chunks prVW, mkBF, mkTS, mkBS and mkBT.
	3922516	f97370b	6	2	5.	2	0	1	1	1	0	0	2	7	1.8	8	Added vpAg structure.
	f97370b	3780274	6	2	4.9	2	0	1	1	1	0	0	2	7	1.8	8	Added oFFs structure.
	3780274	cc7f2f3	6	2	4.8	2	0	1	1	1	0	0	2	7	1.7	8	Added tpNG structure.
	cc7f2f3	7c32673	6	1	4.1	2	0	1	1	0	0	0	2	6	1.4	7	Added bBPn structure.
	7c32673	454152a	10	2	6.8	4	0	1	2	1	0	0	4	12	2.8	14	Added cmOD and cpIp structures.
	454152a	bdbf985	6	2	4.3	2	0	1	1	1	0	0	2	7	1.6	8	Added meTa structure.
	bdbf985	3caa428	6	2	4.2	2	0	1	1	1	0	0	2	7	1.5	8	Added eXIF structure.
	3caa428	6b0cca9	2	2	2.1	0	0	1	0	1	0	0	0	2	0.4	2	Modified sequence to allow the oFFs structure to occur after the bKGD structure.
	6b0cca9	ec33a53	2	2	2.1	0	0	1	0	1	0	0	0	2	0.4	2	Modified sequence to allow the bKGD to occur before the PLTE structure.
	ec33a53	fddce35	2	2	2.1	0	0	1	0	1	0	0	0	2	0.4	1	IEND is now optional.
	fddce35	20b63f0	6	2	4.1	2	0	1	1	1	0	0	2	7	1.5	8	Added gIFg structure.
	20b63f0	b8cd1d9	6	2	4.1	2	0	1	1	1	0	0	2	7	1.5	8	Added tpNG structure.
	b8cd1d9	f096d6c	6	2	4.	2	0	1	1	1	0	0	2	7	1.4	8	Added cmPP structure.
	f096d6c	cff3430	10	2	5.9	4	0	1	2	1	0	0	4	12	2.4	14	Added acTL and fcTL structures.
	cff3430	a691cde	2	2	1.9	0	0	1	0	1	0	0	0	2	0.4	2	Modified sequence to allow the vpAg to occur before the PLTE structure.
	a691cde	bdc85e9	6	2	3.8	2	0	1	1	1	0	0	2	7	1.4	8	Added pRVW structure.
	bdc85e9	399fb54	2	2	1.8	0	0	1	0	1	0	0	0	2	0.4	2	Modified sequence to allow the cmOD, cpIp and meTa structures to occur before the IDAT structure.
jpeg.derric	590a396	c1b3578	7	2	10.3	3	0	2	1	2	0	0	3	11	3.8	28	Added APP0Picasa.
	c1b3578	6ebbad4	2	2	4.3	0	0	2	0	2	0	0	0	4	1.3	18	Modified sequence to allow APP0JFXX to appear as first APP structure.
	6ebbad4	ef0329b	10	2	13.	5	0	2	1	2	0	0	5	15	4.9	37	Added APP14Adobe.
	ef0329b	d679520	10	2	12.	5	0	2	1	2	0	0	5	15	4.5	37	Added APP13Photoshop.
	d679520	fce26b3	2	2	3.7	0	0	2	0	2	0	0	0	4	1.1	19	The APP-only sequence is now optional.
	fce26b3	bbe0bf1	4	2	5.6	0	0	2	1	1	0	0	0	4	1.1	3	EOI is no longer required, but SOS is now required.
	bbe0bf1	13f1e56	4	3	6.4	2	0	3	1	3	0	0	2	11	2.9	23	Added SOF1 structure.
	13f1e56	6a8b0d7	14	8	19.8	5	0	6	4	11	0	0	5	31	7.9	65	Added 0xFF padding.
	6a8b0d7	acfab2d	5	3	6.8	2	0	3	1	3	0	0	2	11	2.3	59	Added SOF3 structure.
	acfab2d	712e583	7	1	6.7	2	0	3	1	1	0	0	2	9	1.8	47	Added COMElanGmk variant of COM.
	712e583	afb17f7	8	1	7.2	3	0	2	1	0	0	0	3	9	1.6	15	Added COMASC variant of COM.

The ratios of changes per total units of change (i.e. lines resp. AST nodes) show that TMDIFF deltas are consistently smaller that the ordinary textual deltas. It is also not the case that a single operation InsertTree operation replaces large parts of the model in one go. The before-last column shows that the number of nodes literally contained in a delta is reasonable. The largest number is 65 (fourth from below). As comparison, the average number of nodes across all revisions in Table 1 is 432.

Figure 10 shows a typical delta computed by TMDIFF on a Derric description. It involves adding a new structure (COMASC) and its two fields (length and data). They are initialized in three InsertTree operations. The last three operations wire the newly created elements into the existing model.

```
format gif d0               format gif
sequence                    sequence
  (Header87a Header89a)        (Header87a Header89a)
  LogicalScreenDesc           LogicalScreenDesc
  GraphicControlExtension?    GraphicControlExtension?
  (                           (
    [TableBasedImage CompressedDataBlock*]     [TableBasedImage CompressedDataBlock*]
    [PlainTextExtension DataBlock*]            [PlainTextExtension DataBlock*]
    [ApplicationExtension DataBlock*]          [ApplicationExtension DataBlock*]
    [CommentExtension DataBlock*]              [CommentExtension DataBlock*]
  )                           )
  ZeroBlock?                  ZeroBlock?
  (                           (
    [GraphicControlExtension?                  [GraphicControlExtension?
      TableBasedImage CompressedDataBlock*       TableBasedImage CompressedDataBlock*
      ZeroBlock]                                 ZeroBlock]
    [GraphicControlExtension?                  [GraphicControlExtension?
      PlainTextExtension DataBlock* ZeroBlock]   PlainTextExtension DataBlock* ZeroBlock]
    [ApplicationExtension DataBlock* ZeroBlock]  [ApplicationExtension DataBlock* ZeroBlock]
    [GraphicControlExtension? CommentExtension   [GraphicControlExtension? CommentExtension
      DataBlock* ZeroBlock]                      DataBlock* ZeroBlock]
  )*                          )*
  Trailer?                    [CommentExtension DataBlock]?
  ...                         Trailer?
CommentExtension d1  = ...    ...
DataBlock d2  = ...
```

d0.sequence[6] = Optional(Seq([d1, d2]))

Fig. 9. A minimal change to the sequence part of a Derric description of GIF. A single line is added on right (underlined). At the bottom the edit script computed by TMDIFF (between 9b3f919 and 872cd67)

```
format d4  jpeg          create Field d0
sequence                 create Field d1
  SOI                    create Term d2
  PADDING*               d0 = Field("data",[Exps([
  COMASC?                  Str("Created_by_AccuSoft_Corp."),
  ...                       Num(0)])])
                         d1 = Field("length",[Exps([d0]),
PADDING d5  = ...          Qualifier(Size(Num(2)))])
COM d3  = ...            d2 = Struct("COMASC",d3,[d1,d0])
                         d4.sequence[1] = Iter(d5)
COMASC d2  = COM {       d4.sequence[2] = Optional(d2)
  length d1 : lengthOf(data) size 2;   d4.structs[21] = d2
  data d0 : "Created by AccuSoft Corp.", 0;
}
```

Fig. 10. Fragment of revision afb17f7 of jpeg.derric (left, added lines are underlined), and the relevant part of the TMDIFF delta from revision 712e583 to afb17f7 (right).

5   Discussion and Related Work

The case-study of the previous section shows that TMDIFF computes reasonable deltas on realistic evolution scenarios on DSL programs. In this section we discuss a number of limitations of TMDIFF and directions for further research.

The matching of entities uses textual deltas computed by diff as a guiding heuristic. In rare cases this affects the quality of the matching. For instance, diff works at the granularity of a line of code. As a result, *any* change on a line defining a semantic entity will incur the entity to be marked as added. The addition of a single comment may trigger this incorrect behavior. Furthermore, if a single line of code defined multiple entities, a single addition or removal will trigger the addition of all other entities. Nevertheless, we expect entities to be defined on a single line most of the time.

If not, the matching process can be made immune to such issues by first pretty-printing a textual model (without comments) before performing the textual comparison. The pretty-printer can then ensure that every definition is on its own line. Note, that simply projecting out all definition names and performing longest common subsequence (LCS) on the result sequences abstracts from a lot of textual context that is typically used by diff-like tools. In fact, this was our first approach to matching. The resulting matching, however, contained significantly more false positives.

Another factor influencing the precision of the matchings is the dependence on the textual order of occurrence of names. As a result, when entities are moved around without any further change, TMDIFF will not detect it. We have experimented with a simple move detection algorithm to mitigate this problem, however, this turned out to be too computationally expensive. Fortunately, edit distance problems with moves are well-researched, see, e.g., [15]. A related problem is that TMDIFF will always see renames as an addition and removal of an entity. Further research is needed if renames of entities can be detected, for instance by matching up additions and removals of entities, where the deleted node and the added node are the same, modulo the renaming.

Much work has been done in the research area of model comparison that relates to TMDIFF. We refer to a survey of model comparison approaches and applications by Stephan and Cordy for an overview [14]. In the area of model comparison, *calculation* refers to identifying similarities and differences between models, *representation* refers to the encoding form of the similarities and differences, and *visualization* refers to presenting changes to the user [9,14]. Here we focus on the calculation aspect.

Calculation involves matching entities between model versions. Strategies for matching model elements include matching by (1) *static identity*, relying on persistent global unique entity identifiers; (2) *structural similarity*, comparing entity features; (3) *signature*, using user defined comparison functions; (4) *language specific algorithms* that use domain specific knowledge [14]. With respect to this list, our approach represents a new point in the design space: matching by textual alignment of names.

The differencing algorithm underlying TMDIFF is directly inspired by Alanen and Porres' seminal work [1]. The identification map M between model elements is explicitly mentioned, but the main algorithm assumes that model element identities are stable. Additionally, TMDIFF supports elements without identity. In that case, TMDIFF performs a structural diff on the containment hierarchy (see, e.g.,[20]).

TMDIFF's differencing strategy resembles the model merging technique used Ensō [18]. The Ensō "merge" operator also traverses a spanning tree of two models in parallel and matches up object with the same identity. In that case, however, the objects are identified using primary keys, relative to a collection (e.g., a set). This means that matching only happens between model elements at the same syntactic level of the spanning tree of an Ensō model. As a result, it cannot deal with "scope travel" as in Fig. 2c, where the locked state moved from the global state to the locking scope. On the other hand, the matching is more precise, since it is not dependent on the heuristics of textual alignment.

Epsilon is a family of languages and tools for model transformation, model migration, refactoring and comparison [10]. It integrates HUTN [13], the OMG's Human Usable Text Notation, to serialize models as text. As result, which elements define semantic identities is known for each textual serialization. In other words, unlike in our setting, HUTN provides a fixed concrete syntax with fixed scoping rules. TMDIFF allows languages to have custom syntax, and custom binding semantics.

6   Conclusion

Accurately differencing models is important for managing and supporting the evolution of models. Representing models as text, however, poses a challenge for model differencing algorithms, because the identity of model elements is not stable across revisions.

In this paper we have shown how this challenge could be addressed by constructing the mapping between model elements using origin tracking and traditional textual differencing. Origin tracking traces the identity of an element back to the symbolic name that defines it in the textual source of a model. Using textual differencing these names can be aligned between versions of a model. Combining the origin relation and the alignment of names is sufficient to identify the model elements themselves. It then becomes possible to apply standard model differencing algorithms.

Based on these techniques, we have presented TMDIFF, a fully language parametric approach to textual model differencing. A prototype of TMDIFF has been implemented in the RASCAL meta programming language [8]. The prototype was used to illustrate the feasibility of TMDIFF by reconstructing the version history of existing textual models. The models in question are file format descriptions in an independently developed DSL in the domain of in digital forensics [16].

Although the work presented in this paper shows promise, important directions for further research remain. First of all, it is unclear if the deltas produced by TMDIFF are on average smaller than the deltas produced by, for instance, EMFCompare [3], for languages which have scoping aligned with the containment hierarchy. Further evaluation should also include benchmarking the size and speed of differencing against a broader set of practical examples.

References

1. Alanen, M., Porres, I.: Difference and union of models. In: Stevens, P., Whittle, J., Booch, G. (eds.) UML 2003. LNCS, vol. 2863, pp. 2–17. Springer, Heidelberg (2003)
2. Brun, C., Pierantonio, A.: Model differences in the eclipse modeling framework. UPGRADE Eur. J. Inform. Prof. **9**(2), 29–34 (2008)
3. Eclipse Foundation: EMF Compare Project. https://www.eclipse.org/emf/compare/
4. Erdweg, S., et al.: The state of the art in language workbenches. In: Erwig, M., Paige, R.F., Van Wyk, E. (eds.) SLE 2013. LNCS, vol. 8225, pp. 197–217. Springer, Heidelberg (2013)
5. Eysholdt, M., Behrens, H.: Xtext: implement your language faster than the quick and dirty way. In: Proceedings of the ACM International Conference Companion on Object Oriented Programming Systems Languages and Applications Companion, OOPSLA 2010, pp. 307–309. ACM, New York (2010)
6. Goldschmidt, T., Becker, S., Uhl, A.: Classification of concrete textual syntax mapping approaches. In: Schieferdecker, I., Hartman, A. (eds.) ECMDA-FA 2008. LNCS, vol. 5095, pp. 169–184. Springer, Heidelberg (2008)
7. Inostroza, P., van der Storm, T., Erdweg, S.: Tracing program transformations with string origins. In: Di Ruscio, D., Varró, D. (eds.) ICMT 2014. LNCS, vol. 8568, pp. 154–169. Springer, Heidelberg (2014)
8. Klint, P., van der Storm, T., Vinju, J.: Rascal: a domain-specific language for source code analysis and manipulation. In: SCAM, pp. 168–177 (2009)
9. Kolovos, D.S., Di Ruscio, D., Pierantonio, A., Paige, R.F.: Different models for model matching: an analysis of approaches to support model differencing. In: ICSE Workshop on Comparison and Versioning of Software Models (CVSM 2009), pp. 1–6. IEEE (2009)
10. Kolovos, D.S., Paige, R.F., Polack, F.A.C.: The epsilon transformation language. In: Vallecillo, A., Gray, J., Pierantonio, A. (eds.) ICMT 2008. LNCS, vol. 5063, pp. 46–60. Springer, Heidelberg (2008)
11. Miller, W., Myers, E.W.: A file comparison program. Softw. Pract. Exper. **15**(11), 1025–1040 (1985)
12. Myers, E.W.: An $O(ND)$ difference algorithm and its variations. Algorithmica **1**(1–4), 251–266 (1986)
13. Rose, L.M., Paige, R.F., Kolovos, D.S., Polack, F.A.C.: Constructing models with the human-usable textual notation. In: Czarnecki, K., Ober, I., Bruel, J.-M., Uhl, A., Völter, M. (eds.) MODELS 2008. LNCS, vol. 5301, pp. 249–263. Springer, Heidelberg (2008)
14. Stephan, M., Cordy, J.R.: A survey of model comparison approaches and applications. In: MODELSWARD, pp. 265–277 (2013)
15. Tichy, W.F.: The string-to-string correction problem with block moves. ACM Trans. Comput. Syst. **2**(4), 309–321 (1984)

16. van den Bos, J., van der Storm, T.: Bringing domain-specific languages to digital forensics. In: ICSE 2011, ACM (2011). Software Engineering in Practice
17. van den Bos, J., van der Storm, T.: A case study in evidence-based DSL evolution. In: Van Gorp, P., Ritter, T., Rose, L.M. (eds.) ECMFA 2013. LNCS, vol. 7949, pp. 207–219. Springer, Heidelberg (2013)
18. van der Storm, T., Cook, W.R., Loh, A.: The design and implementation of object grammars. Sci. Comput. Program. **96**(4), 460–487 (2014). Selected Papers from the Fifth International Conference on Software Language Engineering (SLE 2012)
19. van Deursen, A., Klint, P., Tip, F.: Origin tracking. Symbolic Comput. **15**, 523–545 (1993)
20. Yang, W.: Identifying syntactic differences between two programs. Softw. Pract. Exper. **21**(7), 739–755 (1991)

CoWolf – A Generic Framework for Multi-view Co-evolution and Evaluation of Models

Sinem Getir[1]([⊠]), Lars Grunske[1], Christian Karl Bernasko[2],
Verena Käfer[2], Tim Sanwald[2], and Matthias Tichy[3]

[1] Reliable Software Systems, University of Stuttgart, Stuttgart, Germany
{sinem.getir,lars.grunske}@informatik.uni-stuttgart.de
[2] University of Stuttgart, Stuttgart, Germany
{st106732,swt74174,swt80243}@stud.uni-stuttgart.de
[3] University of Gothenburg, Gothenburg, Sweden
matthias.tichy@cse.gu.se

Abstract. Agile and iterative development with changing requirements lead to continuously changing models. In particular, the researchers are faced with the problem of consistently co-evolving different views of a model-based system. Whenever one model undergoes changes, corresponding models should co-evolve with respect to this change. On the other hand, domain engineers are faced with the huge challenge to find proper co-evolution rules which can be finally used to assist developers in the co-evolution process. In this paper, we introduce the CoWolf framework that enables co-evolution actions between related models and provides a tooling environment. Furthermore, we demonstrate the results of a case study on the developed tool.

Keywords: Model evolution · Multi-view modeling · Model co-evolution · Model synchronization · Model differencing · Quality of service models

1   Introduction

Models are a great aid to reduce the complexity of a software system so that analysis tools and humans can conceive it. Commonly, great parts of the program code are generated from domain specific models and analysis on performance, reliability and safety are completely done on separate models. Consequently, it is desirable to split the information into different views that are all specialized for a specific task allowing a well-founded theory on analysis methods and a rich tool infrastructure. This leads to the problem of co-evolving these different models, to keep them consistent when one of the models evolves over time. A solution to these problems is seen in incremental model transformation [2,9] and synchronization, a process that identifies changes done to a source model and which translates only these changes to the target models.

The CoWolf tool presented in this paper delivers a framework for model development, (incremental) model transformation and analysis. A special focus

© Springer International Publishing Switzerland 2015
D. Kolovos and M. Wimmer (Eds.): ICMT 2015, LNCS 9152, pp. 34–40, 2015.
DOI: 10.1007/978-3-319-21155-8_3

of CoWolf are probabilistic quality attributes like safety, reliability, and performance which CoWolf supports with a common environment with graphical and textual editors. Furthermore, it implements interfaces to external tools to analyse safety, reliability, and performance using the models. While there exist a couple of existing frameworks and approaches for incremental model transformations (see the surveys in [2,9]), our approach specifically addresses quality evaluation models.

2   The CoWolf Framework

CoWolf is an extensible framework for model evolution and co-evolution management and it has mainly two goals. The first goal is conducting the co-evolution process when one of the corresponding models undergoes changes. We denote these corresponding models as *couples*. Currently, CoWolf supports seven different types of models: state charts, component diagrams and sequence diagrams as architectural models; and discrete time markov chains (DTMC), continuous time markov chains (CTMC), fault trees, layered queuing networks (LQN) as QoS models. We use Henshin graph transformations [1] to accomplish the co-evolution process. Implemented transformations and their directions between couples from architectural and QoS models are presented in Fig. 1 (e.g. DTMC-CTMC or CTMC-fault tree are denoted as couples). While there exist bidirectional transformations between state charts and DTMCs, there exist unidirectional transformations from component diagram to fault trees.

The second goal is delivering utilities for the model-driven development and direct support for model analysis. During the continuous development of the models, CoWolf provides a common and user friendly environment with textual (Eclipse Xtext) and graphical editors (Eclipse Sirius) for different model types. Furthermore, it establishes interfaces to external tools to analyse models. In Fig. 1, we display the integrated model solvers to the corresponding QoS models. The tooling environment is enriched with the textual editors to represent the verification properties. Following that the developer can send the model to the analyser with one button.

CoWolf is an Eclipse plug-in designed to be highly extensible for new types of models. We demonstrate the architecture of the tool and used technologies in Fig. 2. In the following, we expand on the working principle of the CoWolf framework and illustrate with the *Stop Watch* example.

2.1   Co-evolution with CoWolf

In the following, we explain the transformation and model difference process in the background of CoWolf, and demonstrate the evolution of a running example afterwards.

Transformation Process. After identifying coupled models, we described Henshin rules between the couples and the rules for the single models. While the Henshin rules can be both manually created and auto-generated in the SiLift [7]

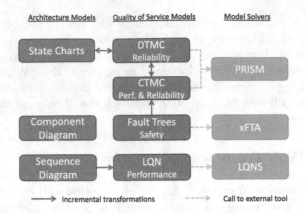

Fig. 1. Couples, transformations and model solvers supported by CoWolf

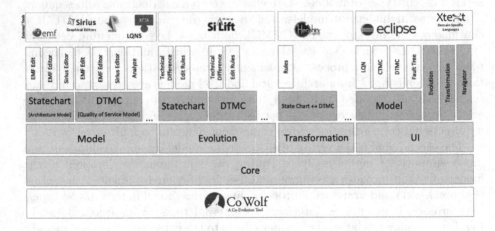

Fig. 2. CoWolf architecture

environment for a single model, the co-evolution rules should be created only manually since it requires mapping between the coupled model elements. Every co-evolution transformation is performed from a source model to a target model, which exposits the co-evolution direction. Defining the co-evolution transformations between the related models is not an easy task and requires domain knowledge. On the other hand, the effort describing the transformations differ from *couple* to *couple*. For example, transforming a state chart to a DTMC can be performed with one to one (assuming that we omit composite states) mapping considering the structure of the models. However, transformations are not straight forward between fault trees and component diagrams [5]. As a result, CoWolf does not claim fully automatic and complete transformations, but aims the utilization of the co-evolution process with user interaction.

When the user wants to apply the co-evolution between couples, the changes between the current version and the last version are calculated for the source model. If it is the first co-evolution between the models, the differences between an empty model and the current model are calculated. We use SiLift [7] for the model difference calculation. After the calculation, we perform the corresponding changes to the target model to accomplish the co-evolution. Note that there has to be a full set of rules for every possible change (predefined) in the source model to do a co-evolution. SiLift produces the difference output in the representation of Henshin rules, which makes the co-evolution process applicable in our framework. After the changes were detected, the rules can be applied and the target model can be co-evolved. There is a high amount of work in the background process. We refer the interested readers to the website http://cowolf.github.io/ for the details and the source code.

Running Example. We demonstrate a running example called *Stop Watch* in Fig. 3 in CoWolf's graphical editor, which enables a drag and drop facility of the model elements from the menu. The source model is a state chart and initially has three states with three transitions. When the user wants to apply a co-evolution, it is possible to have several target models for one source model. For instance in the menu, the user can select DTMC, CTMC as couple models of a state chart. In Fig. 3(a), assuming that the target model is selected as DTMC, we display the DTMC model generated from the state chart on the left side (complete transformations are applied). After the first co-evolution, the two models are now connected with the facility of EMF trace links and if a change happens in the initial model, an out-of-date-warning is shown for the target model. At some point of time, the state chart evolves as shown in Fig. 3(b). A new state *Lap* and its transitions are added to the watch system, and one transition is deleted. The changes are calculated by SiLift, whose output is also visible in CoWolf environment by the user when requested. Based on the corresponding changes, the DTMC co-evolves with incremental transformations. As shown in Fig. 3(c), the applied transformations generate the DTMC with a similar structure with the state chart (topology of the states and transitions). On the other side, the model is incomplete because of the parameters (e.g. transition probabilities), therefore the user interaction is needed for valid models.

Extending CoWolf. CoWolf can be extended for new types of models (new metamodels) with its flexible architecture (Fig. 2). For this, the developer needs to provide four artifacts: (1) Metamodels of the coupled models (2) Henshin rules for the single models to detect changes between two instances (manually created or auto-generated in SiLift environment) (3) Henshin rules for the co-evolutions and (4) a GUI. We refer the readers to https://github.com/CoWolf/CoWolf for the details of the architecture.

2.2   Integrated Model Solvers

Besides the incremental transformation of models, CoWolf is also capable of measuring quality aspects of models. For this, we implemented a user friendly interface to the external solvers for the corresponding QoS models. As presented in Fig. 1, CoWolf supports evaluation over DTMC, CTMC, LQN and fault trees

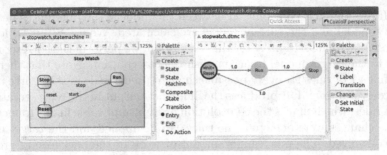

(a) The initial state chart and the co-evolved DTMC

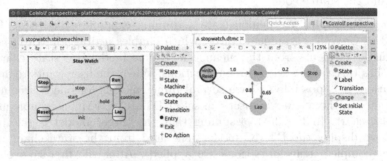

(b) The state chart and DTMC model after the second co-evolution

Fig. 3. A co-evolution from state chart to DTMC in CoWolf

via PRISM [8], LQNSolver [3] and Xfta [11] respectively. The solvers produce analysis results (e.g. measurement and prediction) for availability, performance and safety attributes of the system. With this feature of CoWolf, developers do not have to fully understand the modelling language of the external model solvers (e.g. Prism grammar or Open-PSA script in Xfta) and can run the analysis from CoWolf directly. The developer then only needs to set the properties and trigger the analysis button on the selected model. However, the analysis steps differ from model to model. For example, a fault tree analysis is always performed on the top event in the model. On the other hand, a CTMC model requires property description in PCTL. CoWolf produces a solution for property specification by enabling the user to write the properties in an Xtext textual editor whose design was inspired by ProProST tool [6], being therefore capable of generating the full PCTL.

In the background, whenever the analysis is triggered, CoWolf transforms the model to the language supported by the solver (e.g. Prism) and executes the evaluation with the selected model solver. Afterwards, CoWolf receives and parses the results from the tools and presents them in an Eclipse view. When requested, exporting the models in the language of the external tools is also possible.

3   Evaluation

We evaluate the CoWolf framework on a standard automation case study called Pick & Place Unit (PPU) [10]. The Pick&Place unit has four main components: storage, crane, stamp and sorter, which stores, conveys, processes and sorts the work pieces on the platform respectively. The system has 14 predefined evolution steps (12 of 14 scenarios are system's reliability relevant) and all the steps have different affects on various types of models. We perform co-evolution actions between state charts and the corresponding DTMCs and compare the incremental transformations, which are executed with the co-evolution process, and complete transformations as demonstrated in Fig. 4. While complete transformations run the full set of rules from the scratch at every step, incremental transformations run only the required rules whenever any change occurs in one of the models to maintain the multi-view consistency.

In Fig. 4(a) we present the comparison in terms of the execution time. In general, co-evolution actions are faster than the execution of complete transformation. However at steps such as 4, 5 and 9, the co-evolution process takes much longer than the complete transformation. The reason for this is the calculation of the difference between the models in addition to the execution of the incremental transformations. We observe in the evolution steps that the changes between 3–5 and 8–9 are much bigger compared to the other steps. As aforementioned, we use an external tool (SiLift) to calculate the model differences. Therefore, we provide the second evaluation by only evaluating the number of rules executed with incremental transformations in Fig. 4(b) to support this argument. The number of rules to be executed with incremental transformation is apparently significantly lower than the number of rules to be executed with the complete transformations as expected.

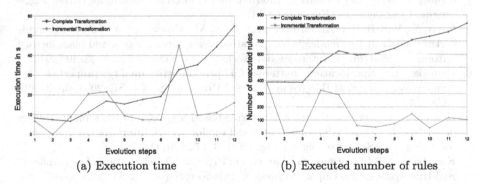

(a) Execution time   (b) Executed number of rules

Fig. 4. Performance comparison between incremental and complete transformations for each step

4   Conclusion

Domain engineers are faced with big challenges to manage co-evolution in multi-view model based systems. In this paper, we have introduced an extensible framework for co-evolution and model analysis to assist the developers. CoWolf is an open source project for the community and extensible for any kind of model. Since it is generic, plug-in based and includes SiLift, we would like to integrate a co-evolution analysis [4] to improve the co-evolution actions between the models as a future work.

Acknowledgments. This work is supported by the DFG (German Research Foundation) under the Priority Programme SPP1593: Design For Future - Managed Software Evolution. The authors would like to thank Christian Karl Bernasko, Manuel Borja, Verena Käfer, David Krauss, Michael Müller, Philipp Niethammer, Tim Sanwald, Jonas Scheurich, David Steinhart, Rene Trefft, Johannes Wolf and Michael Zimmermann for their great work in the CoWolf development.

References

1. Arendt, T., Biermann, E., Jurack, S., Krause, C., Taentzer, G.: Henshin: advanced concepts and tools for in-place EMF model transformations. In: Petriu, D.C., Rouquette, N., Haugen, Ø. (eds.) MODELS 2010, Part I. LNCS, vol. 6394, pp. 121–135. Springer, Heidelberg (2010)
2. Etzlstorfer, J., Kusel, A., Kapsammer, E., Langer, P., Retschitzegger, W., Schoenboeck, J., Schwinger, W., Wimmer, M.: A survey on incremental model transformation approaches. In: Proceedings of the Workshop on Models and Evolution Co-located with ACM/IEEE 16th International Conference on Model Driven Engineering Languages and Systems, pp. 4–13 (2013)
3. Franks, G., Maly, P., Woodside, M., Petriu, D.C., Hubbard, A.: Layered queueing network solver and simulator user manual. Carleton University, Department of Systems and Computer Engineering (2005)
4. Getir, S., Rindt, M., Kehrer, T.: A generic framework for analyzing model co-evolution. In: Model Evolution, International Conference on Model Driven Engineering Languages and Systems (2014)
5. Getir, S., Van Hoorn, A., Grunske, L., Tichy, M.: Co-evolution of software architecture and fault tree models: an explorative case study on a pick and place factory automation system. In: International Workshop on NIM-ALP, pp. 32–40 (2013)
6. Grunske, L.: Specification patterns for probabilistic quality properties. In: Schäfer, W., Dwyer, M.B., Gruhn, V. (eds.) Proceedings of ICSE, 2008, pp. 31–40. ACM (2008)
7. Kehrer, T., Kelter, U., Taentzer, G.: A rule-based approach to the semantic lifting of model differences in the context of model versioning. In: International Conference on Automated Software Engineering, pp. 163–172 (2011)
8. Kwiatkowska, M., Norman, G., Parker, D.: PRISM 4.0: verification of probabilistic real-time systems. In: Gopalakrishnan, G., Qadeer, S. (eds.) CAV 2011. LNCS, vol. 6806, pp. 585–591. Springer, Heidelberg (2011)
9. Leblebici, E., Anjorin, A., Schürr, A., Hildebrandt, S., Rieke, J., Greenyer, J.: A comparison of incremental triple graph grammar tools. ECEASST 67 (2014)
10. Legat, C., Folmer, J., Vogel-Heuser, B.: Evolution in industrial plant automation: a case study. In: Proceedings of IECON 2013. IEEE (2013)
11. Rauzy, A.: Anatomy of an efficient fault tree assessment engine. In: Virolainen, R. (ed.) Proceedings of PSAM'11/ESREL'12 (2012)

Reuse and Industrial Applications

Enabling the Reuse of Stored Model Transformations Through Annotations

Javier Criado[1]([⊠]), Salvador Martínez[2], Luis Iribarne[1], and Jordi Cabot[2,3]

[1] Applied Computing Group, University of Almeria, Almería, Spain
{javi.criado,luis.iribarne}@ual.es
[2] AtlanMod Team (Inria, Mines Nantes, LINA) Nantes, Nantes, France
{salvador.martinez_perez,jordi.cabot}@inria.fr
[3] ICREA - UOC, Barcelona, Spain
jcabot@uoc.edu

Abstract. With the increasing adoption of MDE, model transformations, one of its core concepts together with metamodeling, stand out as a valuable asset. Therefore, a mechanism to annotate and store existing model transformations appears as a critical need for their efficient exploitation and reuse. Unfortunately, although several reuse mechanisms have been proposed for software artifacts in general and models in particular, none of them is specially tailored to the domain of model transformations. In order to fill this gap, we present here such a mechanism. Our approach is composed by two elements (1) a new DSL specially conceived for describing model transformations in terms of their functional and non-functional properties (2) a semi-automatic process for annotating and querying (repositories of) model transformations using as criteria the properties of our DSL. We validate the feasibility of our approach through a prototype implementation that integrates our approach in a GitHub repository.

1 Introduction

Model-to-model (M2M) transformations play a key role in Model-Driven Engineering (MDE) by providing the means to automatically derive new modeling artifacts from existing ones. With the increasing adoption of MDE, these model transformations, difficult to produce as they require not only mastering the transformation tools but also domain specific knowledge, become valuable assets. Consequently, M2M transformations should be described, defined, constructed and then stored in the richest possible manner so that the functional and non-functional properties of each of the implemented transformation operations are easier to identify and query. This is a critical requirement for an efficient exploitation and reuse of the model transformations assets (or some parts of them) when facing similar manipulation tasks.

Unfortunately, although some transformation languages and frameworks provide some reuse facilities like inheritance, imports or Higher-Order Transformations (HOTs) [20] (even if largely unused [14]), they lack mechanisms for

© Springer International Publishing Switzerland 2015
D. Kolovos and M. Wimmer (Eds.): ICMT 2015, LNCS 9152, pp. 43–58, 2015.
DOI: 10.1007/978-3-319-21155-8_4

describing and/or storing information about the inherent properties of model transformations. This makes it difficult to find later the right transformation for the problem at hand unless we dig into the transformation code ourselves to carefully analyze what it does and how it does it [2]. This is specially true considering there are few public M2M transformation repositories (exceptions would be the ATL model transformation ZOO [1] or ReMoDD [5]).

As an example, a very common transformation use case is the translation from *class diagram* models to *relational* models. Being so popular, anybody requiring a transformation between these two domains should easily find an existing transformation to reuse. Even for the concrete case of ATL, a search for a *class to relational* transformation on the Internet yields thousands of results ranging from very minimal ones to complex versions using inheritance between transformations rules. Nevertheless, each variation implies a different trade-off on the properties of the generated relational model, e.g. different transformation strategies can be followed to deal with inheritance (see Fig. 1). While the first strategy could be better for space optimization requirements, the second and third versions improve the maintainability in different degrees. Therefore, beyond its functionality, specific requirements for the task at hand (e.g. having the goal of space optimization) must be considered when choosing the transformation.

Therefore, we believe that a mechanism to facilitate the annotation and search of the transformations in a public repository would be an important step forward towards the reuse of model transformations. Once these annotated repositories are available, a user different from the original transformation developer would be able to select and reuse a transformation (or reuse parts of it) based on its requirements or objectives.

In this paper we propose such mechanism. It is composed by two main elements: (1) a Domain-Specific Language (DSL) to describe functional but also non-functional properties of M2M transformations; (2) a process to semi-automatically tag model transformation with information conforming to our DSL and to query repositories storing these annotated transformations. Functional properties can be calculated in many cases through an static analysis of the transformation code but non-functional properties may require subjective quality metrics or manual analysis in order to be determined.

We demonstrate the feasibility of our approach by developing a prototype implementation specially tailored for ATL [8], including a process to store and query transformations annotated with our DSL in a public GitHub repository. However, we would like to remark that this prototype could be easily extended to deal with other similar rule-based transformation languages like QVT [17], ETL [13] or RubyTL [4] as our approach remains language-independent.

The rest of the paper is structured as follows. Section 2 describes our solution approach. In Sect. 3, our DSL for describing model transformations is detailed while Sect. 4 defines the process to annotate existing transformations and constitute repositories with rich search capabilities. Section 5 provides details about our prototype implementation and Sect. 6 discusses related work. Finally, Sect. 7 presents conclusions and future work.

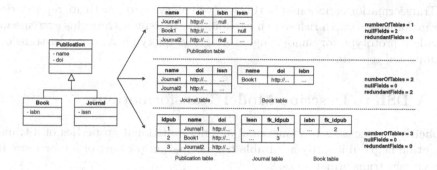

Fig. 1. An example of domain-dependent properties

2 Approach

In order to tackle the aforementioned problems, we propose an approach composed by two main steps (see Fig. 2):

1. A Domain-Specific Language for the description of functional and non functional properties of implemented model transformation. This DSL, which will be further detailed in Sect. 3, is independent from the concrete transformation language. Therefore, it can be used to annotate transformations written in different transformation languages. Along with its abstract syntax, we propose a default catalogue of properties ready-to-use for rule-based model transformations and textual and graphical concrete syntaxes.
2. A semi-automatic process for annotating and reusing existing transformation. This step starts by annotating a given transformation (to be stored) with attributes from a model instance of our proposed DSL. Then, the transformation is stored in a repository of choice. Finally, and transparently to the user, a search engine provides the user with the capability of using the OCL query language to search for model transformations fulfilling a set of given requirements.

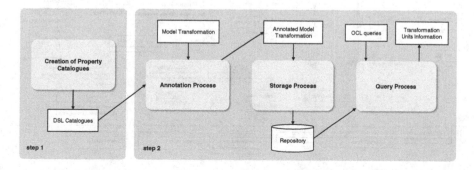

Fig. 2. Annotation and retrieval approach

Transformations annotated in this way will allow us to constitute repositories of transformations with rich search capabilities. To demonstrate this extreme we provide a prototype for annotating, storing and querying ATL model transformations and repositories.

3   A DSL to Describe Model Transformations

Explicitly representing the functional and non-functional properties of a transformation helps to identify a suitable transformation (or part of it) for reuse in a given new transformation task.

In order to allow a precise definition of those properties we have developed a new DSL that allows us to describe properties about a *Transformation unit*, i.e., about a `Module`, or about the `Rules` composing it from a predefined `Catalogue` of properties that can be evolved depending on the transformation domain.

In the following we will provide a detailed description of the abstract syntax of our language, a default catalogue to be used for starting annotate rule-based model transformations out of the box and a concrete syntax for (1) visualizing the annotations and (2) integrate them in transformations languages with textual concrete syntax.

3.1   DSL Specificaton: Abstract Syntax

The metamodel of our DSL is shown in Fig. 3. The main metaclasses are:

Catalogue Metaclass: With the aim of giving more flexibility to the property description and instantiation, we propose to define the properties making use of *Catalogues* instead of hard-wiring a fixed set of properties in the metamodel

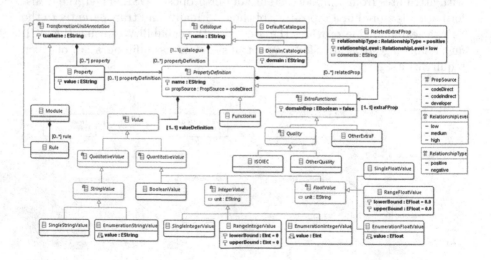

Fig. 3. DSL for describing model transformation properties

itself. Moreover, the catalogues offer (1) a common vocabulary to describe the possible properties which can be annotated and, (2) a common space for the agreement of model transformation developers.

Therefore, the DSL allows us to create domain-independent or dependent catalogues. The first type is used to describe the properties common to all domains while the second type is intended to describe the properties that are only relevant to a particular domain.

For instance, in an example scenario of transformation from a *Class Diagram* to a *Relational* model, there are different transformation strategies for the inheritance relationship (see in Fig. 1). In this sense, it could be useful to define some functional properties specific of this domain, such as the number of tables, the number of "null" fields, or the number of redundant fields generated by the transformation units and some non-functional properties such as maintainability.

Properties: Each catalogue contains a number of *Property* definitions. The *propSource* attribute defines who is responsible for creating the property. A property may be instantiated by an automatic process (calculating its value directly or indirectly from the code), or manually by the developer.

Each property definition is associated with a *Value* definition, which can be qualitative (*Qualitative Value*) or quantitative (*Quantitative Value*). Qualitative definitions can be a single value or an enumeration of string values. Quantitative definitions can be boolean, integer or float. Integer and float types can be instantiated as a single value, a range of values, or an enumeration of values.

Once we have created the catalogues with the property definitions, we can define annotations for transformation modules or rules. Note that each annotation can be related to a property value, but this value must be established according to the property definition of a catalogue.

Non-Functional Properties: Our DSL differentiates between *Functional* (e.g. number of input models, number of helpers, or coverage of target metamodels) and *Non-functional* properties.

As an example, Table 1 lists some non-functional properties defined for ATL transformations but any other property could be adapted as well, e.g. "testability" and "installability" can also be added to our DSL. The former could be used to describe if there exist test models associated with a transformation whereas the "installability" quality attribute could be used to identify if the transformation is implemented in a stable version of the transformation language, if the package references are related with integrated URIs or some packages should be registered previously, etc.

Additionally, we classify *non-functional* properties in two different subtypes. *Quality* related properties or *Other* non-functional properties (e.g. developer name, developer affiliation, or last update) information. Note that within the set of possible *Quality* attributes, we also distinguish between ISO/IEC 25000 (e.g. understandability, reusability, or modifiability) properties, i.e., properties defined in the standard, and *Other quality* properties (e.g. stability, reliability of the developer, or level of updating) not belonging to it.

Relation Between Properties: Functional and Non-functional *properties* can affect the value of related *Non-Functional* properties. In order to represent this relation, a *PropertyDefinition* can contain a collection of *RelatedExtraProperty* definitions describing to which extra-functional *Properties* is related with.

This description can specify a *Type* (positive or negative), a *Level* (low, medium or high), and some *Comments* to this relationship. For example, we can define a functional property named as "ratioOfHelpers" with type "positive" linked (with level "low") to an extra-functional property representing "reusability". This link indicates that this value of the first property has a positive and low effect on the second one. We can also define a extra-functional property named as "understandability" with type "positive" linked (with level "high") to another extra-functional property named as "modifiability", indicating the positive high effect of the first property on the second one.

Table 1. Examples of quality attributes (extracted from [22] and [21])

Property	Description
Understandability	Defines how easy or difficult is to comprehend a model transformation. Negative relationship with the number of input models, output models, unused helpers, or elements per output pattern
Modifiability	Describes how much effort is needed to change a model transformation. Negative relationship with the number of input models, output models, unused helpers, or calls to `resolveTemp()` operations
Completeness	Indicates if the transformation covers all the elements of the input and output models. Positive relationship with coverage of input/output metamodels. Negative relationship with the number of input/output models, unused helpers, or parameters per called rule
Consistency	Describes how coherent and stable is the transformation. Positive relationship with coding convention, number of helpers, or calls to `oclIsUndefined()`. Negative relationship with the number of called rules, calls to helpers, or calls to `oclIsTypeOf()`
Conciseness	Indicates if the transformation is brief and directed to the solution. Positive relationship with number of helpers, rule inheritance, or imported libraries. Negative relationship with the number of input/output models, unused helpers, or the number of called rules
Reusability	Defines if the transformation or some rules could be reused. Positive relationship with number of helpers or imported libraries. Negative relationship with non-lazy matched rules, called rules, or rules with filter

3.2 DSL Specification: Domain-Independent Catalogue

In order to facilitate the adoption of our DSL, we provide a ready-to-use default domain-independent catalogue. This catalogue can be imported when creating a new annotation model for a given transformation. Note that although this catalogue is based on properties and metrics defined for the ATL transformation language [21], it can be reused for other transformation languages just by adapting the metric calculation process to each specific case.

In this sense, we provide the following list of functional and non-functional properties for ATL transformations: *number of input models, number of output models, number of input patterns, ratio of helpers, number of calls to resolveTemp, ocl expression complexity, understandability, modifiability, reusability, completeness, performance, author* and *last update*. As we mentioned, our DSL allows us to establish the value definition for each property. In addition, we can also represent relations between properties. For example, the value definition of the functional property *numberOfInputModels* has been created as a single integer value, and this property is related to three non-functional properties (*understandability, modifiability* and *reusability*) with type *negative* and level *high*.

Note that, as described above, we can also build reusable catalogues for concrete transformation domains. As an example, for the transformation domain of *Class Diagram* to *Relational* models, we have selected three functional properties: *ratio of tables, ratio of null fields* and *ratio of redundant fields*; and 2 non-functional properties: *maintainability* and *storage performance*. These properties arise from the three different transformation strategies depicted in Fig. 1. For example, the second transformation strategy of Fig. 1 has a *medium* value for *ratioOfTables* property, a *low* value for *ratioOfNullFields* and a *high* value for *ratioOfRedundantFields*.

3.3 DSL Specification: Concrete Syntax

Our DSL is intended to be used as an annotation language integrated with existing model transformation languages. As in the vast majority of cases model transformation languages use textual syntaxes as concrete syntax, we propose here a simple textual syntax for our DSL. The grammar of our proposed textual syntax is provided in Listing 1.1.

Basically, our textual syntax allows us to produce annotations that identify the transformation module or rule by name and assign to it couples of properties and the corresponding values (identifying also the catalogue containing the definition of the property as it will help the understandability of the annotation).

As an example, we show an ATL transformation module and a contained rule in Listing 1.2. The rule is annotated with two properties, the ratio of tables functional property with the value of normal (and identifying it as a domain-specific property defined in the catalogue of the Class2Relational domain) and the understandability non-functional property with the value of medium.

Listing 1.1. DSL Grammar

```
Module returns Module:
    rule += Rule*
    '@module' tuaName=EString
    property+=Property*;

Rule returns Rule:
    '@rule' tuaName=EString
    property+=Property*;

Property returns Property:
    '@property' propertyName=EString '=' value=EString
    '(catalogue = ' catalogueName=EString ')';

EString returns ecore::EString:
    STRING | ID;
```

Note that, for simplicity, our annotation language has been integrated in the ATL transformation language by using tags inside comments, which allows us to perform the integration without changing the grammar of the host language. Nevertheless, it would be possible to integrate our annotation language as native tags of the language, which could provide some advantages like syntax highlighting, etc.

Listing 1.2. ATL Class2Relational rule

```
--@module Class2Relational
--@property understandability = medium (catalogue = DefaultCatalogue)
--@property ratioOfTables = normal (catalogue =
    ↪Class2RelationalCatalogue)
--@property reusability = low (catalogue = DefaultCatalogue)
module Class2Relational;
create OUT : Relational from IN : Class;

--@rule Class2Table
--@property understandability = medium (catalogue = DefaultCatalogue)
--@property ratioOfTables = normal (catalogue =
    ↪Class2RelationalCatalogue)
rule Class2Table {
    from
        c : Class!Class
    to
        out : Relational!Table (
            name <- c.name,
            col <- Sequence {key}->union(c.attr->
                select(e | not e.multiValued)),
            key <- Set {key}
        ),
        key : Relational!Column (
            name <- 'objectId',
            type <- thisModule.objectIdType
        )
}
```

Additionally, as graphical information is often easier to grasp at a glance than textual one, we also provide a graphical syntax for our language. In Sect. 5, we show this concrete graphical syntax.

4 Annotating and Searching Model Transformations

We describe in this section the process of annotating existing transformation with models conforming to our DSL and the process of then querying already annotated

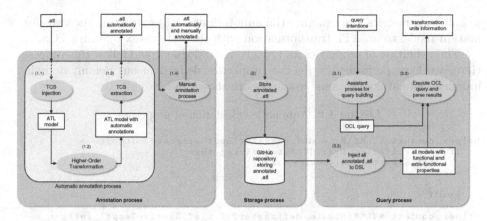

Fig. 4. Process for annotating model transformations and its applications

model transformations. This process is summarized in Fig. 4. Note that the steps 1.1 to 1.4 depend on the transformation language at hand (although the process for others languages will be similar) while the steps 2 to 3.3 are independent of the language.

4.1 Semi-automatic Annotation

The annotation process that we describe here is semi-automatic: (1) functional and non-functional properties that can be derived/extracted from the code itself (including the environment information, like metamodels, etc.) are calculated in an automatic way, and (2) properties that need to be evaluated by a developer are filled manually.

In the case of properties that can be directly derived or extracted from the source code of the transformation (including information about input/output metamodels and models, or about the internal structure of each rule) we have chosen to use Higher-Order Transformations. The uniformity and flexibility of the model-driven paradigm allow us to make use of the same transformation infrastructure to develop the model transformation and the annotation process, since model transformations can be translated into transformation models and be given as objects to a different class of model transformations [20]. The calculation of these properties is based on metrics defined in previous work [21,22].

Note that this process requires having access to the internal structure of the model transformation. Consequently, the concepts of *Module* and *Rule* in our DSL are meant to be linked to the corresponding elements of the metamodel of the transformation language in hand. In the case of ATL, we have linked these concepts to the *Module* and *Rule* concepts of the ATL metamodel so that we are able to inspect all the functional features of the ATL transformation.

Basically, the process of automatically annotating an ATL model transformation follows three steps (see Fig. 4): (1.1) injecting the transformation code to a transformation model by using TCS [9]; (1.2) using a HOT transformation to calculate metrics and generate the annotations; (1.3) extracting the transformation model to an ATL transformation with textual syntax by using TCS.

The definition of properties for any given catalogue would follow this process. Here, we have performed it for the properties defined in our default domain-independent catalogue. Some examples are shown in Listing 1.3.

Listing 1.3. Automatic calculation of properties

```
helper context ATLMM!Rule def:numberOfInputPatterns():Integer =
    if self.oclIsKindOf(ATLMM!MatchedRule) then
        self.inPattern.elements->size()
    else
        0
    endif;

helper context ATLMM!Module def:numberOfCallsToResolveTemp():Integer =
    ATLMM!OperationCallExp->allInstances()->select(oce |
    oce.operationName = 'resolveTemp')->size();

helper context ATLMM!OclExpression def:oclExpComplexity():Integer =
    if(self.oclIsTypeOf(ATLMM!OperatorCallExp))then
        self.oclOperatorCallExpComplexity()
    else
        if(self.oclIsTypeOf(ATLMM!IfExp)) then
            self.oclIfExpComplexity()
        else
            if(self.oclIsTypeOf(ATLMM!LoopExp)) then
                self.oclLoopExpComplexity()
            else
                0
            endif
        endif
    endif;
```

Note that, although some non-functional properties can be derived from the functional information, the intervention of a developer is still necessary for fully documenting model transformations. In this sense, a manual annotation process can be performed by using the textual and the graphical concrete syntax, so that a developer can inspect existing properties and add new ones.

4.2   Queries

In this subsection, we show how our DSL annotations enable rich searching. Our main goal is to be able to query the information from the metadata that have been included into the annotated model transformations (step 3.3. of Fig. 4). This part of the process is completely independent of the transformation language since it relies only on the property annotations and general information about the transformation.

Querying Individual Transformations: Given a single transformation, the process of querying it to check its functional and non functional properties requires injecting the textual representation of the transformation into a model corresponding to our DSL (with preimported and loaded instances of the catalogue/s used to annotate the transformation). Once this model is available, standard OCL queries can be used to retrieve the desired information. For example, the query shown below corresponds to an operation performed on a *module* transformation unit (`self` in the code) that lists all the properties with all their values of a specific rule.

```
self.rule->select(r | r.tuaName = 'Rule1').property->
  collect(p | Tuple{name = p.propertyDefinition.name, value = p.value})
```

Querying Repositories of Transformations: Given a repository of anno-tated transformations, the process of querying it to retrieve transformation units with specific properties requires: (1) executing the previously described injec-tion step for each transformation in the repository and (2) the construction of an index model (this index model, which can be considered equivalent to a megamodel, contains links to instance models of our DSL). It is automatically generated in the step 3.2 of Fig. 4, and it contains links to models created with our DSL.

Once the index model is available, we can use OCL queries over it in order to make rich searches over the repository (step 3.3 in Fig. 4). We can also obtain some information about functional and non-functional properties along with information represented by the transformation models (*e.g.*, metamodels cov-erage or rule structure). Therefore, many different queries can be performed in order to obtain: rules with a specific value (or value range) of a requested property, modules that have some annotations related to an application domain, catalogue properties which are used more often than others, etc.

For example, the following OCL query could be used for obtaining the trans-formation units (modules in this example) in the index model (TUAIndex) that transform UML class diagram models to relational database models.

```
TUAIndex!Index->select(t | t.oclIsTypeOf(tuaproperties::Module))
  ->select(m |m.moduleRef.oclAsType(atl::Module).inModels
  ->exists(inm | inm.metamodel.name = 'ClassDiagram') and
  m.moduleRef.oclAsType(atl::Module).outModels
  ->exists(outm | outm.metamodel.name = 'Relational'))
```

Then, over this collection, it is possible to find which of these selected trans-formation units have annotations about the *ratioOfTables* property with a *low* value and about the *understandability* property with a *high* value.

```
collection->select(t | t.property
  ->exists(p1, p2 | p1.propertyDefinition.name = 'ratioOfTables'
  and p1.value = 'low'
  and p2.propertyDefinition.name = 'understandability'
  and p2.value = 'high'))
```

Note that a library of frequently used OCL queries can be provided in top of our approach in order to simplify the search tasks of developers. Moreover, once the transformations are integrated in an index model, it would be possible to use other query facilities over it, or use other existing infrastructures for the management of megamodels as MoScript [11].

5   Tool Support

In order to validate the feasibility of our approach, here we describe an Eclipse-based prototype implementation (http://acg.ual.es/tua) that includes the cre-ation of textual and graphical editors for our DSL, the adaptation of our DSL to connect it to ATL transformations, the enhancement of the generated *ecore* editor, and facilities for the integration with GitHub and for query execution.

5.1 DSL and Editors

The metamodel shown in Sect. 3 is adapted to the case of ATL in the following way: (1) `Module` elements are linked to the Global Model Management metamodel for ATL [3], in order to store information about input/output metamodels, input/output models, etc. (2) `Rule` elements are connected with the ATL metamodel to represent the internal structure of each rule (type, input/output patterns, conditions, OCL expressions, etc.).

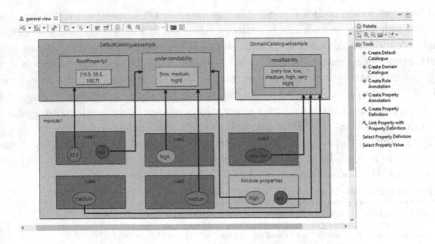

Fig. 5. Snapshot of the graphical editor for our DSL

As discussed in Sect. 3, we have provided textual and graphical syntaxes for our DSL. Editors for these syntaxes are provided by using the Eclipse Xtext[1] and Sirius[2] tools, respectively.

The default generated editors have been modified to assist in the definition of property and annotation values. This helps to create and visualize together the catalogue property definitions, the property annotations, and the relations between properties and property definitions (see Fig. 5). "Recommended" values are automatically represented in green whereas the "not recommended" values are represented in red, and the neutral ones in blue. Finally, our tool allows the user to define OCL queries to search in the repository for transformations (or rules) based on their functional and non-functional properties.

---

[1] https://eclipse.org/Xtext/.

[2] http://eclipse.org/sirius/.

5.2   Integration in GitHub

In order to facilitate the adoption of our annotation approach, we have decided to use a GitHub project as the repository for annotated model transformations. This way, annotated model transformations will be directly stored in GitHub (step 2 in Fig. 4) while a service will be put in place in order to allow the utilization of the metadata. Concretely, we have used the existing Eclipse plugin for "git", which permits the synchronization of the repository with our workspace. Then, from the obtained ATL transformations, we execute an operation in charge of injecting the annotated transformations into the transformation and annotation models (Fig. 6). The "git" plugin also allows us to upload new annotated transformations, commit modifications or perform update proposals.

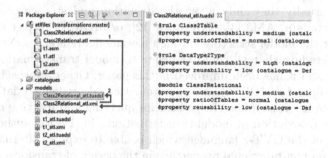

Fig. 6. Inject all annotated transformations from GitHub

Using a GitHub repository for storing the annotated model transformations has some remarkable benefits: (a) it offers a well-known environment that makes very easy to upload or modify transformations, independently of the transformation language, via pull requests; (b) it provides an API to execute basic queries about the stored files, about the contributing users or about other metadata; (c) it gives a tracking system of the problems that may arise in the development of model transformations (through the use of "issues"); (d) it includes the possibility of reviewing the code by adding annotations anywhere in the transformation files; (e) it offers a display of the branches to check the progress and versions of model transformations; and (f) it gathers a lot of information about each user's participation in the development and improvement of the transformations.

This repository is also intended to store the catalogues of properties developed by the community, encouraging the reuse and the collaborative improvement of these elements. However, this kind of repository has some shortcomings. Our repository is intended to store only ATL files, so we must manage the upload operations and limit the repository tracking by using a ".gitignore" configuration file. In addition, GitHub does not implement a specific functionality for managing models or model transformations. Thus, if we want to perform some kind of merge or comparison operation (as our query operations), we have to implement it into a tool or a service outside the repository.

6 Related Work

Storing and searching source code of general purpose languages for reuse is a subject largely studied in the software engineering community. Recent contributions include [18] where the authors present a search approach for retrieving code fragments based on code semantics, [15] where the search is specified by using test cases, or [16] focused on the relation between relevant retrieved functions.

Similar to them, our approach allows us to query the repository for appropriate transformation code fragments. However, we follow a different approach. By storing annotated transformations we take advantage of domain-specific knowledge to perform more complex and complete searches.

Regarding the use of repositories for storing model transformations, most of the existing approaches are focused on the management and storage of models and usually they only allow the definition and storage of very basic structural metadata. AM3 [3], EMFStore [12], or MORSE [6] just store information about the model structure through metamodel references. Nevertheless, the global metadata that [3] could associate to model transformation artifacts is interesting and it has been improved in this paper. Other approaches such as ModelCVS [10] and AMOR [2] extract automatic and predefined data from the metamodels to use it as a knowledge base for querying and merging operations.

As for the description of model transformations, in [19] the authors present an extension of the QVT-r language which is able to express alternatives (and their impact on non-functional properties) in the design of transformations. The concept of quality-driven model transformations is also addressed in [7] where design guides are proposed to define model transformations with "alternatives" based on non-functional properties. Our approach applies these ideas to the problem of model transformation reuse where the alternatives can come from different independent sources.

7 Conclusions and Future Work

We have presented a new DSL specially conceived for describing existing model transformation in terms of their functional and non-functional properties. This DSL along with a semi-automatic annotation process facilitates the reusability of model transformations by enabling the capability of searching for transformation artifacts fulfilling the requirements of a given developer.

As a future work, we would like to explore how our DSL can be used to search for combinations of transformations that may be chained to solve a transformation problem for which a direct transformation is not available Another improvement would be to associate the annotations with weaving models [3] in addition to model transformations. We also intend to reuse existing algorithms for qualitative analysis in goal-oriented requirements engineering to help choose the best possible transformation when none is a perfect match for the designer's goal. At the tool level, we plan to improve the edition and definition of the annotations including code-completion and syntax compilation features as well.

Acknowledgments. This work was funded by the EU ERDF and the Spanish MINECO under Project TIN2013-41576-R, the Spanish MECD under a FPU grant (AP2010-3259), and the Andalusian Regional Government (Spain) under Project P10-TIC-6114.

References

1. The ATL Transformation ZOO. http://www.eclipse.org/atl/atlTransformations/
2. Altmanninger, K., Kappel, G., Kusel, A., Retschitzegger, W., Seidl, M., Schwinger, W., Wimmer, M.: Amor-towards adaptable model versioning. In: 1st International Workshop on Model Co-Evolution and Consistency Management, in Conjunction with MODELS, vol. 8, pp. 4–50 (2008)
3. Bézivin, J., Jouault, F., Rosenthal, P., Valduriez, P.: Modeling in the large and modeling in the small. In: Aßmann, U., Akşit, M., Rensink, A. (eds.) MDAFA 2003. LNCS, vol. 3599, pp. 33–46. Springer, Heidelberg (2005)
4. Cuadrado, J.S., Molina, J.G., Tortosa, M.M.: RubyTL: a practical, extensible transformation language. In: Rensink, A., Warmer, J. (eds.) ECMDA-FA 2006. LNCS, vol. 4066, pp. 158–172. Springer, Heidelberg (2006)
5. France, R.B., Bieman, J., Cheng, B.H.C.: Repository for model driven development (ReMoDD). In: Kühne, T. (ed.) MoDELS 2006. LNCS, vol. 4364, pp. 311–317. Springer, Heidelberg (2007)
6. Holmes, T., Zdun, U., Dustdar, S.: Morse: a model-aware service environment. In: APSCC 2009, pp. 470–477. IEEE (2009)
7. Insfran, E., Gonzalez-Huerta, J., Abrahão, S.: Design guidelines for the development of quality-driven model transformations. In: Petriu, D.C., Rouquette, N., Haugen, Ø. (eds.) MODELS 2010, Part II. LNCS, vol. 6395, pp. 288–302. Springer, Heidelberg (2010)
8. Jouault, F., Allilaire, F., Bézivin, J., Kurtev, I.: Atl: a model transformation tool. Sci. Comput. Program. **72**(1), 31–39 (2008)
9. Jouault, F., Bézivin, J., Kurtev, I.: TCS: a DSL for the specification of textual concrete syntaxes in model engineering. In: GCPE 2006, pp. 249–254. ACM (2006)
10. Kappel, G., Kapsammer, E., Kargl, H., Kramler, G., Reiter, T., Retschitzegger, W., Schwinger, W., Wimmer, M.: On models and ontologies - a semantic infrastructure supporting model integration. In: Modellierung 2006, 22.-24. März 2006, Innsbruck, Tirol, Austria, Proceedings, pp. 11–27 (2006)
11. Kling, W., Jouault, F., Wagelaar, D., Brambilla, M., Cabot, J.: MoScript: a DSL for querying and manipulating model repositories. In: Sloane, A., Aßmann, U. (eds.) SLE 2011. LNCS, vol. 6940, pp. 180–200. Springer, Heidelberg (2012)
12. Koegel, M., Helming, J.: EMFStore: a model repository for EMF models. In: ICSE 2010, pp. 307–308. ACM (2010)
13. Kolovos, D.S., Paige, R.F., Polack, F.A.C.: The epsilon transformation language. In: Vallecillo, A., Gray, J., Pierantonio, A. (eds.) ICMT 2008. LNCS, vol. 5063, pp. 46–60. Springer, Heidelberg (2008)
14. Kusel, A., Schönböck, J., Wimmer, M., Retschitzegger, W., Schwinger, W., Kappel, G.: Reality check for model transformation reuse: The atl transformation zoo case study. In: AMT@ MoDELS (2013)
15. Lemos, O.A.L., Bajracharya, S.K., Ossher, J., Morla, R.S., Masiero, P.C., Baldi, P., Lopes, C.V.: Codegenie: using test-cases to search and reuse source code. In: ASE 2007, pp. 525–526. ACM (2007)
16. McMillan, C., Grechanik, M., Poshyvanyk, D., Xie, Q., Fu, C.: Portfolio: finding relevant functions and their usage. In: ICSE 2011, pp. 111–120. IEEE (2011)

17. OMG. Meta Object Facility (MOF) 2.0 Query/View/Transformation Specification, Version 1.1, January 2011
18. Reiss, S.P.: Semantics-based code search. In: ICSE 2009, pp. 243–253. IEEE (2009)
19. Solberg, A., Oldevik, J., Aagedal, J.Ø.: A framework for QoS-aware model transformation, using a pattern-based approach. In: Meersman, R. (ed.) OTM 2004. LNCS, vol. 3291, pp. 1190–1207. Springer, Heidelberg (2004)
20. Tisi, M., Jouault, F., Fraternali, P., Ceri, S., Bézivin, J.: On the use of higher-order model transformations. In: Paige, R.F., Hartman, A., Rensink, A. (eds.) ECMDA-FA 2009. LNCS, vol. 5562, pp. 18–33. Springer, Heidelberg (2009)
21. van Amstel, M.F., van den Brand, M.: Using metrics for assessing the quality of ATL model transformations. In: MtATL 2011, vol. 742, pp. 20–34 (2011)
22. Vignaga, A.: Measuring atl transformations. MaTE. Department of Computer Science, Universidad de Chile, Technical report, Technical report (2009)

Reusable Model Transformation Components with bentō

Jesús Sánchez Cuadrado$^{(\boxtimes)}$, Esther Guerra, and Juan de Lara

Modelling and Software Engineering Research Group,
Universidad Autónoma de Madrid, Madrid, Spain
jesus.sanchez.cuadrado@uam.es
http://www.miso.es

Abstract. Building high-quality transformations that can be used in
real projects is complex and time-consuming. For this reason, the ability
to reuse existing transformations in different, unforeseen scenarios is very
valuable. However, there is scarce tool support for this task.

This paper presents bentō, a tool which supports the development and
execution of reusable transformation components. In bentō, a reusable
transformation is written as a regular ATL transformation, but it uses
concepts as meta-models. Reuse is achieved by binding such concepts to
meta-models, which induces the transformation adaptation. Moreover,
composite components enable chaining transformations, and it is possible
to convert an existing transformation into a reusable component. Bentō
is implemented as an Eclipse plug-in, available as free software.

Keywords: Model transformation · Transformation reuse · Components · ATL

1 Introduction

Model transformation technology is the enabler of automation in Model-Driven
Engineering (MDE), allowing model refactorings, optimizations, simulations and
language conversions. However, developing a transformation from scratch is complex and error prone, even when specialized languages are used [6]. Thus, the
reuse of existing high-quality transformations should be fostered, to amortize
the effort invested in their development. One way to achieve this goal is to
develop reusable transformation libraries, as it is common with general-purpose
languages (e.g., ready to use Java libraries packaged as a .jar).

There are different reuse approaches for model transformations, ranging from
reusing single rules (e.g., rule inheritance [12]) to reusing complete transformations (e.g.,superimposition [11] or phasing [7]). However, most are type-centric,
in the sense that a transformation cannot be reused for meta-models different
from the ones used by the original transformation, thus limiting the reuse possibilities. There are some exceptions though, like [8] and [10], which use model
subtyping and genericity respectively to define more reusable transformations.

© Springer International Publishing Switzerland 2015
D. Kolovos and M. Wimmer (Eds.): ICMT 2015, LNCS 9152, pp. 59–65, 2015.
DOI: 10.1007/978-3-319-21155-8_5

Other approaches [1] rely on transformation repositories and meta-model match and comparison techniques. However, they do not provide mechanisms to make transformations more reusable. Altogether, reuse of transformations is scarce in practice, as concluded in [3].

In the last few years, we have developed a transformation reuse approach inspired by generic programming [9] (e.g., templates in the C++ style) that we have implemented in a tool called bentō. The tool allows the definition of transformation components consisting of a transformation template, one or more concepts/meta-models, and a description of the component using a dedicated domain-specific language (DSL). *Concepts* are used as a means to describe the struc-

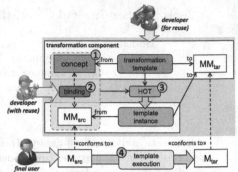

Fig. 1. Component instantiation

tural requirements that a meta-model needs to fulfil to allow the instantiation of the component with the meta-model. In particular, to instantiate the component for a meta-model, a binding mapping the concept elements to concrete meta-model elements (i.e., classes and features) should be written using another DSL. This binding adapts the transformation template to yield a new transformation ready to use with the concrete meta-model. Figure 1 shows this process. In addition, composite components permit combining simpler components using transformation chaining.

Our approach has advantages w.r.t. existing proposals: (i) it is more flexible, since it permits applying components for meta-models that are structurally very dissimilar to the concept; (ii) it does not require adapting the bound meta-models and their instance models, but our template rewriting approach generates a new transformation that can be readily applied to them, improving performance; (iii) no special traceability handling is needed; and (iv) our component model allows the precise description of components and provides a systematic way of reuse.

The aim of this tool-demo paper is to describe the architecture of bentō and its features from the perspective of the tool user. A summary of the concrete demo presented at the conference is available online[1]. The concepts behind the component model underlying bentō have been reported elsewhere [4,5]. Nevertheless, the tool has been improved since its first versions with new features such as support for in-place transformations, validation, integration with a static analyser [6][2], and a REST-based repository to store and retrieve components.

Paper Organization. Section 2 overviews bentō's architecture, and the following ones show its main use cases: developing reusable components (Sect. 3), reusing components (Sect. 4), making a reusable component out of an existing

---

[1] Summary of the demo: http://www.miso.es/tools/bento_demo_icmt2015.pdf.
[2] ANATLYZER: http://www.miso.es/tools/anATLyzer.html.

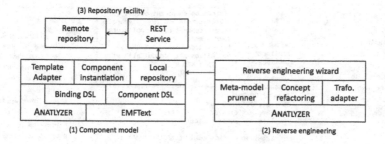

Fig. 2. bentō architecture

Table 1. Features of bentō

Dimension	bentō feature	Description
Abstraction	Concept	Plain Ecore meta-model with optional annotations
Specialization	Binding	A DSL to map concepts and meta-models
	Template adaptation	HOT to rewrite a template according to a binding
	Binding validator	It validates the syntactic correctness of bindings
Selection	Tags, documentation	Markdown documentation and attached tags
	Repository	REST-based repository and search wizard
	Existing artefacts	Reverse engineering process supported by a wizard
Integration	Component definition	A DSL to define components and their dependencies
	Standard structure	Structure and local installation of components
	Composite components	Aggregated components

transformation (Sect. 5), and selecting components (Sect. 6). Section 7 finishes with the conclusions and future work.

2 Tool Architecture

Bentō is an Eclipse-plugin. Its architecture, depicted in Fig. 2, consists of a component model, a reverse engineering wizard, and a remote repository facility. Implementation-wise, the two main elements of the component model are ANAT-LYZER to statically analyse ATL transformations, and the *Template Adapter* which is able to solve non-trivial heterogeneities between concepts and meta-models (see Sects. 3 and 4). The DSLs to specify components and bindings has been defined using EMFText. In addition, bentō includes a reverse engineering wizard to convert an existing transformation into a reusable component (see Sect. 5), and a REST-based repository to share components (see Sect. 6).

As stated by Krueger [2], the practical use of components should consider four dimensions: abstraction, specialization, selection and integration. Table 1 summarizes the features of bentō according to these dimensions.

3 Developing Components

As a running example, let us consider the visualization of object-oriented models by means of a transformation to the DOT format. This transformation will be

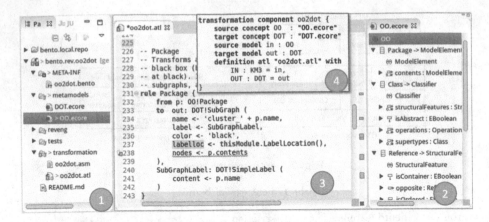

Fig. 3. Definition of component in bentō

similar for a range of object-oriented languages such as Ecore, KM3, UML or even Java. Hence, we create a reusable transformation component called oo2dot that can be specialized for such languages.

A transformation component is made of a transformation template, one or more concepts or meta-models over which the template is defined, and a description of the component. This is shown in Fig. 3. These artefacts are organized according to the structure shown in (1). In this case, the transformation has a source concept (OO.ecore) and a target meta-model (DOT.ecore). A concept is just a regular Ecore meta-model (2), but it only contains the elements required by the transformation, thus removing "accidental elements" for this particular scenario like configuration attributes (e.g., transient in Ecore) or features that we do not intend to visualize (e.g., annotations in Ecore). The transformation template is a regular ATL transformation. Moreover, bentō uses ANATLYZER to statically analyse the transformation templates in order to provide some guarantee of their correctness, as illustrated by the error markers in (3). The component specification, shown in (4), describes the inputs and outputs of the transformation, since it is a single component.

Components can be exported to a remote component repository using the Eclipse export menu (see more details in Sect. 6).

4 Reusing Components

In order to instantiate a component for a concrete meta-model, the component must be specialized by defining a binding from the elements in the concept to elements of the meta-model. Figure 4(1) shows part of the binding from the OO concept to the Ecore meta-model. The binding is used to automatically rewrite the original template, so that it becomes able to transform models conforming to the bound meta-model. A distinguishing feature of our tool is that it allows sophisticated adaptations that bridge many heterogeneities between the concept and the meta-model. This is possible due to the precise typing information gathered by ANATLYZER. A detailed account of the binding features and solvable heterogeneities is given in [4].

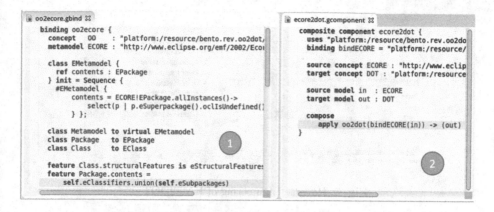

Fig. 4. Binding and composite component definition in bentō

Figure 4(2) shows how to instantiate and execute a component. We need to define a composite component which imports the component to instantiate (oo2dot) and the binding, and uses the apply command to adapt the component according to the binding and execute it on the given source/target models. Composite components also support sequencing components to create transformation chains.

5   Reverse Engineering Existing Transformations

To enable the reuse of existing ATL transformations, bentō provides a reverse engineering facility that converts a transformation whose meta-models are "hard-coded" into a concept-based transformation component. This facility uses ANAT-LYZER to statically determine the elements of the original meta-models that the transformation does not use, and then, it extracts a concept where such elements are pruned. In the process, a set of automated or manual refactorings can be applied to improve the quality of the extracted concept, which may imply the automatic co-evolution of the transformation.

From the user perspective, there is a wizard to configure the process, apply refactorings and automatically generate the component specification.

In the running example, instead of developing the oo2dot transformation from scratch, we could convert the KM32DOT transformation available in the ATL transformation zoo into a reusable component. This transformation has 418 LOC, 18 helpers and 7 rules; thus, its reuse saves a lot of effort. Figure 5 shows the wizard to configure the conversion, which includes links to guide the steps to perform.

6   Selecting Components

The ability to search and select components is important in any reuse approach, being typically enhanced by concise abstractions that can be easily understood

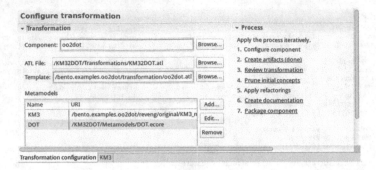

Fig. 5. Reverse engineering of KM32DOT

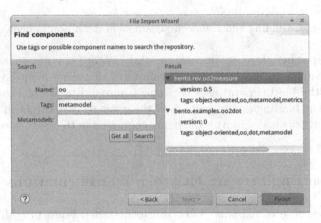

Fig. 6. Searching the repository by name and tags

and compared [2]. In our case, given a transformation component, it is easy to examine its concepts (i.e., its interface) to decide whether they match the meta-models at hand.

In addition, to facilitate the publication and retrieval of components, we have implemented a simple REST service to publish and search components. Components may have tags attached, which can be used in the search. Once a component is selected, it is automatically installed in a local project (bento.local.repo) and can be referenced by other projects using the URI bento:/componentName. When a component uses a URI of this kind, if the corresponding component has not already been installed, it is automatically sought in the remote repository by name. This feature is akin to *Maven* dependency resolution, and is intended to facilitate the maintenance of composite components. Figure 6 shows the Eclipse import wizard to search and install components.

7   Conclusions

In this paper, we have presented bentō, a tool supporting model transformation components. It includes features like flexible template adaptations, reverse engineering of existing transformations into reusable components, a REST-based repository and component validations. To the best of our knowledge, this is the first component model for model transformations.

Bentō is available as free software (http://github.com/jesusc/bento) and as a ready to install Eclipse-plugin (http://www.miso.es/tools/bento.html).

Currently, Java programs can be packaged as bentō components, but these cannot be adapted. We are working on the possibility to package and adapt other MDE artefacts as bentō components, like Acceleo generators.

Acknowledgements. This work was supported by the Spanish Ministry of Economy and Competitivity with project Go-Lite (TIN2011-24139), the R&D programme of the Madrid Region with project (SICOMORO S2013/ICE-3006), and the EU commission with project MONDO (FP7-ICT-2013-10, #611125).

References

1. Basciani, F., Di Ruscio, D., Iovino, L., Pierantonio, A.: Automated chaining of model transformations with incompatible metamodels. In: Dingel, J., Schulte, W., Ramos, I., Abrahão, S., Insfran, E. (eds.) MODELS 2014. LNCS, vol. 8767, pp. 602–618. Springer, Heidelberg (2014)
2. Krueger, C.W.: Software reuse. ACM Comput. Surv. **24**, 131–183 (1992)
3. Kusel, A., Schönböck, J., Wimmer, M., Kappel, G., Retschitzegger, W., Schwinger, W.: Reuse in model-to-model transformation languages: are we there yet? In: SoSyM (2013)
4. Sánchez Cuadrado, J., Guerra, E., de Lara, J.: A component model for model transformations. IEEE Trans. Softw. Eng. **40**(11), 1042–1060 (2014)
5. Sánchez Cuadrado, J., Guerra, E., de Lara, J.: Reverse engineering of model transformations for reusability. In: Di Ruscio, D., Varró, D. (eds.) ICMT 2014. LNCS, vol. 8568, pp. 186–201. Springer, Heidelberg (2014)
6. Sánchez Cuadrado, J., Guerra, E., de Lara, J.: Uncovering errors in ATL model transformations using static analysis and constraint solving. In: 25th IEEE ISSRE, pp. 34–44 (2014)
7. Sánchez Cuadrado, J., Molina, J.G.: Modularization of model transformations through a phasing mechanism. SoSyM **8**(3), 325–345 (2009)
8. Sen, S., Moha, N., Mahé, V., Barais, O., Baudry, B., Jézéquel, J.-M.: Reusable model transformations. SoSyM **11**(1), 111–125 (2010)
9. Stepanov, A., McJones, P.: Elements of Programming. Addison Wesley, Reading (2009)
10. Varró, D., Pataricza, A.: Generic and meta-transformations for model transformation engineering. In: Baar, T., Strohmeier, A., Moreira, A., Mellor, S.J. (eds.) UML 2004. LNCS, vol. 3273, pp. 290–304. Springer, Heidelberg (2004)
11. Wagelaar, D., Straeten, R.V.D., Deridder, D.: Module superimposition: a composition technique for rule-based model transformation languages. SoSyM **9**(3), 285–309 (2010)
12. Wimmer, M., Kappel, G., Kusel, A., Retschitzegger, W., Schönböck, J., Schwinger, W., Kolovos, D.S., Paige, R.F., Lauder, M., Schürr, A., Wagelaar, D.: Surveying rule inheritance in model-to-model transformation languages. JOT **11**(2), 1–46 (2012)

Cost-Effective Industrial Software Rejuvenation Using Domain-Specific Models

Arjan J. Mooij[1]([⊠]), Gernot Eggen[3], Jozef Hooman[1,2],
and Hans van Wezep[3]

[1] Embedded Systems Innovation by TNO, Eindhoven, The Netherlands
{arjan.mooij,jozef.hooman}@tno.nl
[2] Radboud University Nijmegen, Nijmegen, The Netherlands
[3] Philips Healthcare, Best, The Netherlands
{gernot.eggen,hans.van.wezep}@philips.com

Abstract. Software maintenance consumes a significant and increasing proportion of industrial software engineering budgets, only to maintain the existing product functionality. This hinders the development of new innovative features with added value to customers. To make software development efforts more effective, legacy software needs to be rejuvenated into a substantial redesign. We show that partially-automated software rejuvenation is becoming feasible and cost-effective in industrial practice. We use domain-specific models that abstract from implementation details, and apply a pragmatic combination of manual and automated techniques. We demonstrate the effectiveness of this approach by the rejuvenation of legacy software of the Interventional X-ray machines developed by Philips Healthcare.

1 Introduction

Software maintenance is crucial to keep up with technology developments such as technology changes (e.g., the shift from single-core to multi-core processors) and technology obsolescence (e.g., the phasing out of the Microsoft Windows XP operating system). Embedded software is often reused in product lines that are developed over a long period of time, but maintaining the existing functionality consumes an increasing proportion of software engineering budgets. This hinders the development of new innovative features with added value to customers.

In industrial practice, it is often considered too costly and risky to make changes to much of the software. As a consequence, software changes are often made by adding workarounds and wrappers to the legacy software. This increases the technical debt [3], such as the size and incidental complexity of the code base, thus making future development even more costly and risky.

Developers usually understand that, sooner or later, legacy software must be rejuvenated to a redesign with a long-term focus; gradual refactoring [10] is not enough. However, a rejuvenation is typically postponed by individual projects due to the time, risks and costs involved. Manual green-field redesign projects often finish too late, require significant additional resources, and are

© Springer International Publishing Switzerland 2015
D. Kolovos and M. Wimmer (Eds.): ICMT 2015, LNCS 9152, pp. 66–81, 2015.
DOI: 10.1007/978-3-319-21155-8_6

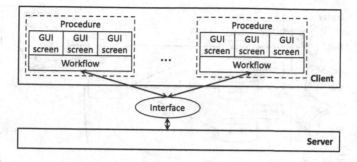

Fig. 1. Software structure of field service procedures for interventional X-ray

difficult to combine with the short-term innovation needs in highly-dynamic businesses.

In this paper we show that partially-automated software rejuvenation is becoming feasible and cost-effective in industrial practice. We demonstrate this using our experiences with the field service procedures of the International X-ray machines developed by Philips Healthcare. The used approach is based on domain-specific models and a pragmatic combination of techniques.

Overview. Sect. 2 introduces the industrial case. The approach is described in Sect. 3, followed by details about reverse engineering in Sect. 4 and forward engineering in Sect. 5. Afterwards, Sect. 6 treats the industrial verification. Section 7 discusses related work, and Sect. 8 draws some conclusions.

2   Industrial Rejuvenation Case

Philips Healthcare develops a product line of interventional X-ray machines. Such machines are used for minimally-invasive cardiac, vascular and neurological medical procedures, such as placing a stent via a catheter. Surgeons are guided by real-time images showing the position of the catheter inside the patient.

The calibration and measurement of the X-ray beams is performed by field service engineers. The machines support their work using an integrated collection of interactive field service procedures. These procedures are based on a workflow, in which some steps are automatically performed by the system, and other steps require manual input or action from the service engineers.

2.1   Legacy Software

The software for the field service procedures is structured based on a common separation between user interface and logic; see Fig. 1. For each procedure, the client consists of one workflow and a collection of screens of a graphical user interface (GUI). Each screen consists of a number of GUI elements. The server provides the logic for the automated workflow steps. As depicted at the left-hand side of Fig. 2, the client is implemented using:

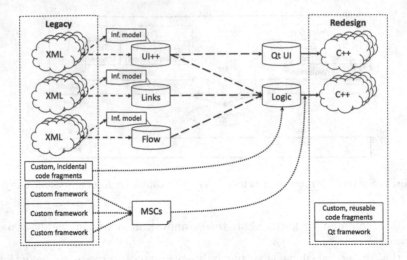

Fig. 2. Rejuvenation chain for the client software from Fig. 1

- three types of XML [2] configuration files (210 kLOC)
- custom, incidental fragments of C# code (10 kLOC)
- stack of custom C++ frameworks (1240 kLOC)

The frameworks are procedure independent and extended over many years. Each specific procedure is configured using the following XML files:

- for each GUI screen, 1 XML file with the static structure (i.e., the placement of GUI elements on the screen) and dynamic behavior (i.e., what should happen if buttons are pressed, items are selected, etc.);
- 1 XML file with links between GUI elements and server identifiers;
- 1 XML file with the workflow and references to associated GUI screens.

The XML files are edited using textual editors, which is time consuming and error prone; see also [9]. The incidental fragments of C# code are procedure specific and are used as workarounds for some framework limitations.

2.2   Rejuvenation Goal

The goal of Philips Healthcare for the rejuvenation of the client software is to make the creation and maintenance of field service procedures more efficient. In particular, there is a wish to eliminate the XML configuration files, and to reduce the large amount of custom framework code (which also needs to be maintained).

The rejuvenated software should be based on well-maintainable C++ code, and off-the-shelf components for common aspects like GUI elements. The main constraint is that the server logic should not be affected by the rejuvenation.

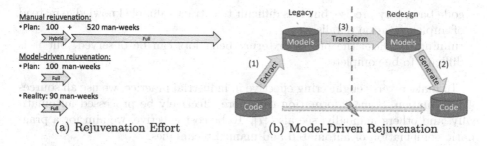

(a) Rejuvenation Effort   (b) Model-Driven Rejuvenation

Fig. 3. Rejuvenation of field service procedures

2.3 Business Case

Philips Healthcare continuously develops new innovations for their products. One of these ongoing developments has an impact on the implementation of the field service procedures. However, experienced developers from Philips Healthcare gave high effort estimations for making the required modifications. To make this manageable, the original plan was to divide them over two manual projects; see Fig. 3(a). The first project takes 100 man-weeks and creates a hybrid solution that fits the new technologies with minimal effort. However, this is a typical workaround solution that increases the incidental complexity. The second project takes 520 man-weeks, and should establish the full rejuvenation.

Based on a model-driven approach (see Sect. 3), we have jointly estimated that the full rejuvenation can be completed in the time that was originally planned for the hybrid solution alone (100 man-weeks). As a result the desired rejuvenation could be combined with a regular development project. Thus a strong cost-effective [12] business case has been made for the rejuvenation.

In industry, rejuvenation projects have the reputation of finishing too late. This project took approximately 90 man-weeks over a period of 1 year. It has been carried out by 1 researcher from TNO and 2 developers from Philips, all working 75 % of their time on this project.

3 Rejuvenation Approach

The rejuvenation approach that we have used is based on three principles. These range from using multiple information sources and extraction techniques, via the use of domain-specific models, to an incremental way-of-working.

3.1 Combination of Information Sources and Techniques

There are various valuable sources of information about legacy software:

- documentation: human-readable descriptions and diagrams, but usually incomplete and outdated;
- developers: undocumented insights and rationales, but the original developers may not be available;

- code base: very precise, but it is difficult to extract valuable knowledge instead of implementation details;
- running software: the precise external behaviors can be observed, but it is difficult to be complete.

To make reverse engineering effective in industrial practice, we use all sources of information. Some information can more effectively be processed automatically, and others manually; see also [7]. To be cost-effective, we aim for a pragmatic combination of automated and manual techniques.

Reverse engineering of code cannot be fully automated [15]. A particular challenge is to distinguish valuable domain-specific knowledge from implementation details. However, users may have started to rely on certain undocumented implementation decisions in the legacy software.

3.2 Domain-Specific Models

Legacy software was usually developed using traditional methods where the initial development stages focus on informal, natural-language documents. Only in the implementation stage, formal artifacts like code are developed [6]. Currently, software can be developed based on models that focus on the valuable business rules. The implementation details are hidden in code generators.

We build a rejuvenation chain that follows the three steps from Fig. 3(b). (1) The first step is to *extract* (Sect. 4) the valuable business rules from the available information sources, and store them in domain-specific models that abstract from implementation details. (2) The second step is to create a model-driven development environment that can *generate* (Sect. 5.2) the redesigned software from redesigned domain-specific models. (3) The last step in our approach is to *transform* (Sect. 5.3) the extracted models into the generation models.

The used domain-specific models and techniques should be tailored to the specific application domain. The extract and generate steps (including the associated models) can be developed in parallel. The transform step links these models, and hence should be developed afterwards. This order helps to avoid that the rejuvenated software resembles the legacy software too much. Such a model-driven approach is now becoming feasible, because of the improved maturity of tools for model-driven software engineering.

3.3 Incremental Approach

The rejuvenation of legacy software requires a large development effort. In our experience it is important to quickly show successful results to all stakeholders, including higher management, system architects and the developers involved. An incremental way-of-working is pivotal in this respect; see also [8,14,18].

In our industrial case, the natural dimension for an incremental approach is the collection of supported procedures. We have addressed procedures in the following order:

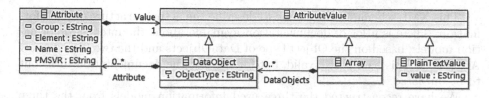

Fig. 4. Schema for all XML files

```
<DataObject ObjectType="PanelProperties">
    <Attribute Group="0x3001" Element="0x652c" PMSVR="IInt16">5</Attribute>
    <Attribute Name="XPosition" Group="0x3001" Element="0x7600" PMSVR="IInt16">0</Attribute>
    <Attribute Name="YPosition" Group="0x3001" Element="0x7601" PMSVR="IInt16">145</Attribute>
    <Attribute Name="Height" Group="0x3001" Element="0x7602" PMSVR="IInt16">35</Attribute>
    <Attribute Name="Width" Group="0x3001" Element="0x7603" PMSVR="IInt16">60</Attribute>
    <Attribute Name="TabOrder" Group="0x3001" Element="0x7609" PMSVR="IInt16">2</Attribute>
    <Attribute Name="LayerType" Group="0x3001" Element="0x77d1" PMSVR="IString">"Data"</Attribute>
</DataObject>
```

Fig. 5. Fragment of an XML file for a GUI

1. some typical procedures (to identify the general patterns);
2. some complex procedures (to identify the variation points);
3. the remaining procedures.

During the first two phases, the complete rejuvenation chain (i.e., steps (1), (2) and (3) of Fig. 3(b)) is developed and extended. In the third phase the rejuvenation chain is quite stable, which leads to an increase in the speed of the rejuvenation project.

4   Reverse Engineering

One of the first steps in software rejuvenation is to reverse engineer the legacy software. The goal is to extract valuable domain-specific knowledge that needs to be preserved, instead of information about how the legacy software works internally.

4.1   Extract Information Model

In the legacy software, the field service procedures are described using many XML files; see Sect. 2.1. The three types of XML files use the same generic XML schema, which is depicted in Fig. 4. A fragment of such a file is shown in Fig. 5. The central element is DataObject, which has an ObjectType and some Attributes. Each Attribute has a data type (called PMSVR) and two identifiers: Name and the combination of Group and Element. The Name is plain text, whereas Group and Element are hexadecimal numbers. The value of each Attribute is described using either a single DataObject, an Array of DataObjects, or a PlainTextValue.

This XML schema is too generic to describe the actual structure of the information. There is a lot of documentation available about the intended information models, based on the ObjectType of DataObjects and the two identifiers of Attributes. This base is still valid, but for the rest the documentation turns out to be outdated.

We have reconstructed the three used information models from the three types of XML files. Using an off-the-shelf XML parser for Java, we have parsed the XML files, and recorded the nesting structure: for each DataObject we record the contained Attributes, and for each Attribute we record the data type and the contained DataObjects. In the terminology of [16], this activity corresponds to "model discovery", although in our case it is not a process model.

The XML files have been edited manually, and hence contain noise. The used XML schema enforces that the information models are duplicated continuously, which naturally leads to inconsistencies. For example, various synonyms were used for the fields ObjectType and PMSVR; the legacy frameworks were robust enough to handle them. Sometimes the two attribute identifiers and the data types were even conflicting. While extracting the information model, we have stored all used patterns, and checked them automatically for inconsistencies. These inconsistencies have been resolved manually in the information model.

Before processing the XML files any further, we have parsed them again and automatically removed the duplicated data about the information model. As a pre-processing step we have also automatically applied the resolutions for the conflicting attribute identifiers, using the combination of Group and Element as the leading identifier. Some other encountered inconsistencies have also been addressed, such as data values of type String where the number of double quotes could be zero, one or two.

The resulting extraction from XML files to pre-processed data is fully automated, but the specific techniques for extracting the information model and addressing the noise and inconsistencies were custom developments. We have developed them incrementally, based on the specific issues that were encountered in the XML files. In Fig. 2, the extracted information models are depicted at the top of the second column. A fragment of the reconstructed information model for the GUI is depicted in Fig. 6.

The extracted information model forms the meta-model of a Domain-Specific Language (DSL [19]) for representing the XML data using Xtext technology. A few fragments of this representation are depicted in Figs. 7(a) and 7(b). This is more compact, and looks more human-friendly than the original XML.

4.2   Identify Behavioral Patterns

The information model from Sect. 4.1 is used by the stack of custom C++ frameworks to define the runtime behaviour of clients at its two external interfaces: the user interface and the server interface. Given the complexity of these frameworks, we doubt that this behaviour can be extracted (manually or automatically) from the code in a cost-effective way. Therefore we have looked for other options.

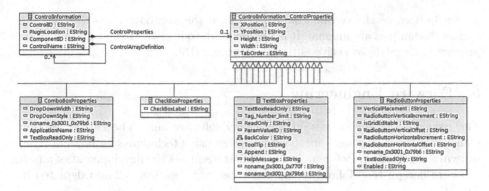

Fig. 6. Fragment of the GUI information model

```
ControlProperties = PanelProperties {
    Dock = 5
    XPosition = 0
    YPosition = 145
    Height = 35
    Width = 60
    TabOrder = 2
    LayerType = "Data"
}
```

(a) Part of the extracted GUI (related to Fig. 5 and Fig. 6)

```
NodeTransitionInformation = NodeTransitionInformation {
    InitializationInformation = NodeTransitionInitialization {
        TransitionInfo = Array {
            TransitionInfo {
                ActionName = "NEXT"
                NodeID = "FULLAUTO"
            }
            TransitionInfo {
                ActionName = "Cancel"
                NodeID = "NULL"
            }
        }
    }
    ComponentCreationInformation = ComponentCreationInformation {
        ComponentID = "GENERICTO"
    }
}
```

(b) Part of the extracted workflow

Fig. 7. DSL representation of the pre-processed data

There is documentation available about the interface between the client and the server. This consists of a small, generic state machine and many Message Sequence Charts (MSCs) to illustrate its intended use. The description of the state machine appears to be up-to-date, but it is too generic to accurately describe the behavior of specific procedures. Therefore we have focused on the MSCs.

Most of the MSCs are still valid, so we have used them as base and extended them in various ways. In the terminology of [16], this is called "model enhancement". As the legacy software is still operational, we have inspected the logs of the running software. In addition we have occasionally performed manual inspections of small code fragments. The few observed deviations from the MSCs have been repaired in the MSCs, as the legacy software is considered to be leading.

The result is a compact and very valuable description of the external behavior of the legacy software, combining information from several sources. These enriched MSCs describe how the information model influences the behavior of the legacy software at both external interfaces. In Fig. 2, the MSCs are depicted at the bottom of the second column. To keep the approach cost-effective, the applied techniques are manual. It is further work to investigate automation using process mining [16] or active automata learning [13].

5 Forward Engineering

The previous section focuses on the legacy software only. The current section transforms the legacy software to a new design using techniques for model-driven software engineering. Before doing so, it first discusses the development of a new software design; thus following the order described in Sect. 3.2 and depicted in Fig. 3(b).

5.1 New Software Design

When developing the new software design, the challenge is to avoid being biased too much by known concepts from the legacy software. Otherwise the rejuvenation may lead to almost a copy of the legacy design. This requires a good knowledge of both modern software designs and the real software requirements (not just the specific implementation decisions of the legacy software).

As described in Sect. 2.2, the redesign aims for plain C++ code and off-the-shelf frameworks. For the GUI we have decided to use the Qt framework, which leads to a design with one class for the static structure of each GUI screen. For each field service procedure, we use one class that contains the dynamic behavior and closely follows the structure of its workflow. To keep the code clean, we have created a small library with reusable code fragments for functionality such as setting up the client-server interface. This structure is sketched at the right-hand side of Fig. 2.

As the field service procedures are based on a notion of workflow, we have considered using a Workflow Management System [17]. We have not done so, because our focus is on a good integration with the existing server, and our goal is to reduce the number of frameworks with a limited contribution. In particular the used workflows are completely sequential and the typical collaboration aspects of workflow management systems, for example, are not relevant in this case.

5.2 Code Generation for the New Software Design

Our aim was to generate the code for the new software design from models; see the third column of Fig. 2. For the static GUI structure, we have used Qt models from which the corresponding code can be generated. The remaining part of the information model describes the logic that is specific for field service procedures: the dynamic behavior of GUI elements, the link between GUI elements and server identifiers, and the workflow. To generate code for that part, we first describe the essential information by means of a DSL. Using modern technology such as Xtext, DSLs can be developed quickly; this confirms observations by [21].

```
// --- node FULLAUTO (stage FullAutomatic) -------
node
    name = "FULLAUTO"
    transitions
        OK -> "STATIC"
        Cancel -> "FINALIZATION"
    stage = FullAutomatic
        part = ""
    UIResource
        assembly = "FSCGeneratorUIDefinitions"
        id = "FSCXGNTubeAdaptationAdjustmentFullAutoUIDef"
    mapping
        event id 21: element "C24"
        event id 20: element "C25"
        event id 10: element "C33" ScrollToLatest
        event id 22: element "C23"
```

Fig. 8. Fragment of a redesigned DSL model

Before developing the DSL and code generators, it is useful to first manually develop a prototype implementation in plain code for a small number of
simple cases, without worrying about models and transformations. Based on the
prototype code and the required external software behavior (described in the
MSCs from Sect. 4.2), the information model for the new design can be identified. Instead of directly reusing the information models from the legacy software,
this is an opportunity to eliminate unnecessary complexity. The legacy models
are likely to include details about old technologies, workarounds for technology
limitations, unnecessary case analysis, and unnecessary inhomogeneity.

Additionally, the new information model might be simplified by making a
minor change in the interfaces with adjacent components. In the case of the field
service procedures, we have made minor changes in the server from Fig. 1 to solve
issues like inhomogeneous data formats. Such changes reduce the complexity of
the redesigned client software, without making the server software more complex.

A fragment of such a redesigned DSL model is depicted in Fig. 8. We have
aimed for a clean separation between information models with domain-specific
knowledge, and code generators with general implementation patterns. This provides a kind of technology independence. After a number of field service procedures had already been migrated, we received the request to change the GUI
framework into Qt. The technology independence has enabled us to address this
request with very limited effort.

5.3 Model Transformation for the Legacy Software

Finally the legacy models must be transformed into the redesigned models. Parts
of these models are closely related, but not all. For example, the legacy models include concepts that deal with internal configuration issues of the custom
frameworks; these are ignored in the transformation. Another big difference is
the link between GUI elements and server identifiers. The legacy models combine
multiple mechanisms for this concept; in some cases there is a direct mapping,

and in other cases it is a combination of two subsequent mappings (described in different XML files). The redesigned models simplify these mechanisms by enforcing the use of direct mappings only.

In a few cases, there was an intricate interplay between the legacy models and the incidental C# fragments. It would have been costly to develop a general transformation for these cases. We have manually provided suitable transformations for these few cases, which turned out to be very effective.

Developing the model transformation is a manual task, but its execution is automated. Instead of a model-to-model transformation, we have used a model-to-text transformation (using Xtext), because the textual representation of the generated models is better readable than their object-oriented structure; see also [8]. By generating text, we can also easily exploit the target DSL's reference resolution mechanism instead of creating explicit references within models.

6   Industrial Confidence

Having finished the rejuvenation, there are three pressing questions. First of all how to verify that the legacy and redesigned software have the same external behavior, secondly the effect on maintainability of the code base, and thirdly how to continue software development from this moment onward.

6.1   Verification

The rejuvenation approach from Sect. 3 does not guarantee correctness by construction. To gain confidence, we exploit an incremental way of working, which enables early feedback. In particular we ensure that all generated artifacts (both models and code) are well-structured; this holds both for final and for intermediate results. In all stages, the generated artifacts can easily be inspected by domain experts to monitor their validity and completeness.

After finishing the rejuvenation, we have assessed the redesigned software using three techniques:

- compare logs of the legacy and redesigned software after performing the same field service procedure;
- review the generated models and code base, which is feasible as they are well-structured;
- execute the legacy set of test cases [12] with good and bad weather scenarios on the redesigned software.

Although the legacy software and the redesigned software have the same functionality, the redesigned software behaves much faster thanks to the removal of several frameworks. This performance improvement has exposed a few bugs (such as race conditions) in other existing software components.

	Legacy	Redesign	
		Model-driven	Plain code
Information models for the GUI	120 kLOC	52 kLOC	—
Generated code for the GUI	—	—	14 kLOC
Information models for the logic	90 kLOC	7 kLOC	—
Generated code for the logic	—	—	27 kLOC
Handwritten code generator for the logic	—	3 kLOC	—
Handwritten incidental code	10 kLOC	—	
Handwritten reusable code	1240 kLOC	5 kLOC	
Total	1460 kLOC	67 kLOC	46 kLOC

Fig. 9. Size of the software artifacts

6.2 Maintainability

Maintainability figures are not available yet, but they are often linked to size and complexity. The redesign eliminates incidental complexity from the stack of legacy frameworks; it follows natural domain structures, and the code generation guarantees a consistent style. In Fig. 9 the sizes of the models used in the rejuvenation are summarized, corresponding to the first, third and fourth column of Fig. 2. The sizes in terms of kLOCs are computed using LocMetric; for source code we use SLOC-L, and for the other artifacts we use SLOC-P.

As the Qt and Xtext frameworks are off-the-shelf components, we do not need to maintain them ourselves, and hence they are not mentioned in the table. Concerning the information models, we distinguish GUI models and logic models. In the legacy, the GUI models correspond to one type of XML files that covers both static structure and dynamic behavior; the logic models combine the other two types of XML files. In the redesign, the GUI models are Qt files that cover only the static structure, whereas the logic models are the DSL models.

It is interesting to compare the ratio between various numbers in Fig. 9:

- The XML files for the GUI elements (120 kLOC) have been more than halved to the Qt models (52 kLOC), from which only 14 kLOC code is generated.
- The XML files for the logic of the procedures (90 kLOC) are reduced to 7 kLOC in the Xtext DSL, from which 27 kLOC code is generated.
- The legacy code base (1460 kLOC) is 21 times larger than the model-driven (67 kLOC) and 31 times larger than the plain code redesign (46 kLOC).

6.3 New Software Development Environment

The original rejuvenation aim of the involved managers was to obtain plain maintainable code. However, the rejuvenation chain contains a model-driven development environment for the redesigned software. If further maintenance and development is going to be performed by manually editing the plain code, then it is expected that the situation from Sect. 1 will return.

The developers have decided to continue in a model-driven way. The models that we have introduced can be edited conveniently; for the GUI models there is a graphical editor (Qt designer), and for the logic there is a textual editor (Xtext). By continuing to generate the code from models, the quality of the code will not degrade.

A potential downside is that this requires the introduction of new tools in the existing development environment. Initially, there were concerns about the learning curve for the developers, but this was no barrier given the modern Xtext technology. Also there were concerns about the possibilities for debugging code. In practice, the software developers had no problem in developing at model level, and debugging at code level, because the generated code was well-structured. The developers have even started to make extensions to the code generators. This confirms the observation [21] that successful practices in model-driven engineering are driven from the ground up.

Thus we provide an interesting way to introduce model-driven software engineering in industry. The model-driven environment is developed as a powerful element in a rejuvenation project. Afterwards, without additional investment, its value can be evaluated for further software development. By storing both the models and the generated code in the software repository, the well-structured generated code always provides an exit-strategy [8] from model-driven software engineering, if this would be desired at any moment in the future.

7   Related Work

The evolution of legacy software to software that uses embedded DSLs is studied in [4]. This work uses the Java-based extensible programming language SugarJ, and gradually replaces larger parts of the legacy software. In particular they present a technique to find source code locations at which a given embedded DSL may be applicable. Our work on software rejuvenation focuses on complete redesigns of a software component (not an evolution but a revolution). Moreover, in our work the DSLs are a means towards a goal, not a goal in itself.

A similar context is used in [7], re-engineering families of legacy applications towards using DSLs. In particular they study whether it is worth to invest in harvesting domain knowledge from the code base. To make our approach cost-effective, we decided that some information should be obtained from the code base, and other information from other sources.

The program transformation work in [1] does not aim to introduce DSLs. They use direct code-to-code transformations, similar to the horizontal arrow at the bottom of Fig. 3(b). This commercial tool has been applied to many industrial cases (including real-time applications), in particular in the context of older programming languages such as Cobol and Fortran. Our work aims for major software redesigns, where domain-specific abstraction steps are essential to eliminate the implementation details.

The model-driven software migration approaches from [5, 11, 20] are based on source code as information source. The source code analysis extracts models that are more abstract than code, based on generic structures like syntax trees. Our work uses multiple information sources and analysis techniques. A crucial ingredient of our approach is the use of domain-specific models, which abstract from the code and follow the structure of the specific application domain.

8   Conclusion

We have addressed an industrial instance of the software rejuvenation problem. For the field service procedures, the plan using a model-driven approach was 6 times shorter than the plan using a manual approach. The model-driven plan has been realized with 10 % less effort than estimated, and combined with a regular project. The rejuvenation has changed the software design substantially, and the software developers have embraced the model-driven infrastructure that was developed to generate the implementation code. The model-driven redesign is 21 times smaller than the legacy code base. Thus we have shown that a cost-effective rejuvenation approach is becoming feasible in industrial practice.

The following recommendations form the key ingredients of the applied model-based rejuvenation approach:

1. work in an incremental way;
2. be pragmatic and aim for partial automation;
3. team up with a large required development project;
4. combine multiple types of information sources;
5. use domain-specific models;
6. eliminate non-essential variation points;
7. generate high-quality well-structured software.

The incremental approach first focuses on the general patterns, then on the variation points, and finally on the bad weather behavior. Such an approach helps to avoid introducing too many (non-essential) variation points from the legacy software. To avoid that the rejuvenated software resembles the legacy software too much, we separate the analysis of the legacy software from the development of the new design. In every increment, the transformation between them is developed as the last step.

This rejuvenation approach is now becoming feasible in industrial practice, because of the improved maturity of the required tools. Domain-specific languages, model transformations and code generators can be developed quickly and easily using modern language workbenches such as Xtext.

We expect that this rejuvenation approach can directly be applied to any legacy software that combines large frameworks with many configuration files, possibly also with some small incidental code fragments. As further work we will consider legacy code in conventional programming languages. This requires other techniques for reverse engineering, but we expect that the same overall rejuvenation approach is applicable. We also plan to investigate to which extent the models with external behavior could be extracted automatically.

Acknowledgment. This research was supported by the Dutch national program COMMIT and carried out as part of the Allegio project. The authors thank Dirk Jan Swagerman for his trust in this endeavor, and Aron van Beurden and Martien van der Meij for their technical contributions to the software rejuvenation.

References

1. Baxter, I.D., Pidgeon, C.W., Mehlich, M.: DMS: Program transformations for practical scalable software evolution. In: Proceedings of ICSE 2004, pp. 625–634. IEEE Computer Society (2004)
2. Bray, T., Paolia, J., Sperberg-McQueen, C.M., Maler, E., Yergeau, F.: Extensible Markup Language (XML) 1.0, 5th edn. W3C recommendation, World Wide Web Consortium (2008). http://www.w3.org/TR/2008/REC-xml-20081126/
3. de Groot, J., Nugroho, A., Bäck, T., Visser, J.: What is the value of your software? In: Managing Technical Debt (MTD 2012), pp. 37–44. ACM (2012)
4. Fehrenbach, S., Erdweg, S., Ostermann, K.: Software evolution to domain-specific languages. In: Erwig, M., Paige, R.F., Van Wyk, E. (eds.) SLE 2013. LNCS, vol. 8225, pp. 96–116. Springer, Heidelberg (2013)
5. Fleurey, F., Breton, E., Baudry, B., Nicolas, A., Jézéquel, J.-M.: Model-driven engineering for software migration in a large industrial context. In: Engels, G., Opdyke, B., Schmidt, D.C., Weil, F. (eds.) MODELS 2007. LNCS, vol. 4735, pp. 482–497. Springer, Heidelberg (2007)
6. Hooman, J., Mooij, A.J., van Wezep, H.: Early fault detection in industry using models at various abstraction levels. In: Derrick, J., Gnesi, S., Latella, D., Treharne, H. (eds.) IFM 2012. LNCS, vol. 7321, pp. 268–282. Springer, Heidelberg (2012)
7. Klint, P., Landman, D., Vinju, J.J.: Exploring the limits of domain model recovery. In: Proceedings of ICSM 2013, pp. 120–129. IEEE (2013)
8. Mooij, A.J., Hooman, J., Albers, R.: Gaining industrial confidence for the introduction of domain-specific languages. In: Proceedings of IEESD 2013, pp. 662–667. IEEE (2013)
9. Parr, T.: Soapbox: Humans should not have to grok XML. IBM developerWorks, IBM, August 2001. http://www.ibm.com/developerworks/library/x-sbxml/
10. Pirkelbauer, P., Dechev, D., Stroustrup, B.: Source code rejuvenation is not refactoring. In: van Leeuwen, J., Muscholl, A., Peleg, D., Pokorný, J., Rumpe, B. (eds.) SOFSEM 2010. LNCS, vol. 5901, pp. 639–650. Springer, Heidelberg (2010)
11. Reus, T., Geers, H., van Deursen, A.: Harvesting software systems for MDA-based reengineering. In: Rensink, A., Warmer, J. (eds.) ECMDA-FA 2006. LNCS, vol. 4066, pp. 213–225. Springer, Heidelberg (2006)
12. Sneed, H.M.: Planning the reengineering of legacy systems. IEEE Softw. **12**(1), 24–34 (1995)
13. Steffen, B., Howar, F., Merten, M.: Introduction to active automata learning from a practical perspective. In: Bernardo, M., Issarny, V. (eds.) SFM 2011. LNCS, vol. 6659, pp. 256–296. Springer, Heidelberg (2011)
14. Tolvanen, J.-P.: Domain-specific modeling for full code generation. Softw. Tech News (STN) **12**(4), 4–7 (2010)
15. Tonella, P., Potrich, A.: Reverse Engineering of Object-Oriented Code. Springer, Heidelberg (2005)
16. van der Aalst, W.M.P.: Process Mining: Discovery. Conformance and Enhancement of Business Processes. Springer, Heidelberg (2011)

17. van der Aalst, W.M.P., van Hee, K.M.: Workflow Management: Models. MIT Press, Methods and Systems (2004)
18. Voelter, M.: Best practices for DSLs and model-driven development. J. Object Technol. **8**(6), 79–102 (2009)
19. Voelter, M.: DSL Engineering (2013). http://dslbook.org/
20. Wagner, C.: Model-Driven Software Migration: A Methodology. Springer, Heidelberg (2014)
21. Whittle, J., Hutchinson, J., Rouncefield, M.: The state of practice in model-driven engineering. IEEE Softw. **31**, 79–85 (2014)

Migrating Automotive Product Lines: A Case Study

Michalis Famelis[1]([✉]), Levi Lúcio[2], Gehan Selim[3], Alessio Di Sandro[1],
Rick Salay[1], Marsha Chechik[1], James R. Cordy[3], Juergen Dingel[3],
Hans Vangheluwe[2], and Ramesh S.[4]

[1] University of Toronto, Toronto, ON, Canada
famelis@cs.toronto.edu
[2] McGill University, Montreal, QC, Canada
[3] Queens University, Kingston, ON, Canada
[4] General Motors, Warren, USA

Abstract. Software Product Lines (SPL) are widely used to manage
variability in the automotive industry. In a rapidly changing industrial
environment, model transformations are necessary to aid in automat-
ing the evolution of SPLs. However, existing transformation technologies
are not well-suited to handling industrial-grade variability in software
artifacts. We present a case study where we "lift" a previously developed migration transformation so that it becomes applicable to realistic
industrial product lines. Our experience indicates that it is both feasible
and scalable to lift transformations for industrial SPLs.

1 Introduction

The sprawling complexity of software systems has lead many organizations to
adopt *software product line techniques* to manage large portfolios of similar products. For example, modern cars use software to achieve a large variety of functionality, from power train control to infotainment. To organize and manage the
huge variety of software subsystems, many car manufacturers, such as General
Motors (GM), make extensive use of software product line engineering techniques [13].

At the same time, *model-based techniques* are also actively used by companies,
especially in domains such as automotive and aerospace, as a way to increase
the level of abstraction and allow engineers to develop systems in notations they
feel comfortable working with [24]. That also entails the active use of *model
transformations* – operations for manipulating models in order to produce other
models or generate code.

Currently, GM is going through the process of migrating models from a legacy
metamodel to AUTOSAR [2]. In previous work, we have presented the transformation GmToAutosar [30]. Given a single GM legacy model, GmToAutosar produces a single AUTOSAR output model, based on a set of requirements followed
by GM engineers. In order to study its correctness, GmToAutosar was implemented in DSLTrans [20,29], a model transformation language that specializes
in helping developers create provably correct transformations.

D. Kolovos and M. Wimmer (Eds.): ICMT 2015, LNCS 9152, pp. 82–97, 2015.
DOI: 10.1007/978-3-319-21155-8_7

Because of the extensive use of product lines, the entire product line of legacy models needs to be migrated to a new product line of AUTOSAR models. To do this, GM engineers need to create purpose-specific migration transformations. Yet transforming product lines is inherently difficult: the relationships between the products need to be preserved, and a variety of properties between the input and output models in the transformation need to be established. Thus, the task of a product-line level transformation is not only to maintain relationships between the features and relationships between the products but also to make sure that the transformation maintains certain properties, expressed in terms of pre- and post- conditions. Existing tools and methodologies do not facilitate model transformations in the context of product lines.

In our earlier work [26], we presented a technique for *"lifting"* a class of model transformations so that they can be applied to software product lines. *Lifting* here means *reinterpretation* of a transformation so that instead of a single product, it applies to the entire product line. This requires lifting of the transformation *engine* to implement lifting semantics. Thus, existing transformations can be applied without modification to product lines using the lifted transformation engine.

The goal of this paper is to demonstrate, using an empirical case study from an automotive domain, that it is tractable to lift industrial-grade transformations. Specifically, we report on an experience of lifting a previously published transformation [30], GmToAutosar, used in the context of automotive software and applying it to a realistic product line. We lifted GmToAutosar using the theory of lifting presented in [26]. In order to do this, we had to adapt parts of the existing model transformation engine, DSLTrans. The resulting lifted version of GmToAutosar is capable of transforming product lines of legacy GM models to product lines of AUTOSAR models, while preserving the correctness of individual product transformations. We also stress-tested the lifted GmToAutosar to investigate the effect of the size of the model and the variability complexity on the lifted transformation. Due to limitations to publication of sensitive industrial data, the product line we analyzed was created using publicly available data and calibrated with input from GM engineering.

The rest of the paper is organized as follows: we introduce background on to software product lines in Sect. 2. The GmToAutosar transformation is described in Sect. 3 and its lifting – in Sect. 4. We discuss the experience of applying the lifted transformation in Sect. 5. In Sect. 6 we present lessons learned and Sect. 7 discusses related work. We conclude in Sect. 8 with a summary of the paper and discussion of future work.

2   Product Lines in the Automotive Industry

Product Lines in GM. Modern cars at GM can contain tens of millions of lines of code, encompassing powertrain control, active and passive safety features, climate control, comfort and convenience systems, security systems, entertainment systems, and middleware to interconnect all of the above. In addition to

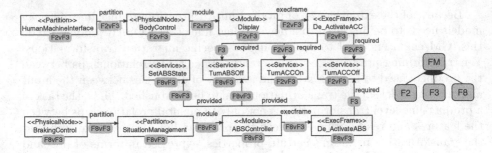

Fig. 1. A fragment of the exemplar automotive product line model. The left side shows the domain model annotated with presence conditions and the right side shows the feature model.

software complexity, the variability is high – over 60 models with further variation to account for requirements differences in 150+ countries. The number of product variants produced is in the low tens of thousands. GM is re-engineering its variability tooling to use the commercial product line tool Gears by BigLever Software[1] [13]. To help manage the complexity, product lines will be decomposed into modules corresponding to the natural divisions in the automotive system architecture to produce a hierarchical product line. For example, the subsystems dealing with entertainment, climate control, etc. will have their own product lines, and these will be merged into parent product lines to represent the variability for an entire vehicle.

Case Study Product Line. We applied a transformation on a realistic product line exemplar (as opposed to the actual product line used in GM) due to reasons of confidentiality. We started with publicly available models [1] and built an exemplar model conforming to the GM metamodel in Fig. 2 and consisting of six features and 201 elements. With the help of our industrial partners, we validated that our exemplar is realistic in terms of its structure and size. Since our goal is to do transformation lifting, the product line we produced is *annotative* [10,17,25]. We formally review the definition of the annotative product line approach below.

Definition 1 (Product Line). A product line P consists of the following parts: (1) A *feature model* that consists of a set of features and the constraints between them; (2) a *domain model* consisting of a set of model elements; and, (3) a mapping from the feature model to the domain model that assigns to each element of the domain model a propositional formula called its *presence condition* expressed in terms of features. We call any selection of features that satisfy the constraints in the feature model to be a *configuration* and the corresponding set of domain elements with presence conditions that evaluate to $True$ given these features is called a *product*. We denote the set of all configurations of P by $\mathsf{Conf}(P)$.

---

[1] www.biglever.com.

Note that the Gears product lines used at GM are annotative but use a slightly different terminology than in Definition 1. Figure 1 shows a fragment of the exemplar product line to illustrate the components of an annotative product line. It shows three of the six features: feature *F2* representing Adaptive Cruise Control (ACC), *F8* representing Anti-lock Braking System (ABS), and *F3* representing Smart Control (SC), an integrated system for assisted driving. The relevant fragment of the feature model is shown on the right of the figure and the solid bar connecting the three features expresses the constraint that the features are mutually exclusive.

The domain model is a class diagram showing the architectural elements. The *BodyControl PhysicalNode* runs *Partitions* such as the *HumanMachineInterface*. The *HumanMachineInterface Partition* contains the *Display Module* which runs multiple *ExecFrames* at the same or different rates. The *De_ActivateACC* Exec Frame allows controlling the ACC feature by invoking Services for variable updates (e.g., *TurnACCon* and *TurnACCoff Services*). The *BrakingControl PhysicalNode* runs the *SituationManagement Partition*. The *SituationManagement Partition* contains the *ABScontroller Module* which runs the *De_activateABS ExecFrame*. The *De_activateABS ExecFrame* provides the *TurnABSoff* and *SetABSstate* Services to control the ABS feature. The *De_activateABS ExecFrame* provides a *Service* (i.e., *TurnABSoff*) that is required by the *De_ActivateACC ExecFrame*, and the two *ExecFrames* require a common *Service* (i.e., *TurnACCoff*).

The presence conditions mapping the features to the elements of the domain model are shown directly annotating the architecture elements. For example, the element *BodyControl* has the presence condition *F2 or F3*. Configuring the product line to produce a particular product involves selecting the features that should be in the product and then using these features with the presence conditions to extract the domain elements that should be in the product. For example, assume that we want to configure the product that has only feature *F2*. In this case, the product will contain the element *BodyControl* because its presence condition says that it is present when the product contains feature *F2* or if it contains *F3*. However, it will not contain element *SetABState* because its presence condition is *F8 or F3*.

3 Migrating GM Models to AUTOSAR

Previously, we reported on an industrial transformation that maps between subsets of a legacy metamodel for General Motors (GM) and the AUTOSAR metamodel [30]. This GmToAutosar transformation manipulated subsets of the metamodels that represent the deployment and interaction of software components. We summarize the source and target metamodels of the GmToAutosar transformation and its implementation in DSLTrans. More details on the source and target metamodels can be found in [30].

The GM Metamodel. Figure 2 shows the subset of a simplified version of the GM metamodel manipulated by our transformation in [30]. A *PhysicalNode* may contain multiple *Partitions* (i.e., processing units). Multiple *Modules* can be deployed

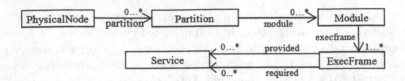

Fig. 2. Subset of the source GM metamodel used by our transformation in [30].

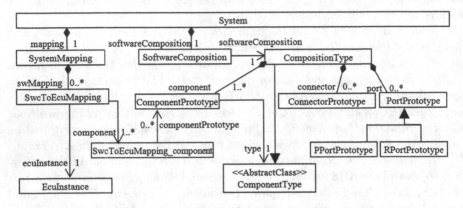

Fig. 3. Subset of the target AUTOSAR metamodel used by our transformation in [30].

on a single *Partition*. A *Module* is an atomic, deployable, and reusable software element and can contain multiple *ExecFrames*. An *ExecFrame*, i.e., an execution frame, is the basic unit for software scheduling. It contains behavior-encapsulating entities, and is responsible for providing/requiring *Services* to/from these behavior-encapsulating entities.

The AUTOSAR Metamodel. In AUTOSAR, an Electronic Control Unit (ECU) is a physical unit on which software is deployed. Figure 3 shows the subset of the AUTOSAR metamodel [2] used by our transformation. In AUTOSAR, the ECU configuration is modeled using a *System* that aggregates *SoftwareComposition* and *SystemMapping*. *SoftwareComposition* points to *CompositionType* which eliminates any nested software components in a *SoftwareComposition*. *SoftwareComposition* models the architecture of the software components (i.e., *ComponentPrototypes*) deployed on an ECU and their ports (i.e., *PPortPrototype*/ *RPortPrototype* for providing/ requiring data and services). Each *ComponentPrototype* has a type that refers to its container *CompositionType*.

SystemMapping binds software components to ECUs using *SwcToEcuMappings*. *SwcToEcuMappings* assign *SwcToEcuMapping_components* to an *EcuInstance*. *SwcToEcuMapping_components*, in turn, refer to *ComponentPrototypes*.

The GmToAutosar Transformation. Although originally implemented in ATL [30], the GmToAutosar transformation was later reimplemented in

Table 1. The rules in each layer of the GmToAutosar transformation, and their input and output types.

Layer	Rule name	Input types	Output types
1	MapPhysNode2FiveElements	PhysicalNode, Partition, Module	System, SystemMapping, SoftwareCom-position, CompositionType, EcuInstance
	MapPartition	PhysicalNode, Partition, Module	SwcToEcuMapping
	MapModule	PhysicalNode, Partition, Module	SwCompToEcuMapping_component, ComponentPrototype
2	MapConnPhysNode2Partition	PhysicalNode, Partition	SystemMapping, EcuInstance, SwcToEcuMapping
	MapConnPartition2Module	PhysicalNode, Partition, Module	CompositionType, ComponentPrototype, SwcToEcuMapping, SwCompToEcuMapping_component
3	CreatePPortPrototype	PhysicalNode, Partition, Module, ExecFrame, Service	CompositionType, PPortPrototype
	CreateRPortPrototype	PhysicalNode, Partition, Module, ExecFrame, Service	CompositionType, RPortPrototype

DSLTrans for the purpose of a study where several of its properties where automatically verified [29]. This allowed us to increase our confidence in the correctness of the transformation. Table 1 summarizes the rules in each transformation layer of the GmToAutosar transformation after reimplementing it in DSLTrans, and the input/output types that are mapped/generated by each rule. For example, rule MapPhysNode2FiveElements in Layer 1 maps a *PhysicalNode* element in the input model to five elements in the output model (i.e., *System*, *SystemMapping*, *SoftwareComposition*, *CompositionType*, and *EcuInstance* elements). A detailed explanation of the mapping rules and the reimplementation of the transformation in DSLTrans can be found in [29,30]. DSLTrans and the notion of rule layers is described in Sect. 4.1.

4 Lifting GmToAutosar

4.1 Background: DSLTrans

DSLTrans is an out-place, graph-based and rule-based model transformation engine that has two important properties enforced by construction: all its computations are both *terminating* and *confluent* [6]. Besides their obvious importance in practice, these two properties were instrumental in the implementation of a verification technique for pre- / post-condition properties that can be shown to hold for all executions of a given DSLTrans model transformation, independently of the provided input model [20,21,29].

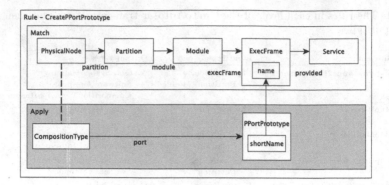

Fig. 4. The *CreatePPortPrototype* rule in the GmToAutosar DSLTrans transformation.

Model transformations are expressed in DSLTrans as sets of graph rewriting rules, having the classical left- and right-hand sides and, optionally, negative application conditions. The scheduling of model transformation rules in DSLTrans is based on the concept of *layer*. Each layer contains a set of model transformation rules that execute independently from each other. Layers are organized sequentially and the output model that results from executing a given layer is passed to the next layer in the sequence. A DSLTrans rule can match over the elements of the input model of the transformation (that remains unchanged throughout the entire execution of the transformation) but also over elements that have been generated so far in the output model. The independence of the execution of rules belonging to the same layer is enforced by allowing matching over the output of rules from previous layer but not over the output of rules of the current layer. Matching over elements of the output model of a transformation is achieved using a DSLTrans construct called *backward links*. Backward links allow matching over traces between elements in the input the output models of the transformation. These traces are explicitly built by the DSLTrans transformation engine during rule execution.

For example, we depict in Fig. 4 the *CreatePPortPrototype* rule in the GmToAutosar DSLTrans transformation, previously introduced in Table 1. The rule is comprised of a *match* and an *apply* part, corresponding to the usual left- and right-hand sides in graph rewriting. When a rule is applied, the graph in the match part of the rule is looked for in the transformation's input model, together with the match classes in the apply part of the rule that are connected to *backward links*. An example of a *backward link* can be observed in Fig. 4, connecting the *CompositionType* and the *PhysicalNode* match classes. During the rewrite part of rule application, the instances of classes in the apply part of the rule that are not connected to backward links, together with their adjacent relations, are created in the output model. In the example in Fig. 4, the *CreatePPortPrototype* rule creates a *PPortPrototype* object and a *port* relation per matching site found. Note that the vertical arrow between the *shortName* attribute of *PPortPrototype* and the *name* attribute of *ExecFrame* implies that the value of attribute *name* is copied from its matching site to the *shortName* attribute of the *PPortPrototype* instance created by the rule.

In addition to the constructs presented in the example in Fig. 4, DSLTrans has several others: *existential matching* which allows selecting only one result when a match class of a rule matches an input model, *indirect links* which allow transitive matching over containment relations in the input model, and *negative application conditions* which allow to specify conditions under which a rule should not match, as usual. The GmToAutosar transformation does not make use of these constructs, and thus we leave the problem of lifting them for future work.

4.2   Lifting DSLTrans for GmToAutosar

Lifting of Production Rules. When executing a DSLTrans transformation, the basic operation (called here a *"production"*) is the application of a individual rule at a particular matching site. The definition and theoretical foundation of lifting for productions are given in [26]. Below, we describe how they apply in the case of GmToAutosar using the model fragment in Fig. 1 and the *CreatePPortPrototype* rule in Fig. 4.

When a DSLTrans rule R is lifted, we denote it by $R^\uparrow$. Intuitively, the meaning of a $R^\uparrow$-production is that it should result in a product line with the same products as we would get by applying R to all the products of the original product line at the same site. Because of this, we do not expect a $R^\uparrow$-production to affect the set of allowable feature combinations in the product line. Formally:

Definition 2 (Correctness of Lifting a Production). Let a rule R and a product line P, and a matching site c be given. $R^\uparrow$ is a *correct lifting* of R iff (1) if $P \overset{R^\uparrow|c}{\Longrightarrow} P'$ then $\mathsf{Conf}(P') = \mathsf{Conf}(P)$, and (2) for all configurations $\mathsf{Conf}(P)$, $M \overset{R|c}{\Longrightarrow} M'$, where M can be derived from P and M' from P' under the same configuration.

An algorithm for applying lifted rules at a specific site is given in [26], along with a proof of production correctness that is consistent with the above definition. In brief, given a matching site and a lifted rule, the algorithm performs the following steps: (a) use a SAT solver to check whether the rule is applicable to at least one product at that site, (b) modify the domain model of the product line, and (c) modify the presence conditions of the changed domain model so the rule effect only occurs in applicable products.

For example, consider the match c={*BodyControl, HumanMachineInterface, Display, De_ActivateACC, TurnABSoff, BodyControlCT*} in the fragment in Fig. 1. In this match, we assume that an element named *BodyControlCT* of type *CompositionType* and its corresponding backward link have been previously created by the rule *MapPhysNode2FiveElements* (see Table 1) and therefore have the presence condition $F2 \lor F3$. To apply the rule *CreatePPortPrototype*$^\uparrow$ to c, we first need check whether all of c is fully present in at least one product.

We do so by checking whether the formula $\Phi_{apply} = (F2 \lor F3) \land (F8 \lor F3)$ is satisfiable. Φ_{apply} is constructed by conjoining the presence conditions of all the domain elements in the matching site c. According to the general lifting algorithm in [26], the construction of Φ_{apply} for arbitrary graph transformation rules is more complex; however, rules in GmToAutosar do not use Negative Application Conditions and do not cause the deletion of any domain element. Therefore, the construction of Φ_{apply} follows the pattern we described for all rules in GmToAutosar$^\top$.

Because Φ_{apply} is satisfiable, $CreatePPortPrototype^\top$ is applicable at c. Therefore, the rule creates a new element called $De\_ActivateACC$ of type $PPortPrototype$, a link of type $port$ connecting it to $BodyControlCT$, as well as the appropriate backward links. Finally, all created elements are assigned Φ_{apply} as their presence condition. In other words, the added presence conditions ensure that the new elements will only be part of products for which the rule is applicable. By construction, this production satisfies the correctness condition in Definition 2. Thus, according to the proofs in [26], the lifting of productions preserves confluence and termination.

Lifting the Transformation. We define the notion of global correctness for GmToAutosar$^\top$ to mean that, given an input product line of GM models, it should produce a product line of AUTOSAR models that would be the same as if we had applied GmToAutosar to each GM model individually:

Definition 3 (Global Correctness of GmToAutosar$^\top$). The transformation GmToAutosar$^\top$ is *correct* iff for any input product line P, it produces a product line P' such that (a) $\mathsf{Conf}(P) = \mathsf{Conf}(P')$, and (b) for all configurations $\mathsf{Conf}(P)$, $M' = GmToAutosar(M)$, where M and M' can be derived from P and P', respectively, under the same configuration.

In order to lift GmToAutosar, we use the DSLTrans engine to perform the identification of matching sites and scheduling of individual productions, and use the lifting algorithm in [26] to lift individual productions, as described above. Since each production is correct with respect to Definition 2, then, by transitivity, the lifted version GmToAutosar$^\top$ is globally correct. Also by transitivity, since the lifting of individual productions preserves confluence and termination, it is confluent and terminating, like GmToAutosar. Because of global correctness, and because it preserves confluence and termination, GmToAutosar$^\top$ also preserves the results of the verification of pre- and post-condition properties using the techniques in [20,21,29]. In other words, GmToAutosar$^\top$ satisfies the same set of pre- and post-condition properties as GmToAutosar.

Implementation. Adapting the DSLTrans engine for GmToAutosar$^\top$ required adding functionality to the existing codebase. We had to write code to extend it to enable the following functionality: (a) Reading and writing presence conditions from and to secondary storage, expressed as Comma-Separated Values

(CSV) and attach them in memory to EMF [15] models. (b) Interfacing with the API of the Z3 SMT solver [12], used for checking the satisfiability of Φ_{apply}. (c)Associating presence conditions to elements belonging to the output model of the transformation and updating those presence condition as the transformation unfolds. These changes required an addition of less than 300 lines of code to an existing codebase of 9250 lines.

5   Applying the Lifted Transformation GmToAutosar†

The aim of this case study is to investigate the feasibility of applying industrial-grade transformations to product lines via lifting [26]. We thus lifted GmToAutosar and applied it to various input product lines with the goal to answer the following research questions:

RQ1: Does GmToAutosar† scale to industrial-sized SPLs?
RQ2: How sensitive is it to the complexity of the product line?

To answer RQ1, we generated realistic product lines, based on input from our industrial partners. We then applied GmToAutosar† to them and measured two variables: (a) total runtime, and (b) complexity of presence conditions of the output. We used the clause-to-variable ratio as a measure of the complexity of presence conditions because it is a well-known metric for evaluating the complexity of queries to SAT solvers. To answer RQ2, we varied the size of the generated product lines in terms of the size of the domain model and the number of features in the feature model.

Setup. Due to limitations of publication of sensitive industrial data, we opted to use a *realistic* rather than *real* product lines, constructed as follows:

1) Using publicly available examples [1], we created the exemplar product line described in Sect. 2. As described earlier, its domain model consists of 201 elements and its feature model has 6 features. 50 % of domain model elements in the model had a single feature presence condition, whereas the presence conditions of the other 50 % consisted of conjunctive clauses of 2-3 features. The overall product line was validated with input from our industrial partners.

2) We consulted our industrial partners regarding the characteristics of a typical product line. We were given the following parameters for a typical product line of DOORS requirements: (a) domain model size is 400 elements, (b)the number of feature variables is 25, (c)1/8th of elements are variation points, (d)an average clause-to-variable ratio of the presence conditions is $^2/_{25} = 0.08$, i.e. an average presence condition consists of 2 clauses containing any of the 25 feature variables.

3) We used the exemplar model built in step 1 as a seed to create product lines of varying sizes for the model and the set of features, i.e., varying parameters (a) and (b) from step 2 while keeping parameters (c) and (d) constant. Therefore, models of increasing sizes were obtained by cloning the exemplar domain model to create models of 200, 400, 800, 1600 and 3200 elements. To obtain product lines with different numbers of feature variables, we cloned the feature model of the exemplar, creating feature models with 6, 12, 24, 48, and 96 features. The product line with 400 elements and 24 features corresponds to the parameters reported by our industrial partners in the previous step. Each variation point was assigned a randomly generated presence condition based on the presence conditions of the exemplar.

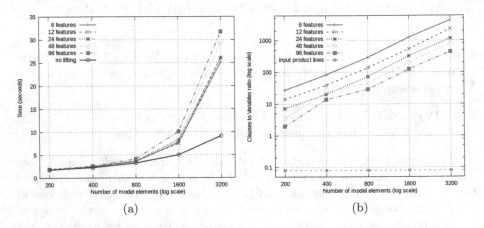

(a)   (b)

Fig. 5. (a) Observed increase in running time. (b) Observed increase in the size of presence conditions.

We executed the experiments on a computer with Intel Core i7-2600 3.40GHz ×4 cores (8 logical) and 8GB RAM, running Ubuntu-64.

Results. Figure 5(a) shows the observed runtimes of applying GmToAutosar[†] to product lines with domain models of increasing size. One line is plotted for each feature set size. For comparison, we also include the runtime of applying GmToAutosar to models (not product lines) of different sizes. Figure 5(b) shows the clause-to-variable ratio of output product lines for inputs of varying size of domain model. One line is plotted for each feature set size. For comparison, we also include the clause-to-variable ratio of the input product line.

With respect to RQ2, we note that runtime grows exponentially with the size of the domain model, while product lines with larger feature sets take longer to transform. The size of presence conditions also grows exponentially with increasing domain model sizes, and is two to three orders of magnitude larger than the input. Applying GmToAutosar[†] to product lines with smaller size of the feature set results in a larger increase to the clause-to-variable ratio. With regard to the sensitivity of GmToAutosar[†] to size of the domain model, we observe that runtime follows the expected pattern of exponential increase. Since the non-lifted version also grows exponentially, we conclude that this exponential increase is not solely due to the use of a SAT solver but also due to the inherent complexity of graph-rewriting-based model transformations. With regard to the sensitivity of GmToAutosar[†] to the size of presence conditions, we again observe an expected pattern of exponential increase. However, the increase is orders of magnitude large which is explained by the fact that our current implementation of GmToAutosar[†] does not perform any propositional simplification.

With respect to RQ1, we observe that for sizes of domain model and feature set that correspond to the description of real GM product lines, the observed runtime of GmToAutosar[†] is 3.59 seconds, compared to 3.25 for GmToAutosar. These differences in runtime indicate that GmToAutosar[†] scales well in terms of runtime. On the other hand we observe that the clause-to-variable ratio increased from 0.08 to 293.53, meaning that the output presence conditions contained a very large number of clauses. This points to the need to further optimize the DSLTrans engine, taking care to strike a balance between runtime and propositional simplification. Additionally, we note that the observed clause-to-variable ratio is not close to 4.26, which is considered to be the hardest for automated SAT solving [23].

Threats to Validity. There are two main threats to validity: First, the seed model was constructed using non-GM data, but rather publicly available automotive examples. Second, product lines of different sizes of domain model and feature set were artificially constructed by cloning the seed model. Both these issues stem from the fact that we could not access to real product lines due to limitations to publication of sensitive industrial data. To mitigate the first concern, we asked industrial partners to validate that our exemplar is realistic in terms of structure and size. To mitigate the second concern, we ensured that our cloning process resulted in product lines that had characteristics that were consistent with the parameters given by our industrial partners (number of variation points, average clause-to-variable ratio, shape of the presence conditions).

6   Lessons Learned and Discussion

The goal of this case study was to study the tractability of transformation lifting for industrial-grade transformations. In this section, we reflect on the experience of lifting GmToAutosar and describe the lessons learned from it.

We note that applying GmToAutosar to product lines fulfils a real industrial need to migrate legacy product lines to a new format. This validates the basic premise of our theory that lifting transformations for product lines is an industrially relevant endeavour. The observed results in Sect. 5 indicate that using GmToAutosar[†] is tractable for industrial-sized product lines, even if some additional optimization is required. It thus adds more evidence to the evaluation results obtained using experimentation with random inputs in [26]. This strengthens the claim that transformation lifting scales to real-world models.

A claimed benefit of transformation lifting is that transformations do not need to be rewritten specifically for product lines. Instead, what is required is the lifting of the transformation engine. This case study did not contradict this claim: we were able to migrate legacy GM product lines to AUTOSAR without having to rewrite the GmToAutosar transformation for product lines. Instead, we lifted the DSLTrans engine.

In [26], lifting was implemented using the Henshin graph transformation engine [5]. Specifically, we implemented lifting for graph transformations while *using* some capabilities of Henshin (e.g., matching) as a black box. However, lifting GmToAutosar required *adapting* part of the underlying transformation engine (DSLTrans) itself. The reason why this was possible was because the DSLTrans language is (a) based on graph-rewriting and (b) uses graph rewriting productions as atomic operations. It is thus possible to lift the entire engine by lifting just these atomic operations while leaving the rest of the matching and scheduling untouched. On the other hand, since GmToAutosar does not make use of certain more advanced language constructs in DSLTrans (e.g., indirect links), we were only required to make very targeted interventions to the DSLTrans engine. Lifting DSLTrans for arbitrary transformations will require more extensive changes. For some language features, most notably, existential matching, this also requires rethinking parts of the lifting algorithm from [26].

7   Related Work

There is extensive work on adapting software engineering techniques to product lines in order to avoid having to explicitly manipulate individual products [31]. Lifting has been applied to model checking [8], type checking [18], testing [19], etc. Our work fits in this category, focusing on lifting transformations.

The combination of product lines and model transformations has been extensively studied from the perspective of using transformations for configuring and refining product lines [10,11,14,16], and merging products and feature models [3,9,25], A theory of product line refinement along with a classification of commonly used refinement approaches is presented in [7]. Transformation lifting differs from these works because it is about adapting existing product-level transformations to the level of entire product lines, as opposed to creating transformations specifically for product lines.

Variant-preserving refactoring, aimed to improve the structure of source code, is presented in [27], for feature-oriented product lines [4]. This is accomplished by extending conventional refactoring with feature-oriented programming. Our lifting approach focuses on *annotative, model-based* product lines instead, and is not limited to structural improvement.

Approaches to product line evolution [22,28] focus on scenarios such as merging and splitting product lines, and changing the feature set or the domain model. The aim is usually to create templates for manually evolving the product line in a safe way. Our approach is to automatically evolve product lines by lifting product-level translation transformations, such as GmToAutosar. Safety is thus ensured by reasoning about the properties of the transformation at the product level [20,21,29].

8 Conclusion and Future Work

In this paper, we presented an empirical case study where we lifted GmToAutosar, a transformation that migrates GM legacy models to AUTOSAR, so that it can be used to transform product lines as opposed to individual products. Lifting required us to adapt the execution engine of DSLTrans, the model transformation language in which GmToAutosar is written. We experimented with the lifted transformation GmToAutosar$^\uparrow$, using realistic product lines of various sizes to study the effect of lifting to the execution time and the complexity of the resulting product line. The observations confirm our theory that lifted model transformations can be applied to industrial-grade product lines. However, more optimization is required in order to strike a balance between keeping the runtime low and avoiding the growth of the size of presence conditions. Our experience with lifting GmToAutosar indicates that lifting is feasible for transformation languages like DSLTrans, where individual productions can be lifted while reusing the engine for matching and scheduling. However, lifting the full range of language features (not used in GmToAutosar) requires rethinking our lifting method. In the future, we intend to lift the entire DSLTrans engine, to take into account its full range of advanced language features such as existential matching and transitive link matching. We also intend to leverage the experience of lifting an entire model transformation language to apply our approach to more complex and powerful transformation languages.

References

1. Automotive Simulink Examples. http://www.mathworks.com/help/simulink/examples.html#d0e477
2. AUTOSAR Consortium. AUTOSAR System Template (2007). http://AUTOSAR.org/index.php?p=3&up=1&uup=3&uuup=3&uuuup=0&uuuuup=0/AUTOSAR_TPS_SystemTemplate.pdf
3. Acher, M., Collet, P., Lahire, P., France, R.: Comparing approaches to implement feature model composition. In: Kühne, T., Selic, B., Gervais, M.-P., Terrier, F. (eds.) ECMFA 2010. LNCS, vol. 6138, pp. 3–19. Springer, Heidelberg (2010)
4. Apel, S., Kästner, C.: An overview of feature-oriented software development. J. Object Technol. 8(5), 49–84 (2009)
5. Arendt, T., Biermann, E., Jurack, S., Krause, C., Taentzer, G.: Henshin: advanced concepts and tools for in-place EMF model transformations. In: Proceedings of MODELS 2010, pp. 121–135 (2010)
6. Barroca, B., Lúcio, L., Amaral, V., Félix, R., Sousa, V.: DSLTrans: a turing incomplete transformation language. In: Malloy, B., Staab, S., van den Brand, M. (eds.) SLE 2010. LNCS, vol. 6563, pp. 296–305. Springer, Heidelberg (2011)
7. Borba, P., Teixeira, L., Gheyi, R.: A theory of software product line refinement. J. Theor. CS 455, 2–30 (2012)
8. Classen, A., Heymans, P., Schobbens, P.Y., Legay, A., Raskin, J.F.: Model checking lots of systems: efficient verification of temporal properties in software product lines. In: Proceedings of ICSE 2010, pp. 335–344 (2010)
9. Classen, A., Heymans, P., Tun, T.T., Nuseibeh, B.: Towards safer composition. In: Proceedings of ICSE'2009, Companion Volume, pp. 227–230 (2009)

10. Czarnecki, K., Antkiewicz, M.: Mapping features to models: a template approach based on superimposed variants. In: Glück, R., Lowry, M. (eds.) GPCE 2005. LNCS, vol. 3676, pp. 422–437. Springer, Heidelberg (2005)
11. Czarnecki, K., Helsen, S.: Staged configuration using feature models. In: Nord, R.L. (ed.) SPLC 2004. LNCS, vol. 3154, pp. 266–283. Springer, Heidelberg (2004)
12. de Moura, L., Bjørner, N.S.: Z3: an efficient SMT solver. In: Ramakrishnan, C.R., Rehof, J. (eds.) TACAS 2008. LNCS, vol. 4963, pp. 337–340. Springer, Heidelberg (2008)
13. Flores, R., Krueger, Ch., Clements, P.: Second-generation product line engineering: a case study at general motors. In: Capilla, R., Bosch, J., Kang, K.C. (eds.) Systems and Software Variability Management, pp. 223–250. Springer, Heidelberg (2013)
14. Garcés, K., Parra, C., Arboleda, H., Yie, A., Casallas, R.: Variability management in a model-driven software product line. Rev. Av. en sistemas e Informática 4(2), 3–12 (2007)
15. Gronback, R.: Eclipse Modeling Project. Addison Wesley, New York (2009)
16. Haugen, Ø., Moller-Pedersen, B., Oldevik, J, Olsen, G.K., Svendsen, A.: Adding standardized variability to domain specific languages. In: Proceedings of SPLC 2008, pp. 139–148 (2008)
17. Kästner, C., Apel, S.: Integrating compositional and annotative approaches for product line engineering. In: Proceedings of McGPLE Workshop at GPCE 2008, pp. 35–40 (2008)
18. Kästner, C., Apel, S., Thüm, T., Saake, G.: Type checking annotation-based product lines. ACM TOSEM 21(3), 14 (2012)
19. Kästner, C., von Rhein, A., Erdweg, S., Pusch, J., Apel, S., Rendel, T., Ostermann, K.: Toward variability-aware testing. In: Proceedings of FOSD 2012, pp. 1–8 (2012)
20. Lúcio, L., Barroca, B., Amaral, V.: A technique for automatic validation of model transformations. In: Petriu, D.C., Rouquette, N., Haugen, Ø. (eds.) MODELS 2010, Part I. LNCS, vol. 6394, pp. 136–150. Springer, Heidelberg (2010)
21. Lúcio, L., Oakes, B.J., Vangheluwe, H.: A Technique for Symbolically Verifying Properties of Graph-Based Model Transformations. Technical report SOCS-TR-2014.1, McGill University (2014). http://msdl.cs.mcgill.ca/people/levi/30_publications/files/A_Technique_/for_Symbolically_Verifying_Properties_of_Model_Transf.pdf
22. Neves, L., Teixeira, L., Sena, D., Alves, V., Kulezsa, U., Borba, P.: Investigating the safe evolution of software product lines. ACM SIGPLAN Not. 47(3), 33–42 (2011)
23. Nudelman, E., Leyton-Brown, K., Hoos, H., Devkar, A., Shoham, Y.: Understanding random SAT: beyond the clauses-to-variables ratio. In: Proceedings of CP 2004, pp. 438–452 (2004)
24. Pretschner, A., Broy, M., Kruger, I.H., Stauner, T.: Software engineering for automotive systems: a roadmap. In: Proceedings of FOSE 2007, pp. 55–71 (2007)
25. Rubin, J., Chechik, M.: Combining related products into product lines. In: de Lara, J., Zisman, A. (eds.) Fundamental Approaches to Software Engineering. LNCS, vol. 7212, pp. 285–300. Springer, Heidelberg (2012)
26. Salay, R., Famelis, M., Rubin, J., Di Sandro, A., Chechik, M.: Lifting model transformations to product lines. In: Proceedings of ICSE 2014, pp. 117–128 (2014)
27. Schulze, S. Thüm, T., Kuhlemann, M., Saake, G.: Variant-preserving refactoring in feature-oriented software product lines. In: Proceedings of VAMOS 2012, pp. 73–81 (2012)
28. Seidl, C., Heidenreich, F., Aßmann, U.: Co-evolution of models and feature mapping in software product lines. In: Proceedings of SPLC 2012, pp. 76–85 (2012)

29. Selim, G.M.K., Lúcio, L., Cordy, J.R., Dingel, J., Oakes, B.J.: Specification and verification of graph-based model transformation properties. In: Giese, H., König, B. (eds.) ICGT 2014. LNCS, vol. 8571, pp. 113–129. Springer, Heidelberg (2014)

30. Selim, G.M.K., Wang, S., Cordy, J.R., Dingel, J.: Model transformations for migrating legacy models: an industrial case study. In: Vallecillo, A., Tolvanen, J.-P., Kindler, E., Störrle, H., Kolovos, D. (eds.) ECMFA 2012. LNCS, vol. 7349, pp. 90–101. Springer, Heidelberg (2012)

31. Thüm, T., Apel, S., Kästner, C., Kuhlemann, M., Schaefer, I., Saake, G.: Analysis strategies for software product lines. School of Computer Science, University of Magdeburg, Technical report FIN-004-2012, (2012)

New Paradigms for Model Transformation

VIATRA 3: A Reactive Model Transformation Platform

Gábor Bergmann[1], István Dávid[3]([⊠]), Ábel Hegedüs[2], Ákos Horváth[1,2],
István Ráth[1,2], Zoltán Ujhelyi[2], and Dániel Varró[1]

[1] Department of Measurement and Information Systems,
Budapest University of Technology and Economics,
Magyar Tudósok Krt. 2, 1117 Budapest, Hungary
{bergmann,varro}@mit.bme.hu
[2] IncQuery Labs Ltd., Budapest, Hungary
{hegedus,horvath,rath,ujhelyi}@incquerylabs.com
[3] Modelling, Simulation and Design Lab, University of Antwerp,
Middelheimlaan 1, 2020 Antwerp, Belgium
istvan.david@uantwerpen.be

Abstract. Model-driven tools frequently rely on advanced technologies to support model queries, view maintenance, design rule validation, model transformations or design space exploration. Some of these features are initiated explicitly by domain engineers (batch execution) while others are executed automatically when certain trigger events are detected (live execution). Unfortunately, their integration into a complex industrial modeling environment is difficult due to hidden interference and unspecified interaction between different features. In this paper, we present a reactive, event-driven model transformation platform over EMF models, which captures tool features as model queries and transformations, and provides a systematic, well-founded integration between a variety of such tool features. VIATRA 3 offers a family of internal DSLs (i.e. dedicated libraries) to specify advanced tool features built on top of existing languages like EMF-INCQUERY and Xtend. Its main innovation is a source incremental execution scheme built on the reactive programming paradigm ssupported by an event-driven virtual machine.

Keywords: Event-driven transformation · Virtual machine · Reactive programming · Source incremental transformations

1 Introduction

With the increasing adoption of model-driven engineering in critical systems development, the increasing complexity of development processes and modeling artefacts poses new challenges for tool developers, especially in collaboration and scalability. Nowadays, such challenges are typically addressed with dedicated

This work was partially supported by the MONDO (EU ICT-611125) project.

D. Kolovos and M. Wimmer (Eds.): ICMT 2015, LNCS 9152, pp. 101–110, 2015.
DOI: 10.1007/978-3-319-21155-8_8

problem-specific solutions such as on-the-fly constraint evaluation engines [1,2] (to improve the scalability of model validation), incremental model transformation tools [3] for scalable model synchronization, or design space exploration tools [4] (to synthesize optimal models wrt some objectives). Some of these scenarios are initiated explicitly by domain engineers (*batch execution*) while others are executed automatically upon certain trigger events (*live execution*).

Unfortunately, integrating different technologies into a complex industrial modeling environment is often difficult and costly. This is due to hidden interference and unspecified interaction between different tool features. For instance, a notification originating from a model change may easily trigger conflicting actions in different plugins. As a consequence, complex tool platforms such as the Eclipse Modeling Framework (EMF) [5] are known to suffer from severe performance and quality issues caused e.g. by the concurrent asynchronous execution of various model indexing and validation mechanisms.

In this paper, we present a *source incremental event-driven model transformation platform based on the reactive programming paradigm* [6] to drive the systematic, well-founded integration of tool features in various scenarios over EMF models. The VIATRA 3 *Event-driven Virtual Machine* (EVM) provides basic executional building blocks and primitives with clearly defined event-based semantics. EVM also enables to combine various advanced tool features so that complex interactions can be constructed easily and executed consistently.

VIATRA 3 offers a family of internal DSLs (i.e. dedicated libraries and APIs) built on top of existing languages to specify advanced tool features as model queries and transformations. The EMF-INCQUERY language is seamlessly integrated to capture any conditions and constraints for a transformation. Furthermore, Java and Xtend-based internal DSLs (APIs) are used to specify transformations rules as well as complex interactions between different tool features.

While VIATRA 3 is designed to support a wide spectrum of tooling scenarios, our case study focuses on a typical scenario including incremental deployment to present challenges that arise in the interaction between *batch and live model transformations*. The aim of the example is to illustrate to what an extent the integration complexity is reduced by capturing and handling all tool features and their interactions based on a uniform event-driven virtual machine.

The rest of the paper is structured as follows: first, we overview modeling scenarios that motivate the development of the generalized virtual machine architecture and introduce the case study in Sect. 2. Then we present our virtual machine for reactive event-driven transformations (Sect. 3). Related work is discussed in Sects. 4 and 5 concludes the paper.

2   Motivating Example

In our motivating example[1], we investigate batch and incremental model-to-model transformations. The source domain describes a generic infrastructure

---

[1] The complete source code, documentation and performance evaluation results are available from https://github.com/IncQueryLabs/incquery-examples-cps.

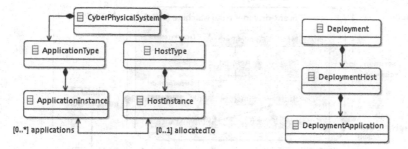

(a) Hosts and Applications of the CPS.   (b) Deployed Hosts and Applications.

Fig. 1. Source and target models

for cyber-physical systems (CPS) where applications (services) are dynamically allocated to connected hosts. The target domain represents the system deployment configuration with stateful applications deployed on hosts. Initially, we aim to derive a deployment model from the CPS model, and then incremental model transformations are used to propagate changes in the CPS model to the deployment model and the traceability model.

Metamodel. Due to space considerations, we present a limited fragment of the metamodel in Fig. 1, the description of the domain is adopted from [4]. The simplified CPS source model (Fig. 1a) contains *HostInstances* and *Application-Instances*, typed by *HostTypes* and *ApplicationTypes*, respectively. *Application-Instances* are allocated to a *HostInstance*. In the Deployment model (Fig. 1b), *DeploymentHosts* and *DeploymentApplications* are derived from their instance counterparts in the CPS model, respectively; and the hosts are associated with the hosted applications. Finally, the mappings between the two domains are persisted in a traceability model.

Scenarios. In the original case study, we had to provide integrated tooling to cover the following use cases:

1. **Batch transformations** are used to map *HostInstances* of a given *HostType* to a *DeploymentHost* (the mapping is stored in an explicit trace model);
2. **Live transformations** are used to automatically map *ApplicationInstances* to *DeploymentApplications* in an event-driven way (i.e. fired upon changes to the source model to keep the target and trace models consistent).
3. **On-the-fly validation** is continuously performed (i.e. before and after model synchronization) to ensure the correctness of the mapping.

   Due to (data and control) dependencies, model synchronization phases should only be initialized once the batch transformations have completely terminated and when the (source) model is free of errors as indicated by validation results.

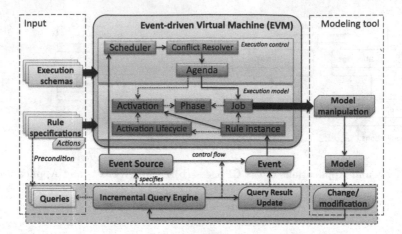

Fig. 2. Architecture of the EVM for model transformations

In a traditional MDE toolchain, separate tool features would be used to describe the various phases, requiring an external orchestrator to facilitate the coordination. Complex features in real MDE tools (like model indexing or file operations) add further complexity to the integration of tool features. The current paper presents how an event-driven virtual machine can reduce such complexity.

3   An Event-Driven Virtual Machine (EVM)

Event-driven model transformations are executed continuously as *reactions* to changes of the underlying model. To facilitate this sort of execution, we adopted reactive programming principles. The core concept of reactive programming is the *event-driven behavior*: components are connected to event sources and their behavior is determined by the event instances observed on *event streams*. Compared to sequential programming, the benefits of reactive programming are remarkable especially in cases when continuous interaction with the environment has to be maintained by the application based on external events without a priori knowledge on their sequence [6].

Figure 2 presents the architecture of the Event-driven Virtual Machine (EVM), the novel execution engine of the VIATRA 3 platform[2]. Although this paper demonstrates its use in model transformation scenarios, EVM is an engine for executing reactive programs in general.

The *specification* of an EVM program consists of two parts. First, the *Rule specifications* are defined as *Queries* over a given *Model*(s) and serve as a precondition to the transformation. Second, the *Actions* to be executed are specified, which in this case are *Model manipulation*s over the input models. Furthermore, *Execution schemas* are defined in order to orchestrate the reactive behavior. Now we briefly describe the behavior of other core components of Fig. 2 in the sequel.

---

[2] http://wiki.eclipse.org/EMFIncQuery/DeveloperDocumentation/EventDrivenVM contains the complete technical documentation.

3.1   Events

In batch transformation scenarios[3], the sequence of executing actions associated with a batch transformation is usually determined solely by the activations initiated from the transformation program. However, the core features of EVM enable reactions to events. We distinguish between two kinds of events.

– *Controlled* events are initiated explicitly by the transformation program, and involve the *firing* of a selected rule with concrete values substituted for its parameters. Thus a controlled event is characterized by a rule activation.
– *Observed* events are caused by external behavior, and the time of their occurrence may not be determined by the transformation program. Such observed events include elementary model notifications and updated results of model queries. However, more complex ways of detecting changes in the model (see change patterns [7]) or aggregating temporal behavior of changes in the past (see complex event processing [8]) are also possible over the EVM platform.

3.2   Activation Lifecycles

Listing 1 presents an event-driven transformation to keep already mapped *ApplicationInstances* of the CPS model in sync with their *DeploymentApplication* counterpart in the Deployment model.

The actions of event-driven transformations (in Lines 10-12, 14-24 and 26-28) are associated with a specific *events* reflecting the current state of the activation. As opposed to simple batch transformations, these events suggest that in addition to executing an action on the *appearance* of an activation, *updates* and the *disappearance* of the same activation might be also relevant from transformation point of view and can also serve as triggers for executing actions.

Events reflecting the current state of the activation constitute a transition system called the *Activation Lifecycle* (Line 8), serving as the centerpiece of the reactive paradigms supported by EVM. An Activation Lifecycle consists of different (1) *Phases* (see Fig. 2) an *Activation* can be associated with during its existence; and (2) event-triggered transitions between the Phases. Optionally, (3) a transition may be associated with a *Job*, which represents the executable *Actions* of an input rule specification. Figure 3 presents two typical Activation Lifecycles.

Figure 3a illustrates the lifecycle of an event-driven transformation rule. Apart from the initial phase, we distinguish between enabled and disabled phases depending on the presence or absence of a *Fire* transition. Event-driven transformations define executable actions for enabled states of the lifecycle. If an activation enters that specific phase, it may fire and upon the transition, the associated job (defined by the action in the transformation rule) gets executed.

For example, the first time a match of the *MappedApplicationInstance* model query is found, an activation of the rule will occur in the *APPEARED* state. If the EVM fires that activation, the *appearJob* will be executed.

---

[3] https://github.com/IncQueryLabs/incquery-examples-cps/wiki/
Alternative-transformation-methods#Batch.

Listing 1. Event-driven transformation rule for maintaining *ApplicationInstances*

```
1   //finds every every transformed and allocated deploymentApp
2   pattern mappedApplicationInstance(
3       appInstance, deploymentApp, hostInstance, deploymentHost) {...}

5   CPSToDeployment mapping //reference to the mapping model val
6   applicationUpdateRule = createRule().name("application update")
7       .precondition(mappedApplicationInstance) //a graph pattern as precondition
8       .lifeCycle(ActivationLifecycles.default)
9       //action to be executed when a pattern match appears
10      .action(ActivationStates.APPEARED) [
11          debug("Starting monitoring mapped application with ID: "+ appInstance.id)
12      ]
13      //action to be executed when a pattern match gets updated
14      .action(ActivationStates.UPDATED) [
15          debug("Updating application with ID: "+ appInstance.id)
16          //case 1: ID changed
17          if (appInstance.id != deploymentApp.id) {
18              deploymentApp.set(id, appInstance.id)
19          }
20          //case 2: host changed
21          if (!deploymentHost.applications.contains(deploymentApp)) {
22              deploymentHost.set(deploymentHost_Applications, deploymentApp)
23          }
24      ]
25      //action to be executed when a pattern match disappears
26      .action(ActivationStates.DISAPPEARED) [
27          debug("Stopped monitoring mapped application with ID: " + appInstance.id)
28      ].build
```

To unify the behavior of model transformations over the EVM platform, both event-driven and batch transformations are executed as reactive programs (using the the activation lifecycle of Fig. 3b for the batch case). The enabled phases of an activation lifecycle represent outstanding reactions to *observed* events, but the firing of the actual reactive jobs is tied to *controlled* events.

3.3   Scheduler

External observed events influence activation phases according to the lifecycle, and the active phase selects the job to be executed (if any). However, it is the chosen *Scheduler* component that determines when EVM can fire these controlled events (i.e. execute the jobs).

Practical examples for the scheduling event include (1) the signal of the query engine indicating that the updating of query results after an elementary model manipulation has concluded; (2) the successful commit of a model editing transaction; or (3) some combination of the former events with a timer. The choice of scheduling event has to take into account the following factors:

- The rules may require a certain level of consistency in the model, e.g. some rules are inefficient to execute while a large-scale transaction is incomplete;
- Otherwise, the rules should be executed as soon as possible thus their effects are observed by the user or by further transformation steps.

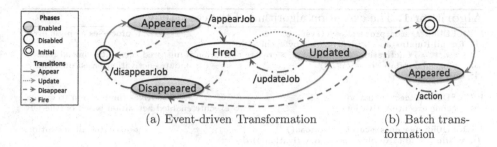

(a) Event-driven Transformation

(b) Batch transformation

Fig. 3. Typical rule lifecycles

Event driven transformation rules may also explicitly invoke other rules, which is a direct rule dependency. However, indirect rule dependency may also exist when model manipulation in a job causes observed changes which, in turn, enable activations and trigger the scheduler.

3.4 Agenda

The *Agenda* stores the current phases (states) of all activations of each rule. Its role is dual: it helps maintain the phase of activations in reaction to events, and it supplies the set of rule activations being in an enabled phase, i.e. activations that can be fired. The core operation of EVM is intrinsically tied to the agenda: in case of an observed or controlled event, the rule activation corresponding to the specific event will change phase according to the transition in the lifecycle model defined for the rule that starts at the current phase and is labeled with the event type token. Afterwards, if there is a job associated with the transition, it is invoked with the activation providing the input parameters.

As the set of all possible activations is practically infinite (as each rule parameter may point to any memory address), the implementation considers only those activations that are currently not in their initial phase. This makes the agenda finitely representable, since a finite number of events may have moved only a finite number of activations out of their initial phases.

3.5 Conflict Resolution

At any point in time, the rules (or a selected subset of rules in a common case of batch transformations) might have multiple activations in an enabled state, which is called a *conflict*. If the transformation is to invoke a rule firing, a single enabled activation has to be selected from the conflicting ones (mainly due to the single threaded manipulation of EMF models). This selection can be done manually by the transformation code, but EVM also provides an automated mechanism that delegates this decision to a user-specified *Conflict Resolver* (see Fig. 2). Built-in conflict resolvers include FIFO, LIFO, fair random choice, rule priority (with a secondary conflict resolver within priority levels), interactive

Algorithm 1. The execution algorithm of the case study

PROCEDURE Agenda.processEvent(Event e)   ▷ processes a single event
1: **for all** RuleInstance ri if triggered by event e **do**
2:      $act := ri$.activationForEvent(e)   ▷ creates activation if unstored (i.e. in the initial phase)
3:      agenda.updatePhase(act, e)   ▷ updates activation based on event e
4: **end for**

PROCEDURE Scheduler.main()   ▷ drives the reaction to events
5: Agenda.executeActivations()   ▷ execute enabled activation based on the CR

PROCEDURE Agenda.executeActivations()   ▷ executes all activations
6: **while** (ConflictResolver.hasNextActivation()) **do**
7:      $act :=$ ConflictResolver.nextActivation()   ▷ gets next activation
8:      Executor.fire(act)   ▷ fires the activation
9: **end while**

choice (e.g. on the user interface), but it is possible to implement arbitrary conflict resolution strategies.

3.6 Execution

The execution of event-driven transformations is handled by the EVM. We present the process by walking through the execution Algorithm 1 using an example scenario. The scenario presents an update of ApplicationInstance *a1* where its associated HostInstance is replaced.

Step 1 The HostInstance reference of ApplicationInstance *a1* is removed. The matched precondition of the rule generates an *updates* event.

Step 2 In the EVM, the *Agenda* processes the event. The activation of the transformation rule is updated (Line 3).

Step 3 When the notifications are processed, the *Scheduler* initiates the rule execution by notifying the *Agenda* (Line 5). The *Agenda* attempts to acquire the next transformation activation from the ConflictResolver (Line 7) and fire it (Line 8).

4   Related Work

Virtual machines for model queries and transformations. The ATL virtual machine was the first to provide execution primitives on which different transformation languages (like, ATL and QVT) can be executed. Recently introduced new features include lazy evaluation [9], incremental [10] combined into the ReactiveATL transformation engine. As a main conceptual difference, this approach is target incremental, i.e. a transformation is executed only when its result is needed — unlike our source incremental virtual machine.

EMFTVM [11] is an execution engine for EMF models that provides both a very low-level language and execution primitives to have a more simple compiler architecture. Similarly, T-Core [12] is based on the same concept for providing an execution engine for graph transformation rules. Their main advantage is that they provide better performance for the low-level primitives and optimization capabilities in case of translation from high-level languages. Model transformation chains [13] aim at composing different transformations proposing a loosely coupled integration between existing transformation steps.

Our virtual machine is unique in combining different best practices: (1) it provides tight integration between many heterogeneous tool features (queries, transformations, validation, exploration, etc.) built upon (2) a source-incremental reactive event-driven paradigm to provide well-founded integration.

Event-driven techniques and model transformations. Event-driven techniques have been used in many fields. In relational database management systems, even the concept of triggers can be considered as simple operations whose execution is initiated by events, which have been utilized for event-driven model transformation purposes previously [14]. These approaches provided the basics for event-driven model transformation techniques.

Our approach presented in the this paper can be regarded as a foundation for previous work on incremental well-formedness validation [1], live and change-driven transformations [7], design space exploration [4] and streaming model transformations [8]. Despite not having been published previously, EVM has been a hidden component of EMF-INCQUERY since 2013, and has already proven to be an efficient execution platform for incremental transformations [15].

5   Conclusion

In this paper, we have proposed a novel execution infrastructure for model processing chains, based on an event-driven reactive virtual machine architecture. Its primary design principle is *flexibility*: through the customizability of rules and execution strategies, it can provide the foundations to a wide range of applications, it supports both stateless and stateful systems, and its internal DSLs (based on Xtend and Java) provide a uniform integration platform for complex model processing programs. As we have shown through the case study, VIATRA 3 is capable of unifying several previously separated advanced modeling aspects into an integrated system, which can address challenging issues such conflict management.

As a main direction for future development, we plan to externalize the DSLs into a family of extensible, yet easy-to-use languages.

Acknowledgements. The authors wish to thank all the contributors of the VIATRA 3 and EMF-INCQUERY projects, in particular Tamás Szabó.

References

1. Ujhelyi, Z., Bergmann, G., Hegedüs, Á., Horváth, Á., Izsó, B., Ráth, I., Szatmári, Z., Varró, D.: EMF-IncQuery: an integrated development environment for live model queries. Sci. Comput. Program. **98**, 80–99 (2015)
2. Willink, E.D.: An extensible OCL virtual machine and code generator. In: Proceedings of the 12th Workshop on OCL and Textual Modelling, pp. 13–18. ACM (2012)

3. Giese, H., Wagner, R.: From model transformation to incremental bidirectional model synchronization. Softw. Syst. Model. (SoSyM) **8**(1), 21–43 (2009)
4. Abdeen, H., Varró, D., Sahraoui, H., Nagy, A.S., Hegedüs, Á., Horváth, Á., Debreceni, C.: Multi-objective optimization in rule-based design space exploration. In: 29th IEEE/ACM International Conference on Automated Software Engineering (ASE 2014), pp. 289–300. IEEE, Vasteras, Sweden (2014)
5. The Eclipse Project: Eclipse Modeling Framework. Accessed: (2007)
6. Bainomugisha, E., Carreton, A.L., Cutsem, T.V., Mostinckx, S., Meuter, W.D.: A survey on reactive programming. ACM Comput. Surv. **45**(4), 52:1–52:34 (2012)
7. Bergmann, G., Ráth, I., Varró, G., Varró, D.: Change-driven model transformations. Software and Systems Modeling **11**, 431–461 (2012)
8. Dávid, I., Ráth, I., Varró, D.: Streaming model transformations by complex event processing. In: Dingel, J., Schulte, W., Ramos, I., Abrahão, S., Insfran, E. (eds.) MODELS 2014. LNCS, vol. 8767, pp. 68–83. Springer, Heidelberg (2014)
9. Tisi, M., Martínez, S., Jouault, F., Cabot, J.: Lazy Execution of Model-to-Model Transformations. In: Whittle, J., Clark, T., Kühne, T. (eds.) MODELS 2011. LNCS, vol. 6981, pp. 32–46. Springer, Heidelberg (2011)
10. Jouault, F., Tisi, M.: Towards incremental execution of ATL transformations. In: Tratt, L., Gogolla, M. (eds.) ICMT 2010. LNCS, vol. 6142, pp. 123–137. Springer, Heidelberg (2010)
11. Wagelaar, D., Tisi, M., Cabot, J., Jouault, F.: Towards a general composition semantics for rule-based model transformation. In: Whittle, J., Clark, T., Kühne, T. (eds.) MODELS 2011. LNCS, vol. 6981, pp. 623–637. Springer, Heidelberg (2011)
12. Syriani, E., Vangheluwe, H., LaShomb, B.: T-core: a framework for custom-built model transformation engines. Softw. Syst. Model. 1–29 (2013)
13. Yie, A., Casallas, R., Deridder, D., Wagelaar, D.: Realizing model transformation chain interoperability. Softw. Syst. Model. **11**(1), 55–75 (2012)
14. Bergmann, G., Horváth, D., Horváth, A.: Applying incremental graph transformation to existing models in relational databases. In: Ehrig, H., Engels, G., Kreowski, H.-J., Rozenberg, G. (eds.) ICGT 2012. LNCS, vol. 7562, pp. 371–385. Springer, Heidelberg (2012)
15. van Pinxten, J., Basten, T.: Motrusca: interactive model transformation use case repository. In: 7th York Doctor Symposium on Computer Science & Electronics, vol. 57 (2014)

Towards Functional Model Transformations with OCL

Frédéric Jouault[✉], Olivier Beaudoux, Matthias Brun,
Mickael Clavreul, and Guillaume Savaton

ESEO, Angers, France
{frederic.jouault,olivier.beaudoux,matthias.brun,
mickael.clavreul,guillaume.savaton}@eseo.fr

Abstract. Several model transformation approaches such as QVT and
ATL use OCL as expression language for its model-querying capabilities.
However, they need to add specific and incompatible syntactic constructs
for pattern matching as well as model element creation and mutation.

In this paper, we present an exploratory approach to enable the
expression of whole model transformations in OCL. This approach leverages some OCL extensions proposed for inclusion in the upcoming OCL
2.5: pattern matching and shadow objects. It also relies on a specific
execution layer to enable traceability and side effects on models.

With model transformations as OCL functions, it becomes possible to use a single, standard, well-known, functional, and formalized
model querying language to perform tasks traditionally assigned to model
transformation languages. Thus, functional techniques such as function composition and higher-order become directly applicable to model
transformations.

Keywords: Model transformation · OCL · Functional transformation

1 Introduction

The Object Constraint Language [6] (OCL) progressively evolved from a language focused on the expression of constraints (invariants, pre- and post- conditions) on UML models to a more general metamodel-independent language for
model query and navigation. Some model transformation approaches (such as
QVT and ATL) started making use of these capabilities by integrating (or host-
ing) OCL as an expression languages. These *host* languages typically leverage
OCL to express *guards* (i.e., predicates selecting elements that match transformation rules) and for navigation (i.e., path expressions over models).

Because OCL is a purely functional language, it cannot be directly used to
perform changes on models or their elements. Therefore, host languages must
define specific syntax and semantics around OCL for these purposes. However,
recent OCL extension proposals [3,5] considered for inclusion in the next version
of OCL [12] give even more capabilities to OCL. For instance, structural *pattern*

© Springer International Publishing Switzerland 2015
D. Kolovos and M. Wimmer (Eds.): ICMT 2015, LNCS 9152, pp. 111–120, 2015.
DOI: 10.1007/978-3-319-21155-8_9

matching enables declarative data analysis, and *shadow objects* enable creation and processing of immutable versions of model elements. Making use of shadow objects does not require performing any side effect such as creating elements in models. This constraint is mandatory to keep OCL purely functional.

In this paper, we explore the possibility of directly using OCL as a transformation language. For this purpose, we define our own variant of OCL called OCLT (where the T stands for transformation). OCLT is based on OCL 2.4 [6] and integrates pattern matching and shadow objects extensions in a way that is similar to the work presented in [5], but with syntax closer to the one used in [3]. These custom extensions are likely to become unnecessary when they actually become standard by being integrated in OCL 2.5. In the mean time, OCLT lets us start investigating their capabilities. In addition to these extensions, OCLT also needs some means to actually create elements in models. To this end, we additionally integrate to OCLT a specific layer that can translate shadow objects to actual model elements. This layer is also responsible for *trace link* resolution, which consists in linking elements created separately by using traceability links between source and target elements.

Model transformations expressed in OCLT are pure functions taking as arguments a collection of source model elements, and returning a collection of target elements. Transformation composition thus becomes function composition. Other functional techniques such as partial application and higher-order functions also become applicable to model transformation. We illustrate our approach on the well-known *ClassDiagram2Relational* model transformation case-study.

The paper is organized as follows. Section 2 gives an overview of the shadow objects and pattern matching OCL extensions. Section 3 presents the specific execution layer of OCLT, and shows how our approach can be applied to the well-known *ClassDiagram2Relational* transformation. Section 4 discusses the merits of the OCLT approach. Relation to some related works is given in Sect. 5. And finally Sect. 6 concludes.

2   Overview of Proposed OCL Constructs

Over the years, many different OCL extensions have been proposed and discussed (notably in the OCL Workshop series since the year 2000). We focus here on two extensions that facilitate functional model transformation: *shadow objects*, and *pattern matching*. They are both considered for inclusion in the next version of OCL, as explained in [12]. They were first introduced in [5], and are also discussed in [3] along with other extensions such as lambda expressions and active operations [1]. Although these other extensions could be useful, they are not strictly necessary for the approach presented in this paper. This section presents shadow objects and pattern matching with emphasis on their application to model transformation.

2.1   Shadow Objects

OCL already offers immutable tuples with labeled components. These tuples notably help with complex computations by enabling the construction of temporary data structures. The following example shows a possible tuple-based representation of class named C owning an attribute named a:

```
1 Tuple {name = 'C', attr = OrderedSet {Tuple {name = 'a'}}}
```

The outermost tuple is a class, and the innermost tuple an attribute. One can note that these facts are not captured in the tuple representation. Although it would be possible to add an explicit *type* component to both tuples, shadow objects extend tuples with an attached model element type, as illustrated below:

```
1 Class {name = 'C', attr = OrderedSet {Attribute {name = 'a'}}}
```

Like tuples, shadow objects are immutable and can be processed by OCL expressions. The semantics of OCL is only modified so that they are mostly indistinguishable from actual model elements. Shadow objects can be useful in side effect-free OCL expressions (e.g., as metamodel-typed tuples). But they are especially convenient when explicitly supported by a host language. For instance, a model transformation language may create an actual element in a model when a shadow object is assigned to a property of an existing model element. Model element creation can thus use the same standard OCL syntax in all host languages.

2.2   Pattern Matching with OCL

Pattern matching is a construct found in several successful functional languages (e.g., Haskell, ML, Scala), but not in OCL. It is typically used to analyze the structure of data. Existing OCL-based model transformation languages typically heavily rely on OCL guards for rule matching. For instance, to match all `Attribute`s named `'id'` and not multivalued, one may write (in ATL-like syntax):

```
1 a : Attribute (
2     a.name = 'id' and not a.multiValued
3 )
```

To each `Attribute` in turn a variable named a is bound (line 1), and then a guard (line 2) is evaluated to test if `Attribute` a matches or not. The guard becomes more verbose when the values of more properties need to be examined. With pattern matching, one may write:

```
1 a@Attribute {
2     name = 'id',
3     multiValued = false
4 }
```

The @ character (line 1) denotes an as-pattern (like in Haskell and Scala), which binds the matched value to the variable. The pattern we have here is an object pattern that matches model elements (or shadow objects). It consists of a type: `Attribute` (line 1), and a set of slots (lines 1-2) between curly braces. Each slot details the value (right of equal symbol) that its associated property (named on the left of the equal symbol) must have for a match. More complex pattern matching can be performed: all values can be matched (e.g., `Tuples`, `Collections`), and multiple variables may be bound in a single pattern.

Moreover, in the context of this paper, we decide to support non-linear patterns (i.e., patterns in which a given variable may be bound several times). Nonetheless, guards are still useful, and can be combined with pattern matching.

3 Application to Model Transformation

3.1 Traceability and Side Effects

As mentioned earlier, OCL is purely functional and does not permit side effects on mutable data structures. However, models and their elements are often represented as such. This is notably the case in EMF[1]-based tools. Whether they should rather be represented as immutable data structures or not is beyond the scope of this paper. We want to find a solution that plays well with mutable models as well. The resolution of trace links is another issue: it typically works by linking (and therefore updating) elements created at different places.

In order to address these problems, we add a specific layer to OCLT. After the execution of an OCLT transformation, this layer translates shadow objects into actual model elements, and performs trace links resolution. These actions are only performed at the end of each transformation before their results can be reused (e.g., by another transformation). We also impose that whole models are created by OCLT transformations (i.e., no update to existing models). Therefore, model creation can happen atomically, models as seen from OCLT can be considered as immutable, and the purely functional property of OCLT can be preserved. We add a new type of OCL expression called *transfo* in order to identify which OCLT functions require this specific layer to kick in. This is its only syntactically visible aspect. The workings of trace link resolution are best explained on a case study. They are therefore explained in the next section.

3.2 ClassDiagram2Relational in OCLT

This section shows how the *ClassDiagram2Relational* transformation can be encoded in OCLT, as given in Listing 1. The source and target metamodels are given in Fig. 1. They were adapted from [9].

The transformation is written as OCLT function *classDiagram2Relational* with type *transfo* (line 1). It is composed of three parts similar to model transformation rules: *Class2Table* (line 4), *SingleValuedAttribute2Column* (line 14), and *MultiValuedAttribute2ColumnsAndTable* (line 17). Each *rule* is encoded as a *case* in a single *collect* over the whole source model contents (line 2). Although the syntax of *cases* is different from the one presented in [5], it is equivalent. *collect* ignores elements that do not match any pattern, like an implicit *select*.

Rule *Class2Table* selects instances of *Class* from the source and binds them to variable *a* since they trivially match the empty object pattern (line 4). A shadow object instance of *Table* is then created before being collected to the target (lines 5 to 12). The mapping between the class and the relational table is defined

---

[1] Eclipse Modeling Framework: https://www.eclipse.org/modeling/emf/.

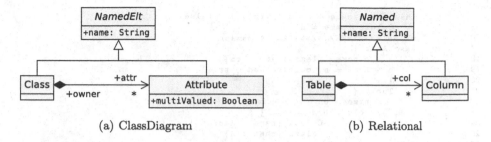

(a) ClassDiagram   (b) Relational

Fig. 1. Metamodels for the *ClassDiagram2Relational* transformation.

within the shadow object directly by setting its properties. The name of the table matches exactly the name of the class (line 6), and its columns consist of a column defining the primary key (line 8) union the set of columns representing the single-valued attributes of the class (line 10).

According to the Relational metamodel, the *cols* property of Table only accepts Columns as values. Therefore, trying to put Attributes in this property is an issue. OCLT relaxes the type system for shadow object so as to temporarily allow it to happen, until trace link resolution kicks in. Once the whole transformation has been executed, all source elements stored in the properties of target elements (such as Attributes being stored in property *cols* of Table here) are resolved into their corresponding target elements. The trace links between source elements and target elements required for resolution are automatically created during the execution of every *collect* iterator that has a collection of source elements as input, and a collection of target elements as output. Therefore, our single-valued Attributes stored in property *cols* are ultimately replaced by the Columns created in the *case* labeled *SingleValuedAttribute2Column*. This mechanism is similar to the implicit trace link resolution of ATL.

The next two rules follow a similar construct based on the use of pattern matching and shadow objects. They however differs from the first rule by introducing variables *n* and *on* (lines 14 and 18) directly within the pattern expression for capturing the values of object properties, rather than using a single variable representing the matched object *c* (line 4). This example illustrates the two styles that can be used for writing pattern expressions (navigation or deconstruction), but using a single style for a whole transformation may be preferable.

Listing 1. *ClassDiagram2Relational* in OCLT.

```
1  transfo: classDiagram2Relational(sourceModelContents:
2  OrderedSet(NamedElt)): OrderedSet(Named)=sourceModelContents->collect(
3          -- Class2Table
4          case c@Class {} |
5              Table {
6                  name = c.name,
7                  cols = OrderedSet {
8                      Column {name = 'id'}
9                  }->union(
10                     c.attrs->select(a | not a.multiValued)    -- resolving!
11                 )
12             }
13         -- SingleValuedAttribute2Column
```

```
14          case Attr {name = n, multiValued = false} |
15              Column {name = n}
16          -- MultiValuedAttribute2ColumnsAndTable
17          case Attr {
18                  owner = Class {name = on},
19                  name = n, multiValued = true
20              } |
21              Table {
22                  name = on + '_' + n,
23                  cols = OrderedSet {
24                          Column {name = 'idref'},
25                          Column {name = n}
26                  }
27              }
28      )
```

4 Discussion

The previous sections presented the OCLT approach, and its application to a well-known case-study. In this section, we briefly discuss five points: model transformations seen as functions in Sect. 4.1; interoperability with model transformation languages in Sect. 4.2; performance benefits of pattern matching in Sect. 4.3; an alternative *rule* structuring in Sect. 4.4; and some limitations of the OCLT approach in Sect. 4.5.

4.1 Model Transformations as Functions

When model transformations are functions, functional programming techniques become usable. External model transformation composition [11] is simply achievable via function composition.

Considering model transformations as functions is not a new idea. For instance, the type system introduced in [10] gives a function type to every model transformation. It thus enables type checking of model transformation compositions. However, this type system only considers black-box functions. With OCLT, even the internals of transformations are expressed in a functional language.

The case of higher-order transformations [8] (HOTs) is similar: existing techniques are closer to transformation generation. It is the black-box view of these transformations as functions, which has a higher-order functional type. Adding lambda expressions and partial application to OCLT would enable HOTs as high-order functions.

4.2 Interoperability with Model Transformation Languages

We consider two different motivations for interoperability between model transformation languages. (1) *Reusing* transformations written in other languages. (2) *Leveraging capabilities* of several languages.

Motivations 1 and 2 can be achieved by existing transformation composition approaches. Moreover, OCLT could be extended to support functional composition of transformations written in several languages. In this case, these transformations are considered as black-box functions.

However, sometimes only part of a transformation may need to be written in a different language. Because OCL is used in several existing model transformation languages, internal composition [11] with OCLT becomes possible by integrating the OCL extensions of OCLT into these transformation languages. Concretely, partial OCLT transformations could be integrated anywhere the host language allows OCL expressions. The host language could then benefit from OCLT capabilities (motivation 2).

Finally, OCLT could also be compiled into existing model transformation languages, which would achieve motivations 1 and 2. This would also be one way to implement OCLT. Pattern matching can be relatively easily transformed into regular OCL guards for languages that do not support complex patterns such as ATL. Thus, flat OCLT transformations such as the one presented in Sect. 3.2 would be relatively trivial to compile to QVT or ATL. Nonetheless, it may be more difficult to compile complex rule dependencies such as could potentially be achieved in more complex OCLT transformations. There may also be some issues if the target language only offers declarative rules with specific scheduling incompatible with OCLT.

4.3   Performance Benefits of Pattern Matching

Pattern matching can make OCL expressions more readable and less verbose [5]. But it can also have a positive impact on performance. For instance, to match a Class with an Attribute it owns, one may write (in ATL-like syntax):

```
1 c : Class,
2     a : Attribute (
3     c.attr->includes(a)
4 )
```

Naive execution is very expensive because the cartesian product of the sets of all Classes and of all Attributes must be filtered with the guard (line 3). Deep guard analysis can result in a significant optimization: given a Class, only the Attributes it owns need to be considered. But it relies on extracting the intent behind the guard, which is not a trivial task in the general case. With pattern matching, the intent is directly expressed at the right level of abstraction:

```
1 c@Class {
2     attr = Set {a : Attribute, ...}
3 }
```

The dots at the end of the set denote that the matched set may contain other elements than the matched attribute. With such a pattern, it is relatively simple for each Class c to iterate only on Attributes it owns.

Of course, pattern matching cannot express all relationships between model elements. Therefore, guards must still be permitted. In OCLT as presented here, guards may be encoded using pre-filtering (using the *select* iterator) or with the *if-then-else-endif* expression. A possibly better solution would be to integrate the *selectCollect* iterator proposed in [12] into OCLT.

4.4 ClassDiagram2Relational Without Cases

Listing 2 gives a different version of the *ClassDiagram2Relational* transformation that does not make use of cases. It relies on the implicit selection performed by *collect* when patterns do not match. If a guard is required, then *selectCollect* could be used. A drawback of this new version is that a naive implementation would traverse the whole source model three times instead of once. However, it has the advantage that each *collect* may traverse different collections. This may prove useful to apply different *rules* to different models. Another potential use is to *collect* on a cartesian product of model element collections (with multiple iterators). This is one possibility to express model transformation rules that take multiple source elements.

Another way to express rules without relying on cases is to follow an approach similar to the definition of functions with equations, which is used in functional programming languages like Haskell. However, such an approach would not easily support rules with different numbers of source elements.

Listing 2. *ClassDiagram2Relational* in OCL without cases.

```
1  transfo: classDiagram2Relational_WithoutCases(sourceModelContents:
2  OrderedSet(NamedElt)): OrderedSet(Named) = sourceModelContents->collect(
3  sourceModelContents->collect(
4              [...]     -- Class2Table
5      )->union(
6          sourceModelContents->collect(
7              [...]     -- SingleValuedAttribute2Column
8          )
9      )->union(
10         sourceModelContents->collect(
11             [...]  -- MultiValuedAttribute2ColumnsAndTable
12 )
```

4.5 Limitations of the Approach

The OCL extensions presented in this paper enable writing whole transformations in OCLT. We have nonetheless identified the three following limitations:

- **Explicit trace link resolution** is not currently possible. All trace link resolution is performed entirely automatically by the specific layer of OCLT. However, our experience with ATL has shown that explicit trace link resolution (with *resolveTemp*) is sometimes useful.
- **Model refining** transformations leave most of a model unchanged, and only perform few changes. This is notably what the refining mode is for in ATL. OCLT does not currently offer such a capability. This mostly becomes an issue when in-place changes must be performed. Otherwise, it is always possible to copy all unchanged elements.
- **MxN rules** transform *M* source elements into *N* target elements. OCLT can currently handle multiple source elements by *collect*ing over cartesian products as discussed in Sect. 4.4. However, multiple target elements is not currently supported. It would be possible to return a collection of elements for matched source element. This may work because *collect* automatically

flattens collections. However, such rules may need to be specified separately (e.g., using *union* as in Listing 2). A more critical issue would be to enable trace link resolution to one target element among several. This would be difficult to support without explicit trace link resolution.

5   Related Work

In [5], Clark proposes to add pattern matching and object expressions (similar to shadow objects) to OCL and already addresses the similarities with functional programming languages and graph-based transformation languages. While Clark tackles the issue of navigation expressions and their verbosity for expressing constraints, our proposal focuses on model transformation. Of course, all advantages noted by Clark also apply to OCLT.

In [7], Pollet et al. propose new constructs for implementing model manipulation in OCL using the concept of actions where navigation through the elements of the models is available. Our approach extends OCL to enable similar declaration of model manipulation actions. Pollet et al. and Cariou et al. also propose to express contracts [4,7] on OCL actions. This is currently not a concern for OCLT.

In [2], Bergmann proposes to tranform OCL constraints into EMFQuery to improve the performance of querying models. In [13], Winkelmamm et al. propose to transform a subset of OCL constraints into graph constraints. The intent of this approach is to generate valid instances of model for a given metamodel for testing purposes. While the generation of instances might be considered as a specific kind of model transformation, our approach focuses on the definition of model transformation rules. The use of these rules for model synthesis could be investigated in further research. These two works show that translation of OCL guards into patterns is possible in some cases.

6   Conclusion

This paper has presented OCLT, an OCL-based approach to express model transformations. OCLT relies on two OCL extensions (pattern matching and shadow objects) that are considered for inclusion in OCL 2.5 [12]. Therefore, the only lasting difference with OCL may be the new *transfo* type of expressions along with its semantics. *transfo* expressions are post-processed by instantiating shadow objects in actual models, and by resolving trace links.

The *ClassDiagram2Relational* transformation written in OCLT looks similar to, and is as readable as with more traditional rule-based model transformation languages. Because OCLT transformations are purely functional, they can directly use techniques such as functional composition. Partial application and higher-order functions have not been deeply investigated yet but look promising.

As an exploratory work, OCLT still need further work to become actually usable. Notably, its specific *transfo* type and associated layer should be given clear and precise semantics. Then, a full implementation should be created.

Finally, the addition of other proposed OCL extensions should be evaluated. For instance, adding an active operations semantics [1,3] to OLCT has the potential of enabling incremental synchronization, with at least partial bidirectional updates. However, such an addition may be difficult to reconcile with the purely functional aspect of OCLT.

References

1. Beaudoux, O., Blouin, A., Barais, O., Jézéquel, J.-M.: Active operations on collections. In: Petriu, D.C., Rouquette, N., Haugen, Ø. (eds.) MODELS 2010, Part I. LNCS, vol. 6394, pp. 91–105. Springer, Heidelberg (2010)
2. Bergmann, G.: Translating OCL to graph patterns. In: Dingel, J., Schulte, W., Ramos, I., Abrahão, S., Insfran, E. (eds.) MODELS 2014. LNCS, vol. 8767, pp. 670–686. Springer, Heidelberg (2014)
3. Brucker, A.D., Clark, T., Dania, C., Georg, G., Gogolla, M., Jouault, F., Teniente, E., Wolff, B.: Panel Discussion: proposals for Improving OCL. In: Proceedings of the 14th International Workshop on OCL and Textual Modelling, pp. 83–99 (2014)
4. Cariou, E., Marvie, R., Seinturier, L., Duchien, L.: OCL for the specification of model transformation contracts. In: OCL and Model Driven Engineering on UML 2004 Conference Workshop, vol.12, pp.69–83 (2004)
5. Clark, T.: OCL pattern matching. In: Proceedings of the MODELS 2013 OCL Workshop, pp. 33–42 (2013)
6. Object Management Group (OMG). Object Constraint Language (OCL), Version 2.4. February 2014. http://www.omg.org/spec/OCL/2.4/
7. Pollet, D., Vojtisek, D., Jézéquel, J.-M.: OCL as a core uml transformation language. In: Workshop on Integration and Transformation of UML models WITUML (held at ECOOP 2002), Malaga(2002)
8. Tisi, M., Jouault, F., Fraternali, P., Ceri, S., Bézivin, J.: On the use of higher-order model transformations. In: Paige, R.F., Hartman, A., Rensink, A. (eds.) ECMDA-FA 2009. LNCS, vol. 5562, pp. 18–33. Springer, Heidelberg (2009)
9. Tisi, M., Jouault, F., Delatour, J., Saidi, Z., Choura, H.: FUML as an assembly language for model transformation. In: Combemale, B., Pearce, D.J., Barais, O., Vinju, J.J. (eds.) SLE 2014. LNCS, vol. 8706, pp. 171–190. Springer, Heidelberg (2014)
10. Vignaga, A., Jouault, F., Bastarrica, M.C., Brunelière, H.: Typing artifacts in megamodeling. Softw. Sys. Model. 12(1), 105–119 (2013)
11. Wagelaar, D.: Composition techniques for rule-based model transformation languages. In: Vallecillo, A., Gray, J., Pierantonio, A. (eds.) ICMT 2008. LNCS, vol. 5063, pp. 152–167. Springer, Heidelberg (2008)
12. Willink, E.: OCL 2.5 Plans. Presentation given at the 14th International Workshop on OCL and Textual Modelling, September 2014. http://www.software.imdea.org/OCL2014/slides/OCL25Plans
13. Winkelmann, J., Taentzer, G., Ehrig, K., Küster, J.M.: Translation of restricted ocl constraints into graph constraints for generating meta model instances by graph grammars. Electron. Notes Theor. Comput. Sci. 211, 159–170 (2008)

Transparent Model Transformation: Turning Your Favourite Model Editor into a Transformation Tool

Vlad Acretoaie[1](✉), Harald Störrle[1], and Daniel Strüber[2]

[1] Technical University of Denmark, Kongens Lyngby, Denmark
{rvac,hsto}@dtu.dk
[2] Philipps-Universität Marburg, Marburg, Germany
strueber@mathematik.uni-marburg.de

Abstract. Current model transformation languages are supported by dedicated editors, often closely coupled to a single execution engine. We introduce Transparent Model Transformation, a paradigm enabling modelers to specify transformations using a familiar tool: their model editor. We also present VMTL, the first transformation language implementing the principles of Transparent Model Transformation: syntax, environment, and execution transparency. VMTL works by weaving a transformation aspect into its host modeling language. We show how our implementation of VMTL turns any model editor into a flexible model transformation tool sharing the model editor's benefits, transparently.

1 Introduction

The science and practice of model transformation (MT) has made significant progress since it was first identified as the *"heart and soul"* of Model-Driven Engineering (MDE) [12]. A varied array of model transformation languages (MTLs) have been proposed since then, each with its own benefits and drawbacks.

While it has found adoption in specialized domains such as embedded systems development, MDE remains outside the mainstream of software development practice. Empirical evidence identifies the poor quality of tool support as one of the main obstacles in the path of large-scale industrial adoption of MDE [18]. Considering the central role of MT in MDE, as well as the experimental nature of most MT tools, we infer that at least some of the criticism addressed to MDE tool quality directly concerns MT tools.

Most (if not all) executable MTLs currently come with dedicated tools that modelers must learn and use in order to specify and execute transformations. But modelers already have at their disposal at least one mature, production-ready tool which they know how to use: their model editor. This observation leads to our central research question:

Is it possible to explicitly specify model transformations using only existing, conventional model editors as an interface?

In this paper we show that this question can be answered positively by following the three principles of Transparent Model Transformation (TMT):

© Springer International Publishing Switzerland 2015
D. Kolovos and M. Wimmer (Eds.): ICMT 2015, LNCS 9152, pp. 121–130, 2015.
DOI: 10.1007/978-3-319-21155-8_10

1. The MTL can express transformations at the syntax level supported by the model editor. In most cases this is concrete syntax, but abstract syntax, containment tree, and textual interfaces are also common.
2. Users are free to adopt their preferred editor for each transformation artefact: the source and target model(s), as well as the transformation specification.
3. Transformations can be compiled to multiple executable representations.

We propose the Visual Model Transformation Language (VMTL) as the first MTL following the principles of TMT. Fig. 1 positions VMTL in the current model transformation landscape and highlights its key benefits. Namely, VMTL is a declarative language designed to be woven at the syntactic level into any host modeling language, turning that modeling language into a transformation language for models conforming to it. VMTL adopts any editor of the host modeling language as its own, effectively turning it into a transformation editor. Transformations are subsequently executed by compilation to existing MTLs, which we exemplify in this paper by compiling to the Henshin [3] MTL.

The remainder of this paper is structured as follows: Sect. 2 introduces VMTL via a motivating example, Sect. 3 provides an overview of VMTL's main features, Sect. 4 lays out the fundamentals of TMT with VMTL as an application, Sect. 5 describes our implementation of VMTL, Sect. 6 discusses the scope and limitations of VMTL, Sect. 7 summarizes related work, and Sect. 8 concludes the paper.

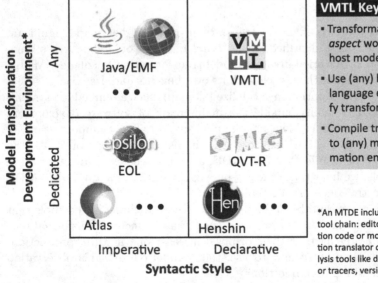

Fig. 1. VMTL and its key benefits in the current model transformation landscape

2 Motivating Example

Consider a UML [10] Use Case model in which an Actor is connected by Associations to two Use Cases, one of which extends the other. The described scenario is a refactoring candidate because the extending Use Case *"typically defines behavior that may not necessarily be meaningful by itself"* [10]. Deleting the Association between the Actor and the extending Use Case is recommended.

A VMTL specification for this transformation is shown in Fig. 2 (top). VMTL employs textual annotations for a number of purposes, such as specifying model manipulation operations. The `delete` annotation is used here to state that the offending Association must be removed from the model. In the case of UML, Comments are an appropriate vehicle for VMTL annotations. Annotation-carrying comments are identified by the `<<VM Annotation>>` stereotype.

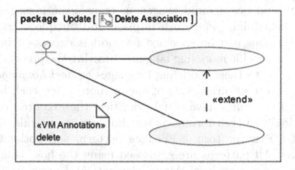

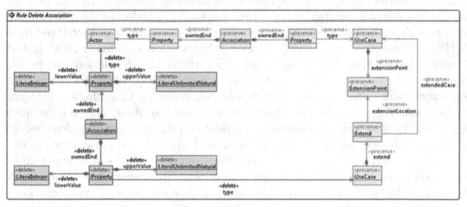

Fig. 2. Example transformation specified using VMTL (top) and Henshin (bottom)

The same transformation could be specified using most existing MTLs, such as Henshin, a graph transformation-based MTL (see Fig. 2, bottom). The Henshin specification is considerably more verbose than its VMTL counterpart, arguably due to the complexity of the UML metamodel. This observation is true for all MTLs exposing the abstract syntax of the host modeling language, since large and complex metamodels are by no means unique to UML and its profiles.

Nevertheless, specifying transformations at the concrete syntax level is not the main argument put forward by VMTL. A more compelling argument is that VMTL allows specifying transformations directly in the model editor. The transformation in Fig. 2 (top) is specified using the MagicDraw model editor (http://www.nomagic.com/products/magicdraw), but any other UML editor could have been used instead, including containment tree and abstract syntax editors. VMTL circumvents the need for a dedicated transformation editor by implementing the principles of Transparent Model Transformation.

3   The Visual Model Transformation Language

VMTL is a usability-oriented MTL descended from the Visual Model Query Language (VMQL [14]). It is a model-to-model, unidirectional transformation language supporting endogenous and exogenous transformations, rule application conditions, rule scheduling, and both in-place and out-place transformations. VMTL transformations can be specified for models expressed in any general-purpose or domain-specific modeling language meeting the preconditions defined in Sect. 4.1. We refer to these modeling languages as *host languages*.

A VMTL transformation consists of one or more *rules*, each having an *execution priority*. If two rules have equal priorities, the executed rule is selected non-deterministically. A transformation terminates when no rules are applicable. Rules consist of a **Find** pattern, a **Produce** pattern, and optional **Forbid** and **Require** patterns. All patterns are expressed using the host language(s), typically at the concrete syntax level. Model elements and meta-attributes that do not have a concrete syntax representation are also included in the transformation specification. VMTL patterns correspond to the notions of Left-Hand Side (LHS), Right-Hand Side (RHS), Negative Application Condition (NAC), and Positive Application Condition (PAC) from graph transformation theory [5]. Some transformations, such as the one in Fig. 2 (top), allow the **Find** and **Produce** patterns to be merged for conciseness, resulting in an **Update** pattern. Strings starting with the "**$**" character represent variables, and can be used wherever the host language accepts a user-defined string. Variables identify corresponding model elements across patterns and support rule parameterization.

Patterns may contain textual annotations expressed as logic programming-inspired clauses. The adoption of logic clauses as an annotation style is motivated by their declarative nature and their composability via propositional logic operators. VMTL provides clauses for pattern specification, model manipulation, and transformation execution control. Apart from the **delete** clause featured in Fig. 2 (top), examples of VMTL clauses include **create** (for creating model elements), **indirect** (for specifying a relation's transitive closure), **optional** (for identifying model elements that can be omitted from successful pattern matches), and **priority** (for specifying rule priorities). A complete list of VMTL clauses and a more detailed presentation of the language are available in [1].

4   The Principles of Transparent Model Transformation

Transparent Model Transformation is defined by three principles: (1) *syntax transparency*, (2) *environment transparency*, and (3) *execution transparency*. The following subsections define these principles and exemplify them on VMTL.

4.1   Syntax Transparency

Consider an MTL capable of specifying transformations on models conforming to metamodel $\mathcal{M}$. The MTL is said to be *syntax transparent* with respect to $\mathcal{M}$ if all such transformation specifications also conform to $\mathcal{M}$. For example, since VMTL is a syntax transparent language, Fig. 2 (top) simultaneously represents a valid UML model and a transformation specification.

VMTL achieves syntax transparency by *weaving a transformation aspect* into the host modeling language. The constructs of VMTL – rules, patterns, and annotations – are mapped to existing elements of the host language using stereotypes or naming conventions. Consider, for instance, the realization of a VMTL Update pattern and a VMTL annotation in UML and Business Process Model and Notation (BPMN [9]). The UML realizations rely on stereotypes (the <<VM Update>> stereotype for Packages and the <<VM Annotation>> stereotype for Comments), while the BPMN realizations rely on naming conventions (the [VM Update] prefix for Package names and the [VM Annotation] prefix for Text Annotation IDs). We refer to these realizations of VMTL as VMTL$_{UML}$ and VMTL$_{BPMN}$, respectively. Similar realizations can be created for other general-purpose or domain-specific modeling languages.

VMTL can only be woven into host modeling languages meeting certain prerequisites. First of all, the host language must support a scoping construct, a role played by Packages in UML and BPMN. Scoping constructs enable VMTL's execution engine to identify which transformation rules or patterns different model elements belong to. Second, all host language elements must support annotations, which are required to act as containers for VMTL clauses. Finally, the availability of a profiling mechanism facilitates the realization of VMTL, since stereotypes can precisely identify model elements as VMTL constructs. A profiling mechanism can be substituted by the adoption of naming conventions.

4.2   Environment Transparency

An MTL is *environment transparent* if it allows users to adopt their preferred editors for interacting with all transformation artefacts: the source model(s), target model(s), and transformation specification. Environment transparency is facilitated by syntax transparency, but can also exist independently. For instance, most textual MTLs allow the use of general-purpose text editors as specification tools, thus exhibiting environment transparency but not syntax transparency.

Since most current MTLs are experimental, few are supported by mature, production-ready editors. The ability to specify transformations using existing model editors is thus beneficial to end-users from two standpoints: (1) avoiding the learning curve imposed by a new editor, and (2) leveraging a tested, mature tool. By promoting loose editor coupling, environment transparency also opens new deployment avenues, such as remote transformation execution.

VMTL is an environment transparent language. For example, $VMTL_{UML}$ transformations are specified using a UML editor, while a $VMTL_{BPMN}$ transformations are specified using a BPMN editor.

4.3   Execution Transparency

An MTL is *execution transparent* if transformations specified using it can be executed by compilation to multiple MTLs operating at a lower abstraction level. Execution transparency gives users the freedom to select a transformation engine appropriate for the task at hand. For instance, in a safety-critical scenario, users might prefer a transformation engine that supports model checking and state-space exploration over one that aims at highly efficient rule execution.

The number and complexity of language constructs included in VMTL is deliberately limited in order to facilitate its compilation to existing MTLs. Since the components of VMTL transformations can be mapped to graph transformation concepts, the most intuitive compilation targets are graph transformation-based MTLs. However, implementations based on imperative MTLs (e.g. EOL [8]), transformation primitive libraries (e.g. T-Core [15]), or general purpose programming languages accompanied by modeling APIs are all possible.

5   Implementation and Deployment

Our implementation of VMTL is based on the Eclipse Modeling Framework (EMF [13]) and the Henshin MT engine. Henshin was selected because its graph transformation-based operational semantics aligns well with VMTL. As a standalone API, it also supports VMTL's syntax and environment transparency. The architecture of our implementation is presented in Fig. 3. As illustrated, the source model and VMTL specification are created using the same editor.

VMTL specifications are compiled by the VM* Runtime[1] into semantically equivalent Henshin specifications to be executed by the Henshin transformation engine. The compilation process can be seen as a Higher-Order Transformation (HOT) consisting of the four steps illustrated in Fig. 3.

In step ❶ model fragments representing transformation components are identified and extracted from the transformation model. These are the transformation's Left-Hand Side (LHS), Right-Hand Side (RHS), Negative Application Conditions (NAC), and Positive Application Conditions (PAC). As these components correspond to VMTL patterns, their identification is informed by VMTL stereotypes or naming conventions.

In step ❷ the extracted model fragments are translated into structurally equivalent Henshin graphs intended to play the same role (LHS, RHS, NAC, or PAC) in the generated Henshin transformation.

---

[1] The VM* Runtime is also capable of evaluating model queries and constraints.

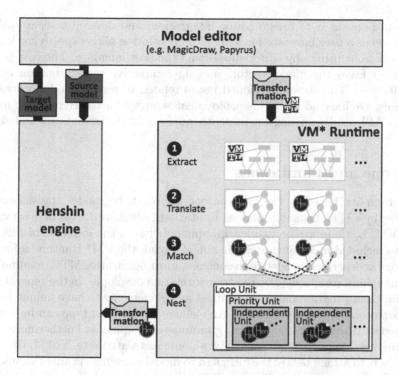

Fig. 3. The architecture of a Henshin-based VMTL implementation. Numbers encircled in black indicate the sequence of steps in the VMTL to Henshin compilation process.

In step ❸ a set of atomic Henshin rules are created by constructing mappings between the nodes of each LHS graph and the corresponding nodes in every other graph belonging to the same rule. As a mapping is a connection between two matching nodes, obtaining the set of mappings between two graphs is equivalent to computing a match between the graphs. The EMFCompare (https://www.eclipse.org/cmf/compare/) API is used for match computation.

In step ❹ the generated rules are nested inside Units, Henshin's control flow specification formalism. The resulting control structure implements the operational semantics of VMTL: The applicable rule with highest priority is executed until no more applicable rules exist, at which point the MT terminates.

The architecture presented in Fig. 3 is compatible with several deployment strategies. In a monolithic plugin-based deployment, a model editor plugin encapsulates the VM* Runtime and the MT engine. This approach offers limited portability, as a full-featured new plugin is required for every editor.

To improve portability without sacrificing editor integration, the VM* Runtime and the MT engine can be deployed remotely and accessed via a REST API[2]. Business logic can be removed from the editor plugin, facilitating its re-implementation. However, transferring models over a network is a performance bottleneck, while remote model processing requires strong security provisions.

---

[2] Any other remote code execution technology may be used.

A third option is to forego editor integration, and develop a separate Web application as a user interface for VMTL. This solution allows specifying VMTL transformations using any editor supporting the host language. The cost is that users must leave the model editor, making interactive transformation execution infeasible. The above-mentioned issues related to remote model processing also apply. We have adopted this deployment strategy for the Hypersonic model analysis API, and provided an in-depth analysis of its advantages and drawbacks [2].

6   Scope and Limitations

Apart from its benefits, the transparent approach to model transformation embraced by VMTL has some inherent limitations, which we discuss in this section.

In VMTL, there are no explicit mappings between the elements of different patterns included in a transformation rule. Instead, the VM* Runtime infers the mappings as described in Sect. 5. In contrast, most declarative MTLs assume that these mappings are specified by the transformation developer. In the general case, inferring them programmatically requires model elements to have unique identifiers corresponding across patterns. An element's name and type can be used to construct such identifiers, but with no guarantee of uniqueness. Furthermore, some host language elements might not have a name meta-attribute. VMTL therefore allows users to attach tags of the form #id to model elements via annotations. It is the developer's responsibility to ensure that corresponding elements have the same name or tag in all patterns. These element identification provisions have the added benefit of allowing the patterns of a rule to conform to different metamodels, thus providing support for exogenous transformations.

One may also argue that VMTL's priority-based rule scheduling is not sufficiently expressive. While not included in the current VMTL specification, control flow structures such as conditional execution and looping constructs could be specified using VMTL's existing textual annotation mechanism.

At the implementation level, incompatibilities between VMTL's operational semantics and the capabilities of its underlying MT engine may appear. One example is the indirect clause, allowing VMTL patterns to express a relation's transitive closure, i.e. a chain of undefined length of instances of this relation. Transitive closure computation is problematic for most graph transformation-based engines, but trivial for, say, a logic programming-based engine.

Employing model editors to carry out a task they were not designed for also brings a series of limitations. The well-formedness and syntactical correctness of VMTL rules cannot be verified inside the editor in the absence of a dedicated plugin, while transformation debugging would also benefit from editor extensions. On the other hand, most model editors will enforce the conformance of VMTL patterns to the host language metamodel. This expressiveness limitation is mitigated by VMTL's textual annotations. Finally, displaying target models in the host editor is complicated due to the fact that diagram layout is typically not part of the host language metamodel. Maintaining a layout similar to that of the source model is therefore only possible for in-place transformations.

7   Related Work

MoTMoT [17] proposes an extensible UML 1.5 profile as a uniform concrete syntax for all graph transformation languages. This approach allows graph transformations to be specified using any UML 1.5 editor, and executed by existing graph transformation engines. Although it offers execution transparency and limited environment transparency, MoTMoT does not address syntax transparency.

Several MT approaches (e.g. PICS [4], AToMPM [16]) include concrete syntax model fragments in their specification languages, taking a first step towards syntax transparency. Some of these approaches (e.g. AToMPM) augment the host modeling language with flowchart-like rule scheduling constructs. Even though they are more expressive than VMTL's priority-based scheduling mechanism, these augmentations preclude full syntax and environment transparency. In the same area, Schmidt [11] proposes a transformation profile for UML models, but does not consider other host modeling languages.

Model Transformation By-Example (MTBE, [7]) is an emerging paradigm aimed at leveraging the concrete syntax of host modeling languages. In MTBE, transformations are *inferred* using machine learning or optimization algorithms from a series of example source and target model pairs. In contrast, VMTL transformations are explicitly *specified* using the host language model editor.

Execution transparency is addressed in the context of the systematic development of model transformations by transML [6]. In the same direction, AToMPM transformations are compiled to a lower-level specification language, namely the T-Core [15] transformation primitive library.

8   Conclusion

The perceived lack of adequate tool support in MDE can be mitigated by leveraging production-ready tools familiar to modelers, such as conventional model editors. Adopting existing model editors as transformation tools requires a new approach to model transformation, which we refer to as Transparent Model Transformation (TMT). The principles of syntax transparency, environment transparency, and execution transparency define TMT. Although a number of MTLs adopt subsets of these principles, they have never been explicitly acknowledged and systematized. Doing so has been the first contribution of this paper.

Our second contribution has been the proposal of VMTL: the first transformation language fully compliant with the principles of TMT. We have introduced VMTL's syntax and high-level semantics, and discussed its scope and limitations.

Finally, we have presented the VM* Runtime as an implementation of VMTL. The VM* Runtime leverages the existing Henshin transformation engine, while supporting both local and distributed deployment. It allows us to conclude that TMT is feasible not only conceptually, but also practically.

Acknowledgments. The authors would like to thank Gabriele Taentzer for her insightful comments on the content and presentation of this paper.

References

1. The VM* Wiki. https://vmstar.compute.dtu.dk/
2. Acretoaie, V., Störrle, H.: Hypersonic: Model analysis and checking in the cloud. In: Proceedings of the 2nd Workshop on Scalability in Model Driven Engineering. CEUR Workshop Proceedings, vol. 1206, pp. 6–13 (2014)
3. Arendt, T., Biermann, E., Jurack, S., Krause, C., Taentzer, G.: Henshin: advanced concepts and tools for in-place emf model transformations. In: Petriu, D.C., Rouquette, N., Haugen, Ø. (eds.) MODELS 2010, Part I. LNCS, vol. 6394, pp. 121–135. Springer, Heidelberg (2010)
4. Baar, T., Whittle, J.: On the usage of concrete syntax in model transformation rules. In: Virbitskaite, I., Voronkov, A. (eds.) PSI 2006. LNCS, vol. 4378, pp. 84–97. Springer, Heidelberg (2007)
5. Ehrig, H., Ehrig, K., Prange, U., Taentzer, G.: Fundamentals of Algebraic Graph Transformation. Springer, Berlin Heidelberg (2006)
6. Guerra, E., de Lara, J., Kolovos, D.S., Paige, R.F., dos Santos, O.M.: Engineering model transformations with transML. Softw. Syst. Model. **12**(3), 555–577 (2013)
7. Kappel, G., Langer, P., Retschitzegger, W., Schwinger, W., Wimmer, M.: Model transformation by-example: a survey of the first wave. In: Düsterhöft, A., Klettke, M., Schewe, K.-D. (eds.) Conceptual Modelling and Its Theoretical Foundations. LNCS, vol. 7260, pp. 197–215. Springer, Heidelberg (2012)
8. Kolovos, D.S., Paige, R.F., Polack, F.A.C.: The epsilon object language (EOL). In: Rensink, A., Warmer, J. (eds.) ECMDA–FA 2006. LNCS, vol. 4066, pp. 128–142. Springer, Heidelberg (2006)
9. Object Management Group: Business Process Model and Notation (BPMN), Version 2.0.2 (2013) http://www.omg.org/spec/BPMN/2.0.2/
10. Object Management Group: Unified Modeling Language (UML), Version 2.5 Beta 2 (2013) http://www.omg.org/spec/UML/2.5/Beta2/
11. Schmidt, M.: Transformations of UML 2 models using concrete syntax patterns. In: Guelfi, N., Buchs, D. (eds.) RISE 2006. LNCS, vol. 4401, pp. 130–143. Springer, Heidelberg (2007)
12. Sendall, S., Kozaczynski, W.: Model transformation: the heart and soul of model-driven software development. IEEE Softw. **20**(5), 42–45 (2003)
13. Steinberg, D., Budinsky, F., Paternostro, M., Merks, E.: EMF: Eclipse Modeling Framework. Addison-Wesley Professional, Boston (2008)
14. Störrle, H.: VMQL: a visual language for ad-hoc model querying. J. Visual Lang. Comput. **22**(1), 3–29 (2011)
15. Syriani, E., Vangheluwe, H., LaShomb, B.: T-Core: a framework for custom-built model transformation engines. Softw. Syst. Model. **13**(3), 1–29 (2013)
16. Syriani, E., Vangheluwe, H., Mannadiar, R., Hansen, C., Van Mierlo, S., Huseyin, E.: AToMPM: a web-based modeling environment. In: Joint Proceedings of MODELS 2013 Invited Talks, Demonstration Session, Poster Session, and ACM Student Research Competition. CEUR Workshop Proceedings, vol. 1115, pp. 21–25 (2013)
17. Van Gorp, P., Keller, A., Janssens, D.: Transformation language integration based on profiles and higher order transformations. In: Gašević, D., Lämmel, R., Van Wyk, E. (eds.) SLE 2008. LNCS, vol. 5452, pp. 208–226. Springer, Heidelberg (2009)
18. Whittle, J., Hutchinson, J., Rouncefield, M., Burden, H., Heldal, R.: Industrial adoption of model-driven engineering: are the tools really the problem? In: Moreira, A., Schätz, B., Gray, J., Vallecillo, A., Clarke, P. (eds.) MODELS 2013. LNCS, vol. 8107, pp. 1–17. Springer, Heidelberg (2013)

Transformation Validation
and Verification

A Sound Execution Semantics for ATL via Translation Validation

Research Paper

Zheng Cheng[✉], Rosemary Monahan, and James F. Power

Computer Science Department, Maynooth University,
Maynooth, Co. Kildare, Ireland
{zcheng,rosemary,jpower}@cs.nuim.ie

Abstract. In this work we present a translation validation approach to encode a sound execution semantics for the ATL specification. Based on our sound encoding, the goal is to soundly verify an ATL specification against the specified OCL contracts. To demonstrate our approach, we have developed the VeriATL verification system using the Boogie2 intermediate verification language, which in turn provides access to the Z3 theorem prover. Our system automatically encodes the execution semantics of each ATL specification (as it appears in the ATL matched rules) into the intermediate verification language. Then, to ensure the soundness of the encoding, we verify that it soundly represents the runtime behaviour of its corresponding compiled implementation in terms of bytecode instructions for the ATL virtual machine. The experiments demonstrate the feasibility of our approach. They also illustrate how to automatically verify an ATL specification against specified OCL contracts.

Keywords: Model transformation verification · ATL · Automatic theorem proving · Intermediate verification language · Boogie

1 Introduction

Model-driven engineering (MDE) has been recognised as an effective way to manage the complexity of software development. Model transformation is widely acknowledged as a principal ingredient of MDE. Two main paradigms for developing model transformations are the operational and relational approaches. Operational model transformations are imperative in style, and focus on imperatively describing **how** a model transformation should progress. Relational model transformations (MTr) have a "mapping" style, and aim at producing a declarative specification that documents **what** the model transformation intends to do. Typically, a declarative specification is compiled into a low level transformation

---

Z. Cheng—Funded by the Doctoral Teaching scholarship, John & Pat Hume scholarship and Postgraduate Travel fund from Maynooth University.

© Springer International Publishing Switzerland 2015
D. Kolovos and M. Wimmer (Eds.): ICMT 2015, LNCS 9152, pp. 133–148, 2015.
DOI: 10.1007/978-3-319-21155-8_11

implementation and is executed by the underlying virtual machine. Because of its mapping-style nature, a MTr is generally easier to write and understand than an operational transformation.

The Atlas Transformation Language (ATL) is one of the most widely used MTr languages in industry and academia [9]. An ATL specification (i.e. an ATL program) is a declarative specification that documents what the ATL transformation intends to do. It is expressed in terms of a list of rules (Sect. 2). These rules describe the mappings between the source metamodel and the target metamodel, using the Object Constraint Language (OCL) for both its data types and its declarative expressions. Then, the ATL specification is compiled into an ATL Stack Machine (ASM) implementation to be executed.

Verifying the correctness of the ATL transformation means proving assumptions about the ATL specification. These assumptions can be made explicitly by transformation developers via annotations, so-called contracts. The contracts are usually expressed in OCL for its declarative and logical nature. Many approaches have been adopted to verify the correctness of an ATL transformation [5,6,8,15]. These approaches usually consist of encoding the execution semantics of an ATL specification in a formal language. Combined with a formal treatment of transformation contracts, a theorem prover can be used to verify the ATL specification against the specified contracts. The result of the verification will imply the correctness of the ATL transformation.

However, existing approaches do not verify that the encoded execution semantics of an ATL specification soundly represents the runtime behaviour provided by the ASM implementation. Therefore, an unsound encoding will yield unsound results after verification, i.e. it will lead to erroneous conclusions about the correctness of the ATL transformation (Sect. 2). In a model transformation verification survey by Rahim and Whittle, this problem is characterised as ensuring the semantics preservation relationship between a declarative specification and its operational implementation, which is an under-researched area in MDE [1].

In this work, we are specifically interested in the core component of ATL, i.e. ATL matched rules. We aim for the sound verification of the total correctness of an ATL transformation. Therefore, we compositionally verify the termination, and the soundness of our encoding of the execution semantics of each ATL matched rule in the given ATL specification (i.e. we verify that the execution semantics of each ATL matched rule soundly represents the runtime behaviour of its corresponding ASM implementation). Consequently, we are able to soundly verify the ATL specification against its specified OCL contracts, based on our sound encodings for the execution semantics of the ATL matched rules.

We have developed our VeriATL verification system in the Boogie intermediate verification language (Boogie) to demonstrate our approach (Sect. 6) [4].

Boogie. Boogie is a procedure-oriented language that is based on Hoare-logic. It provides imperative statements (such as assignment, if and while statements) to implement procedures, and supports first-order-logic contracts (i.e. pre/postconditions) to specify procedures. Boogie allows type, constant, function and axiom declarations, which are mainly used to encode libraries that define data structures, background theories and language properties. A Boogie procedure is verified if its implementation satisfies its contracts. The verification of Boogie procedures is performed by the Boogie verifier, which uses the Z3 SMT solver as its underlying theorem prover. Using Boogie in verifier design has two advantages. First, Boogie encodings can be encapsulated as libraries, which are then reusable when designing verifiers for other languages. Second, Boogie acts as a bridge between the front-end model transformation language and the back-end theorem prover. The benefit here is that we can focus on generating verification tasks for the front-end language in a structural way, and then delegate the task of interacting with theorem provers to the Boogie verifier.

Thus, using Boogie enables Hoare-logic-based automatic theorem proving via an efficient theorem prover, i.e. Z3[1]. The details for performing our proposed verification tasks were far from obvious to us, and articulating them is the main contribution of this work. In particular,

- We adapt a memory model used in the verification of object-oriented programs to explain concepts within MDE. This allows the encoding of both these MDE concepts and the execution semantics of ATL matched rules in Boogie (Sect. 4).
- We use the translation validation approach to compositionally verify the soundness of our Boogie encoding for the execution semantics of an ATL matched rule (Sect. 5). The benefit is that we can automatically verify the soundness of each ATL specification/ASM implementation pair. Our translation validation approach is based on encoding a translational semantics of the ASM language in Boogie, to allow us precisely explain the runtime behaviour of ASM implementations (Sect. 5).

2   Motivating Example

We use the ER2REL transformation as our running example [5]. It transforms the Entity-Relationship (ER) metamodel (Fig. 1(a)) into the RELational (REL) metamodel (Fig. 1(b)). Both the ER schema and the relational schema have a commonly accepted semantics. Thus, it is easy to understand their metamodels.

The *ER2REL* specification is defined via a list of ATL matched rules in a mapping style (Fig. 2). The first three rules map respectively each *ERSchema* element to a *RELSchema* element (*S2S*), each *Entity* element to a *Relation* element (*E2R*), and each *Relship* element to a *Relation* element (*R2R*). The remaining three rules generate a *RELAttribute* element for each *Relation* element created in the *REL* model.

Each ATL matched rule has a *from* section where the source elements to be matched in the source model are specified. An optional OCL constraint may be added as the guard, and a rule is applicable only if the guard passes. Each rule also has a *to* section which specifies the elements to be created in the target

---

[1] Z3. http://z3.codeplex.com/.

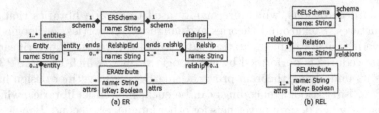

Fig. 1. Entity-Relationship and Relational metamodels

```
1    module ER2REL; create OUT : REL from IN : ER;
2
3    rule S2S {
4      from s: ER!ERSchema
5      to t: REL!RELSchema (relations<-s.relships, relations<-s.entities)}
6
7    rule E2R {
8      from s: ER!Entity to t: REL!Relation ( name<-s.name) }
9
10   rule R2R {
11     from s: ER!Relship to t: REL!Relation ( name<-s.name) }
12
13   rule EA2A {
14     from att: ER!ERAttribute, ent: ER!Entity (att.entity=ent)
15     to t: REL!RELAttribute ( name<-att.name, isKey<-att.isKey, relation<-ent ) }
16
17   rule RA2A {
18     from att: ER!ERAttribute, rs: ER!Relship ( att.relship=rs )
19     to t: REL!RELAttribute ( name<-att.name, isKey<-att.isKey, relation<-rs ) }
20
21   rule RA2AK {
22     from att: ER!ERAttribute, rse: ER!RelshipEnd
23        ( att.entity=rse.entity and att.isKey=true )
24     to t: REL!RELAttribute ( name<-att.name, isKey<-att.isKey, relation<-rse.relship )}
```

Fig. 2. ATL specification for ER2REL model transformation

model. The rule initialises the attribute/association of a generated target element via the binding operator (<-). This binding operator resolves its right hand side before assigning to the left hand side. For example, the binding *relation<-ent* in the *EA2A* rule on line 15 of Fig. 2 assigns the *Relation* element that is created for *ent* by the *R2R* rule to the *relation*.

3 Proving Transformation Correctness

In this work the correctness of an ATL transformation is specified using OCL contracts. These OCL contracts form a Hoare-triple which is used to verify the

```
1  context ERSchema inv entities_unique: —— entity names are unique in the ER schema
2    self.entities->forAll(e1,e2 | e1<>e2 implies e1.name<>e2.name)
3  ------------------------------------------------
4  context RELSchema inv relations_unique: —— relation names are unique in the REL schema
5    self.relations->forall(r1,r2| r1<>r2 implies r1.name<>r2.name)
```

Fig. 3. OCL contracts for ER and REL

correctness of each ATL transformation. For example, using the OCL contracts specified in Fig. 3, we can verify whether the constraint *entities_unique* imposed on the *ER* metamodel, along with the *ER2REL* specification, guarantees that the constraint *relations_unique* holds on the *REL* metamodel.

In order to prove the correctness of the ATL transformation, we encode the OCL transformation contracts, along with the ATL transformation specification into the Boogie language. Figure 4 shows this encoding applied to the *ER2REL* transformation:

- First, the OCL contracts are encoded as a Boogie contract. In particular, the OCL constraints on the source metamodels are encoded as Boogie preconditions (line 2–8), and the OCL constraints on the target metamodels are encoded as Boogie postconditions (line 10–16).

```
1    procedure main();
2    /* precondition: entity names are unique in the ER schema */
3    requires (∀ s: ref • s∈find(srcHeap,ER$ERSchema)⟹
4      (∀ j1,j2: int • 0≤j1<j2<arrayLength(read(srcHeap,s,ERSchema.entities))⟹
5       read(srcHeap,s,ERSchema.entities)[j1] ≠
6       read(srcHeap,s,ERSchema.entities)[j2] ⟹
7        read(srcHeap,read(srcHeap,s,ERSchema.entities)[j1],Entity.name) ≠
8        read(srcHeap,read(srcHeap,s,ERSchema.entities)[j2],Entity.name)));
9    modifies tarHeap;
10   /* postcondition: relation names are unique in the REL schema */
11   ensures (∀ t: ref • t∈find(tarHeap,REL$RELSchema)⟹
12     (∀ j1,j2: int • 0≤j1<j2<arrayLength(read(tarHeap,t,RELSchema.relations))⟹
13      read(tarHeap,t,RELSchema.relations)[j1] ≠
14      read(tarHeap,t,RELSchema.relations)[j2] ⟹
15       read(tarHeap,read(tarHeap,t,RELSchema.relations)[j1],Relation.name) ≠
16       read(tarHeap,read(tarHeap,t,RELSchema.relations)[j2],Relation.name)));
17
18   implementation main() {
19   /* Initialize Target model */
20      call init_tar_model();
21   /* instantiation phase */
22      call S2S_matchAll(); call E2R_matchAll(); call R2R_matchAll();
23      call EA2A_matchAll(); call RA2A_matchAll(); call RA2AK_matchAll();
24   /* initialisation phase */
25      call S2S_applyAll(); call E2R_applyAll(); call R2R_applyAll();
26      call EA2A_applyAll(); call RA2A_applyAll(); call RA2AK_applyAll();
27   }
```

Fig. 4. Verifying the Correctness of the *ER2REL* Transformation

- Second, the execution semantics of the ATL specification is encoded as a Boogie implementation (line 18–27). The body of this Boogie implementation is a series of procedure calls to the encoded Boogie contracts for the execution semantics of each ATL matched rule. Specifically, the execution semantics of a given matched rule involves an **instantiation** step (for matching source elements and allocating target elements) and an **initialisation** step (for initialising target elements) [3]. Each step is encoded as a Boogie contract. These Boogie contracts for ATL rules are scheduled to execute their instantiation steps before their initialisation steps, which ensures the confluence of transformation [3].
- Finally, we pair the Boogie contract that represents the specified OCL contracts, with the Boogie implementation that represents the execution semantics of the

ATL specification. Such a pair forms a verification task, which is input to the Boogie verifier. The Boogie verifier either gives a confirmation that indicates the ATL specification satisfies the specified OCL contracts, or trace information that indicates where the OCL contract violation is detected.

Whether the ER2REL transformation is verified for the given OCL contracts depends on our encoded Boogie contracts for the execution semantics of each ATL matched rule. Our encoding is based on existing documentation of ATL [3,9]. However, the ambiguities in the documentation increase our encoding difficulty. For example, on line 5 of the ER2REL specification (Fig. 2), the *relations* association is bound twice. The ATL documentation does not explicitly specify how to encode the execution semantics of such a case. We can encode it by either assuming that:

- The second binding *overwrites* the first binding. In this case the *relations_unique* constraint holds, since the *relations* of each *RELSchema* element will be resolved from the *entities* of the *ERSchema* element only; or
- The second binding is *composed* with the first binding. In this case the *relations_unique* constraint does not hold, since the *relations* of each *RELSchema* element will come from both the *relships* and *entities* of the *ERSchema* element, and we do not know that the names of *relships* are all unique for each *ERSchema* element, nor that the names of *entities* and *relships* of each *ERSchema* element are different.

Problem Statement. To resolve the ambiguity here, our quest in this work is to ensure our encoded execution semantics of the ATL specification soundly represents the runtime behaviour of its corresponding ASM implementation, i.e. verifying the soundness of our encoding for the execution semantics of the ATL specification. Therefore, in the next sections, we first detail our Boogie encoding for the execution semantics of each ATL matched rule (Sect. 4). Then, we report our translation validation approach to verify the soundness of our encoding (Sect. 5).

4   Encoding Metamodels, OCL and ATL Matched Rules

To begin with, we illustrate how to encode the metamodels and OCL constructs in Boogie, which will be used to encode the execution semantics of ATL matched rules.

Metamodels. Metamodelling concepts share many similarities with object oriented (OO) programming language constructs. Thus, we reuse the encoding of OO programs (specifically the memory model) to encode metamodels in Boogie.

Specifically, each classifier in the metamodel gives rise to a unique constant of type *ClassName*. Inheritance is defined via a partial order between two classifiers (multiple-inheritance is currently not supported by our encoding). Each element of a classifier is abstracted as a reference and generated as a Boogie variable of type *ref*. Each structural feature is mapped to a unique constant of type

Field α, where α is of primitive type (i.e. *int*, *bool* and *string*) for an attribute, and is of *ref* type for an association. Moreover, all these constants generated for attributes or associations are extended with the corresponding classifier name to ensure their uniqueness.

The OO memory model we chose uses an updatable array *heap* to organise the relationships between model elements. The *heap* is of type $ref \times (Field\ \alpha) \rightarrow \alpha$. Thus, it maps memory locations (identified by an element of a classifier, and a structural feature) to values. A memory access expression $o.f$ is now seen as an expression $read(heap,o,f)$. An assignment $o.f := x$ is understood as an expression $update(heap,o,f,x)$, i.e. changing the value of heap at the position given by the element o and structural feature f to the value of x. In addition, the domain of the *heap* includes allocated as well as unallocated elements. To distinguish between these two, we add a structural feature *alloc* of type *Field bool* and arrange to set it to true when an element is allocated.

OCL Constructs. We encode a subset of OCL data types supported in ATL, i.e. OclType, Primitive (*bool*, *int* and *string*), Collection (*set*, *ordered-set*, *sequence*, *bag*) and Map data types. Overall, 32 OCL operations are supported on the chosen data types. This encoding is based on a Boogie library for the theory of *set*, *sequence*, *bag* and *map* provided by the **Dafny** verification system [11]. Twenty-three Boogie functions from this library are directly reused in our encoding. One of them is modified to enhance the verification performance for sequence slicing. On top of these, we further introduce the *ordered-set* collection data type (with 3 OCL operations), and 6 OCL iterators on *sequence* and *ordered-set* data types (i.e. exists, forall, isUnique, select, collect and reject iterators). One subtlety in our encoding of OCL is how to handle the two *Undefined* values (i.e. *null* and *invalid*). To simplify the type system, we decided to support *null* as the *Undefined* value exclusively, and have not encountered verification problems caused by this decision.

ATL Matched Rules. According to the specification of the ATL virtual machine [3], the execution semantics of a given matched rule involves an instantiation step and an initialisation step. The execution semantics of each step is encoded as a Boogie contract.

We introduce three functions to help our encoding. The *dtype* function returns the classifier for a given reference. The *find* function returns all the references for the given classifier allocated on the given *heap*. The *getTarget* function returns the corresponding target element generated for a sequence of source elements. Its inverse function *getTarget_inverse* returns the sequence of source elements used to generate the given target element.

As an example, the instantiation step for the *S2S* rule is shown in Fig. 5. First, it requires that the target element generated for the *ERSchema* source element is not allocated yet (line 2–3). Then, it specifies that the instantiation step will only affect the heaps for the target model (line 4). This is because we use different *heaps* to represent the source and target models, and axiomatise them to be disjoint (an element that is allocated on one heap is not allocated on the other heap). This ensures, for example, a modification made on the target

```
 1  procedure S2S_matchAll();
 2  requires (∀ s: ref • s∈find(srcHeap,ER$ERSchema)⟹
 3    getTarget({s})=null ∨ ¬read(tarHeap,getTarget({s}),alloc));
 4  modifies tarHeap;
 5  ensures (∀ s: ref • s∈find(srcHeap,ER$ERSchema)⟹
 6    read(tarHeap,getTarget({s}),alloc)
 7    ∧ getTarget({s}) ≠ null
 8    ∧ dtype(getTarget({s}))=REL$RELSchema);
 9  ensures (∀ o: ref, f: Field α •
10    (o=null ∨ read(tarHeap,o,f)=read(old(tarHeap),o,f)
11    ∨ (dtype(o)=REL$RELSchema
12    ∧ f=alloc ∧ dtype(getTarget_inverse(o)[0])=ER$ERSchema)));
```

Fig. 5. The auto-generated Boogie contract for the instantiation step of the *S2S* rule

heap will not affect the state of the source heap. Next, it ensures that after the execution of the instantiation step, for each *ERSchema* element, the corresponding *RELSchema* target element is allocated (line 5–8). Finally, it ensures that nothing else is modified, except the *RELSchema* element(s) created from the *ERSchema* element by the instantiation step (line 9–11).

```
 1  procedure S2S_applyAll();
 2  requires (∀ s: ref • s∈find(srcHeap,ER$ERSchema)⟹
 3    read(tarHeap,getTarsBySrcs({s}),alloc)
 4    ∧ getTarget({s}) ≠ null ∧ dtype(getTarget({s}))=REL$RELSchema);
 5  modifies tarHeap;
 6  ... // t.relations ≠ null ∧ t.relations.alloc
 7  ... // dtype(t.relations)=class._System.array
 8  // length(t.relations)=length(s.entities)+length(s.relships)
 9  ensures (∀ s: ref • s∈find(srcHeap,ER$ERSchema)⟹
10    ArrayLength(read(tarHeap,getTarsBySrcs({s}),RELSchema.relations))
11    = ArrayLength(read(srcHeap,s,ERSchema.entities))
12    +ArrayLength(read(srcHeap,s,ERSchema.relships))
13  );
14  // t.relations[j] = resolve(s.entities[j])
15  ensures (∀ s: ref • s∈find(srcHeap,ER$Entity)⟹
16    (∀ j: int • 0≤j<ArrayLength(read(srcHeap,s,ERSchema.entities))⟹
17      read(tarHeap,getTarsBySrcs({s}),RELSchema.relations)[j]
18      =getTarsBySrcs({read(srcHeap,s,ERSchema.entities)[j]})));
19  // t.relations[j+len(s.entities)] = resolve(s.relships[j])
20  ensures (∀ s: ref • s∈find(srcHeap,ER$Entity)⟹
21    (∀ j: int • 0≤j<ArrayLength(read(srcHeap,s,ERSchema.relships))⟹
22      read(tarHeap,getTarsBySrcs({s}),RELSchema.relations)
23      [j+ArrayLength(read(srcHeap,s,ERSchema.entities)]
24      =getTarsBySrcs({read(srcHeap,s,ERSchema.relships)[j]})));
25  ensures (∀ o: ref, f: Field α •
26    o ≠ null ∧ read(old(tarHeap),o,alloc)⟹
27    (dtype(o)=REL$RELSchema ∧ f=RELSchema.relations
28    ∧ dtype(getTarget_inverse(o)[0])=ER$ERSchema)
29    ∨ (read(tarHeap,o,f)=read(old(tarHeap),o,f)));
```

Fig. 6. The auto-generated Boogie contract for the initialisation step of the *S2S* rule

The Boogie contract generated for the initialisation step of the *S2S* rule is shown in Fig. 6. First, it requires that the instantiation step of the *S2S* rule is finished (line 2–4). Then, it specifies that only the heap for the target model will be modified (line 5). Next, it ensures that the corresponding target element is fully initialised, by performing associated binding as specified in the *S2S* rule (line 6–24). In particular, we encode consecutive bindings to the *relations* association as a composition. Finally, it ensures that nothing else is modified, except the binding performed on the created target element (line 25–29).

5 Sound Encoding for the Execution Semantics of ATL Rules

Each ATL matched rule is actually compiled into two ASM operations by the ATL compiler, i.e. a *matchAll* operation (for the instantiation step) and an *applyAll* operation (for the initialisation step). An important contribution of our work is the verification of the soundness of our Boogie encoding for the execution semantics of the ATL rules, i.e. that the encoded execution semantics of each ATL rule soundly represents the runtime behaviour of its corresponding ASM operation. In this section, we first provide a translational semantics of the ASM language in Boogie, which allows the runtime behaviour of the ASM operations to be represented using Boogie implementations. Then, we illustrate our translation validation approach to verify the soundness of our Boogie encoding for the execution semantics of ATL rules.

Translational Semantics of ASM. Each ASM operation has a list of local variables, which are encoded as Boogie local variables. An operand stack is used by each ASM operation to communicate values for local computations, and this is abstracted as an OCL *sequence* data type, which is represented as a list in Boogie called *Stk* in our encodings. Source and target elements are globally accessible by every ASM operation, and they are managed by the disjoint source and target *heaps* as described in Sect. 4.

The ASM language contains 21 bytecode instructions. Apart from the general-purpose instructions for control flow and stack handling, the important feature of the ASM language is the model-handling-specific instructions that are dedicated to model manipulation.

We provide a translational semantics of the ASM language via a list of translation rules to Boogie. Each translation rule encodes the operational semantics of an ASM instruction in Boogie. The only resource we can find to explain the operational semantics of ASM bytecode instructions is the specification of the ATL virtual machine [3]. However, it is imprecise and leaves many issues open. This raises the question of how a correct translation rule, especially for each model handling instruction, should be encoded in Boogie.

Unlike the other two categories of instructions, the model handling instructions might have different operational semantics for different model management systems. This is because ATL aims at interacting with various model management systems which offer different interfaces for model manipulation [9].

Our strategy is to focus on the EMF model management system. Then, we can check the ATL source code (specifically the ATL virtual machine implementation that relates to EMF) for the operational semantics of each ASM instruction, and then design the rule correspondingly.

In what follows, we pick a representative ASM instruction as an example, i.e. the *SET* instruction. We first give an informal description of its operational semantics, and then explain the intuition behind its corresponding translation to Boogie. The full translational semantics of the ASM language can be accessed through our online repository given in Sect. 6.

The *SET* instruction is one of the ASM instructions for model handling (Fig. 7 (left)). The parameter of a *SET* instruction is a structural feature f (either an attribute or an association). Before executing the *SET* instruction, the top two elements on the operand stack are an element o (second-top) and a value v (top) respectively.

The operational semantics of the *SET* instruction forms a case distinction according to the instruction parameter f. If f is an association and its multiplicity has an upper-bound that is greater than one, then compute the union of the value of $o.f$ with v. Otherwise, set $o.f$ to v. Finally, the top two elements are popped.

Thus, the operational semantics of the *SET* instruction explains the unusual behaviour of consecutive bindings to the *relations* association (whose multiplicity has an upper-bound that is greater than one) shown in Sect. 2. Each binding corresponds to a *SET* instruction on the ASM level. Therefore, the two consecutive bindings correspond to two *SET* instruction invocations. The result will be a composition of two bindings.

n: SET f	`let o=hd(tl(Stk)),v=hd(Stk) in`
	`assert size(Stk)>1 ∧ o ≠ null ∧ read(heap,o,alloc);`
	`if(isCollection(f))`
	`    {heap:=update(heap,read(heap,o,f),read(heap,o,f)∪v);}`
	`else {heap:=update(heap,o,f,v);}`
	`Stk:=tl(tl(Stk));`

Fig. 7. *SET* instruction in ASM (left) and its translation rule in Boogie (right)

The translation rule for the *SET* instruction is shown in Fig. 7 (right). It offers no surprise in its operational semantics, except for the auxiliary function *isCollection*. The *isCollection* function (of type *Field* $\alpha \rightarrow bool$) is encoded while mapping the structural features to the Boogie constants. It is axiomatised so that it returns *true* when the given structural feature is an association and its multiplicity has an upper-bound that is greater than one, and returns *false* otherwise.

The translational semantics of the ASM language is encapsulated as a Boogie library, which can be found in our online repository as outlined in Sect. 6.

Translation Validation of Encoding Soundness. In order to verify the soundness of our Boogie encoding for the execution semantics of each ATL matched rule, we define that the execution semantics of an ATL matched rule encoded in Boogie is sound, if,

```
1   procedure S2S_matchAll();        //Contract for instantiation step
2   ...
3   ensures (∀ s: ref • s∈find(srcHeap,ER$ERSchema)⟹
4       dtype(getTarget({s}))=REL$RELSchema);
5
6   implementation S2S_matchAll() //Implementation for matchAll operation
7   { ...
8     #ERSchemas := find(srcHeap,ER$ERSchema);
9     counter:=0;
10
11    while(counter<size(#ERSchemas))
12      invariant (∀ n:int • 0≤n<counter⟹
13        dtype(getTarget({#ERSchemas[n]}))=REL$RELSchema);
14      decreases size(#ERSchemas)−counter;
15    { ... counter:=counter+1; }
16  }
```

Fig. 8. Soundness verification of Boogie encodings for the instantiation step of *S2S* rule

- the Boogie contract that represents the execution semantics of its *instantiation* step is satisfied by the Boogie implementation that represents the runtime behaviour of its *matchAll* operation, and
- the Boogie contract that represents the execution semantics of its *initialisation* step is satisfied by the Boogie implementation that represents the runtime behaviour of its *applyAll* operation.

Each of them forms a verification task, and is sent to the Boogie verifier. If none of the verification tasks generate any errors (from the verifier), we conclude that our Boogie encoding for the execution semantics of the ATL matched rules is sound. Essentially, our approach is based on a translation validation technique used in compiler verification [12]. The benefit is that we do not need to verify that the encoded execution semantics of ATL specifications are always sound with respect to the runtime behaviour of their ASM implementation (which is difficult to automate). Instead, we can automatically verify the soundness of each ATL specification/ASM implementation pair.

We demonstrate our approach on the instantiation step of the *S2S* rule (Fig. 8). Generally, a Boogie implementation that contains loops is difficult to verify because the users cannot generally predict how many times the loop executes, or whether it will terminate.

The key ingredient to prove the correctness of a loop is to provide the **loop invariant** that holds before and after the loop. The general loop invariant for the Boogie implementation is automatically generated. This is demonstrated on the soundness verification of Boogie encodings for the instantiation step of the *S2S* rule as follows (Fig. 8): In the Boogie implementation for its *matchAll* operation, an invariant is generated to ensure that for all the matched source elements that have been iterated, the postcondition of the instantiation step is fulfilled (line 12–13). Thus, by the end of the iteration, all the matched source elements are iterated, and therefore the postcondition of the instantiation step can be established (line 3–4).

We also use a **variant expression** to ensure that the loop terminates. A general variant expression for the Boogie implementation of a *matchAll* operation is the size of the iterated collection minus the increasing loop counter (line 14). Since the counter increases on each iteration and the size of the processed collection remains unchanged, we can deduce that there are less elements in the collection to be iterated.

We can conclude that the execution semantics of an ATL specification encoded in Boogie is sound when the execution semantics of all the relevant ATL matched rules encoded in Boogie are sound.

6   Implementation

We have implemented the **VeriATL** verification system (Fig. 9) to demonstrate our approach. It accepts the source and target ECore metamodels and an ATL specification. The output is a sound execution semantics of the ATL specification encoded in the Boogie intermediate verification language, which soundly represents the runtime behaviour of its corresponding ASM implementation. As a result, the verification of the correctness of the ATL transformation that is based on our output will be sound.

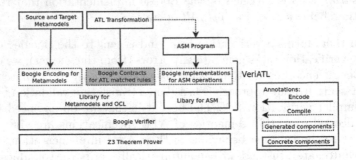

Fig. 9. Overview of our sound verification of the correctness of the ATL transformation

VeriATL automatically serialises its inputs into three kinds of models. Specifically, the KM3 API is used to serialise the ECore metamodels into the KM3 model[2]. The ATL extractor API is used to serialise the input ATL specification as an ATL model. The ATL virtual machine API is used to serialise the ASM program into an ASM model. Next, the corresponding Boogie code is automatically generated for each kind of model by a template-based model-to-text transformation using Xpand[3], i.e. the ATL model generates Boogie contracts, the KM3 model generates Boogie types and constants, and the ASM model produces Boogie implementations. Then, VeriATL sends the generated Boogie code to the Boogie verifier (version 2.2), and relies on the Z3 (version 4.3) to perform automatic theorem proving. Finally, if the Boogie verifier confirms that the execution semantics of an ATL specification encoded in Boogie is sound, then such

---

[2] KM3 is a domain specific language for metamodel specifications.

[3] Xpand. http://wiki.eclipse.org/Xpand/.

an encoding will be output by VeriATL. Otherwise, the trace information from the Boogie verifier, indicating where the encoding unsoundness was detected, will be output.

Evaluation. We evaluate VeriATL on the *ER2REL* transformation. Our *ER2REL* transformation is a modified version of the one originally developed by Büttner et al. [5]. The modification does not cause the ATL specification to behave differently. However, it contains a feature (i.e. consecutive bindings in an ATL matched rule) that is not considered in the previous work.

Our experiment is performed on an Intel 2.93 GHz machine with 4 GB of memory running on Windows. Verification times are recorded in seconds. Table 1 shows the performance on automatically verifying the soundness of our Boogie encoding. The *second* and *third* columns show the size of the Boogie code generated for the instantiation and initialisation step of the ATL matched rule respectively (shown by Lines of Boogie contract/Boogie implementation). Their corresponding verification time is shown in the *fourth* and *fifth* columns.

Table 1. Performance measures for verifying the encoding soundness of *ER2REL*

Rule name	Boogie (LoC)		Veri. time (s)		Automation
	Instantiation	Initialisation	Instantiation	Initialisation	
S2S	13/133	41/200	0.124	0.894	Auto
E2R	13/150	15/79	0.109	0.077	Auto
R2R	13/150	15/79	0.109	0.062	Auto
EA2A	17/202	33/145	0.187	0.328	Auto
RA2A	17/202	33/145	0.187	0.327	Auto
RA2AK	17/225	33/141	0.374	0.311	Auto
Total	90/1062	170/789	1.090	1.999	

We also verify our modified *ER2REL* transformation against the 4 OCL contracts that are specified by Büttner et al., and produce the same verification result. Table 2 shows the performance of our transformation correctness verification. The *second* column shows the size of the Boogie code generated for the OCL contracts. Its corresponding verification time is shown in the *third* column. In addition, we report that 2 out of 4 OCL contracts are verified semi-automatically. This is because of incompleteness issues with our approach, which we analyse in the **threat to validity** section below.

Due to space limitations, we are unable to show the whole case study. We refer to our online repository for the generated Boogie programs for verifying the correctness of *ER2REL* transformation [7].

Threat to Validity. The experiments strongly demonstrate the feasibility of our approach. However, our current approach has some limitations:

Table 2. Performance measures for verifying transformation correctness of *ER2REL*

	Boogie (LoC)	Veri. time (s)	Automation
unique_rel_schema_names	45	0.624	Auto
unique_rel_relation_names	48	1.716	Semi
unique_rel_attribute_names	48	0.608	Auto
exist_rel_relation_iskey	49	0.562	Semi
Total	190	3.510	

- First, the soundness of our approach depends on the correctness of our encodings for metamodels, OCL, ATL language and ASM bytecode. The correctness of these encodings are challenging theoretical problems that require well-defined and commonly accepted formal semantics of each. To our knowledge, none of them are currently available. When there is one, we can adapt existing techniques to reason the correctness of our encodings [2,8]. Moreover, our Boogie encodings are intuitive and available for inspection.
- Second, the completeness of our approach remains one of the major concerns. The incompleteness might be due to known limitations of SMT solvers. It may also be due to our encodings. For example, the *append* operation of *sequence* data type in our OCL library is encoded by the essential axioms to define its meaning. The auxiliary axioms such as "any sequence appended with an empty sequence is the original sequence" are not in our encoding. We think it is better to present the missing auxiliary axioms as lemmas and introduced on demand to make the verification task smaller. Moreover, presenting only the essential axioms is a strategy that helps manual inspection and reduces the possibility of inconsistent axioms.
- Third, our approach only covers the ATL matched rules in this work. Other constructs, such as lazy rules and imperative features (e.g. *resolveTemp* operation), are not considered. We would like to include them in the near future. For example, we are currently considering ATL lazy rules, which are called from the other rules. The lazy rules are not as frequently used as the matched rules, but are the main source of transformation non-termination.
- Last, because of the underlying SMT solver, the expressiveness of our approach is based on first order predicate logic with equality. To ensure this expressiveness power is useful in practice of MTr verification, we need to experiment with more ATL transformations that have OCL contracts specified.

7   Related Work

There is a large body of work on the topic of ensuring model transformation correctness [1]. In this section, we focus on the works that verify the correctness of MTr by applying formal methods.

Troya and Vallecillo provide an operational semantics for ATL based on rewriting logic, and use the Maude system for the simulation and reachability analysis of ATL specifications [15]. Lúcio et al. develop an off-the-shelf model checker that is tied to the DSLTrans language. Their model checker allows the user to check the syntactic correctness (encoded in algebra) of the generated target models [13]. These approaches are bounded, which means that the MTr specification will be verified against its contracts within a given search space (i.e. using finite ranges for the number of models, associations and attributes). Bounded approaches are usually automatic, but no conclusion can be drawn outside the search space.

Calegari et al. use the Coq proof assistant to interactively verify that an ATL specification is able to produce target models that satisfy the given contracts [6]. Inspired by the proof-as-program methodology, further research develops the concept of proof-as-model-transformation methodology [10,14]. At its simplest, the idea is to present the model transformation specification and contract as a theorem. Then, a model transformation implementation can be extracted from its proof. These approaches are unbounded. Therefore, they are preferable when the user requires that contracts hold for the MTr specification over an infinite domain. However, unbounded approaches tend to require guidance from the user.

The situation can be ameliorated by a novel usage of SMT-solvers. The built-in background theories of SMT solvers give enhanced expressiveness to handle constraints over an infinite domain. For example, Büttner et al. translate a declarative subset of the ATL and OCL contracts (for semantic correctness) directly into first-order-logic formulas [5]. The formulas represent the execution semantics of the ATL specification, and are sent to the Z3 SMT solver to be discharged. The result implies the partial correctness of an ATL transformation in terms of the specified OCL contracts. However, their approach lacks an intermediate form to bridge between the ATL and the back-end SMT-solver. This compromises the reusability and modularity of the verifier. In our work, we extend existing Boogie libraries for our metamodel and OCL encodings. We also develop a Boogie library that gives a translational semantics to the ASM language. Each Boogie library is designed modularly, and is made available for public reuse of verifier design (especially for model transformation languages).

Finally, all the approaches we have just described rely on encoding the execution semantics of the model transformation specification. We address a different challenge to verify that the execution semantics of an ATL matched rule encoded in Boogie soundly represents the runtime behaviour of its corresponding ASM implementation, which makes our approach complementary to the existing approaches. We developed our approach in Boogie. The Why3[4] intermediate verification language would also be suitable to implement our approach.

8   Conclusion

In this work, we have encoded a sound execution semantics for ATL specifications, and developed the VeriATL verification system for this task. It is implemented in Boogie which allows Hoare-logic-based automatic theorem proving

---

[4] Why3. http://why3.lri.fr/.

via the Z3 theorem prover. We adapt the memory model used in the verification of object-oriented programs to explain the concepts within MDE. We explain precisely the runtime behaviour of ASM implementations by encoding a translational semantics of the ASM language in Boogie. We also articulate a translation validation approach to verify the soundness of our Boogie encoding for the execution semantics of the ATL matched rule. Consequently, we are able to soundly verify the ATL specification against its specified OCL contracts, based on our sound encodings for the execution semantics of the ATL matched rules.

References

1. Ab.Rahim, L., Whittle, J.: A survey of approaches for verifying model transformations. Soft. Syst. Modeling (2015) (to appear)
2. Apt, K.R., de Boer, F.S., Olderog, E.R.: Verification of Sequential and Concurrent Programs, 3rd edn. Springer, Berlin (2009)
3. ATLAS Group: Specification of the ATL virtual machine. Technical report, Lina & INRIA Nantes (2005)
4. Barnett, M., Chang, B.-Y.E., DeLine, R., Jacobs, B., M. Leino, K.R.: Boogie: a modular reusable verifier for object-oriented programs. In: de Boer, F.S., Bonsangue, M.M., Graf, S., de Roever, W.-P. (eds.) FMCO 2005. LNCS, vol. 4111, pp. 364–387. Springer, Heidelberg (2006)
5. Büttner, F., Egea, M., Cabot, J.: On verifying ATL transformations using 'off-the-shelf' SMT solvers. In: France, R.B., Kazmeier, J., Breu, R., Atkinson, C. (eds.) MODELS 2012. LNCS, vol. 7590, pp. 432–448. Springer, Heidelberg (2012)
6. Calegari, D., Luna, C., Szasz, N., Tasistro, Á.: A type-theoretic framework for certified model transformations. In: Davies, J. (ed.) SBMF 2010. LNCS, vol. 6527, pp. 112–127. Springer, Heidelberg (2011)
7. Cheng, Z., Monahan, R., Power, J.F.: Online repository for VeriATL system (2013). https://github.com/veriatl/veriatl
8. Combemale, B., Crégut, X., Garoche, P., Thirioux, X.: Essay on semantics definition in MDE - an instrumented approach for model verification. J. Softw. 4(9), 943–958 (2009)
9. Jouault, F., Allilaire, F., Bézivin, J., Kurtev, I.: ATL: a model transformation tool. Sci. Comput. Program. 72(1–2), 31–39 (2008)
10. Lano, K., Clark, T., Kolahdouz-Rahimi, S.: A framework for model transformation verification. Formal Aspects Comput. 27(1), 193–235 (2015)
11. Leino, K.R.M.: Dafny: an automatic program verifier for functional correctness. In: Clarke, E.M., Voronkov, A. (eds.) LPAR 16 2010. LNCS, vol. 6355, pp. 348–370. Springer, Heidelberg (2010)
12. Leroy, X.: Formal certification of a compiler back-end or: programming a compiler with a proof assistant. SIGPLAN Not. 41(1), 42–54 (2006)
13. Lúcio, L., Barroca, B., Amaral, V.: A technique for automatic validation of model transformations. In: Petriu, D.C., Rouquette, N., Haugen, Ø. (eds.) MODELS 2010, Part I. LNCS, vol. 6394, pp. 136–150. Springer, Heidelberg (2010)
14. Poernomo, I.H.: Proofs-as-model-transformations. In: Vallecillo, A., Gray, J., Pierantonio, A. (eds.) ICMT 2008. LNCS, vol. 5063, pp. 214–228. Springer, Heidelberg (2008)
15. Troya, J., Vallecillo, A.: A rewriting logic semantics for ATL. J. Object Technol. 10(5), 1–29 (2011)

From UML/OCL to Base Models: Transformation Concepts for Generic Validation and Verification

Frank Hilken[1][✉], Philipp Niemann[1], Martin Gogolla[1], and Robert Wille[1,2]

[1] Computer Science Department, University of Bremen,
28359 Bremen, Germany
{fhilken,pniemann,gogolla,rwille}@informatik.uni-bremen.de
[2] Cyber-Physical Systems, DFKI GmbH,
28359 Bremen, Germany

Abstract. Modeling languages such as UML and OCL find more and more application in the early stages of today's system design. Validation and verification, i.e. checking the correctness of the respective models, gains interest. Since these languages offer various description means and a huge set of constructs, existing approaches for this purpose only support a restricted subset of constructs and often focus on dedicated description means as well as verification tasks. To overcome this, we follow the idea of using model transformations to unify different description means to a *base model*. In the course of these transformation, complex language constructs are expressed by means of a small subset of so-called *core elements* in order to interface with a wide range of verification engines with complementary strengths and weaknesses. In this paper, we provide a detailed introduction of the proposed base model and its core elements as well as corresponding model transformations.

Keywords: Model transformation · UML · OCL · Metamodel · Validation and verification · Base model

1 Introduction

In recent years, *Model-Driven Engineering* (MDE) has become more and more popular, and modeling languages are more and more used in early stages of today's system design. In this context, the *Unified Modeling Language* (UML) and the *Object Constraint Language* (OCL) are de facto standards to describe systems and their behavior. They provide formal descriptions of system models which, besides others, can be applied for purposes of validation and verification. Indeed, identifying flaws and errors early in the design of such systems using validation and verification techniques is an important task. In our work, we focus on automatic (i.e. *push button*) methods which require almost no further knowledge on the underlying verification technique and, thus, can be used by every system designer.

© Springer International Publishing Switzerland 2015
D. Kolovos and M. Wimmer (Eds.): ICMT 2015, LNCS 9152, pp. 149–165, 2015.
DOI: 10.1007/978-3-319-21155-8_12

However, developments in the previous years led to an "inflation" of different verification approaches for designs given in terms of modeling languages (this is discussed in detail later in Sect. 2). Finding an appropriate verification approach is a non-trivial task, since most approaches focus on one particular UML diagram type and additionally restrict the set of supported language constructs. This poses a severe problem, as complex system designs often consist of a variety of different diagram types interacting with each other. Moreover, often these approaches address specific verification tasks only.

In order to overcome this, the idea of a generic verification framework has been presented in [35]. Instead of considering each description mean separately, the underlying idea of this framework is a transformation into a uniform/normalized description: a *base model*. Moreover, in the course of this transformation complex language constructs are expressed by means of a small subset of so-called *core elements* in order to interface with a wide range of verification engines with complementary strengths and weaknesses. The base model is integrated in the validation and verification process in a way that the designer does not need to have knowledge of it. The results of verification engines which are derived using the base model are mapped back to the source model and represented to the developers in their domain.

In this work, we provide a detailed introduction of the proposed base model and its core elements. Roughly speaking, the base model is a UML class diagram enriched with OCL constraints with a reduced feature set that only contains essential and atomic language constructs. However, we will show that this reduced feature set is sufficient to express many complex language constructs by providing the corresponding model transformations. We focus on transformations within class diagrams because transformations from alternative diagram types, e.g. sequence diagrams or activity diagrams, to class diagrams have already been considered, e.g. in [20] and [19], respectively.

The remainder of this work is structured as follows: motivation for the generic verification framework and a discussion about related work is presented in Sect. 2. A detailed introduction of the base model and its core elements is provided in Sect. 3, while the actual transformations of complex class diagram features into the base model are discussed in Sect. 4. Finally, we conclude the paper in Sect. 5.

2   Motivation and Related Work

The development of automated methods for the verification of UML/OCL models has intensely been considered by researchers and engineers in the recent past. For this purpose, several solving techniques have been applied ranging from a guided enumeration, as done e.g. in the *UML-based Specification Environment* (USE, [14]) together with the language ASSL [13], to the application of verification engines such as CSP solvers [5], Alloy [1], or SAT solvers [33,34]. Fig. 1 gives an (incomplete) overview of the current state-of-the-art categorized by their respective support for diagram types and verification task. While this led to a variety of powerful tools and methods for the verification of UML/OCL models, the resulting state-of-the-art suffers from three main drawbacks:

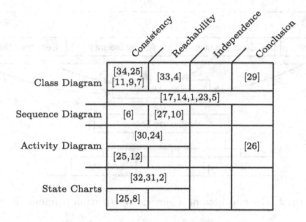

Fig. 1. Overview on related work

1. The resulting solutions often support dedicated verification tasks only. While e.g. [34] allows for consistency checking of class diagrams, this approach does not support sequence diagrams. That is, for each modeling method and each verification task usually a different verification approach has to be applied.
2. Complex systems are usually not modeled by means of single diagrams only, but composed of a variety of different diagram types which interact with each other. For example, while class diagrams specify the structure of a system, the behavior may be defined by a statechart. But again, most of the available verification approaches support single diagram types only.
3. Almost all proposed verification approaches are bound to one particular verification engine. For example, the approach presented in [5] exploits CSP solvers, whereas e.g. in [33] SAT and SMT solvers find application. This is disadvantageous as verification engines may behave differently effective for various models. If additionally, new and better verification engines emerge in the future, existing transformations to the respective solver input have to be re-developed.

   In order to overcome these drawbacks, a generic verification framework for UML/OCL models was envisioned in [35]. The general idea is sketched in Fig. 2: Instead of treating single diagram types separately (as it has mainly been done in the past; see Fig. 1), it was proposed to transform them to a so-called *base model* – a subset of UML/OCL constraints which is expressive enough to describe most constructs of the UML and OCL, but small enough to allow for a flexible further processing.

   Having this generic description, the development of verification approaches can focus on the core constructs available in the base model. This allows for an easier integration of verification engines than before. Moreover, even new solving technologies which may emerge in the future can be exploited more easily since a restricted subset of constructs needs to be considered only. In contrast, transformations from the original description means (class diagrams, sequence

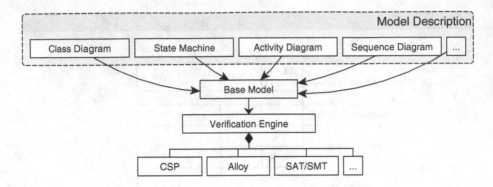

Fig. 2. General idea of a generic verification framework

diagrams, etc.) to the base model have to be provided. But since those would only require a model-to-model transformation to the base model (and e.g. not to the numerous solver-specific inputs), they need to be developed only once. By this separation of concerns, a more generic verification of UML/OCL models relying on a variety of solving techniques as well as supporting a wide range of verification tasks, becomes possible at moderate costs.

However, while the principle feasibility of the vision has been demonstrated on selected examples in [35], no implementation of the generic framework exists yet. In particular, a precise definition of the base model and a corresponding transformation scheme from arbitrary description means are still missing[1]. In the following, we aim for closing this gap. More precisely, we provide a precise proposal for a base model and discuss how general constructs can be transformed into it.

3   A Base Model for UML and OCL Verification

As motivated in the previous section, the purpose of the base model is to provide a generic interface between heterogeneous UML/OCL model descriptions and validation and verification tools. This interface shall be flexible and generic at both the source and the target side. More precisely, it shall be applicable for a large variety of diagram types and verification tasks on the one hand, while, on the other hand, it shall allow for a flexible choice of verification engines for further processing. To this end, the base model needs to be:

- *universal*, i.e. for each construct in a source model, an equivalent formulation in the base model must exist, and
- *atomic*, i.e. the constructs of the base model should be limited to fundamental modeling concepts such that a uniform further processing as well as the flexibility of the overall framework is ensured.

---

[1] First ideas, leaving numerous details open, have been sketched in a preliminary version of this paper which has been discussed at a workshop [21].

Clearly, these are contrary properties as UML and OCL are very powerful languages with a rich set of language constructs – some of which are very complex in nature and can hardly be expressed by simpler means. Consequently, the solution is necessarily a trade-off between universality and atomicity. Nonetheless, we aim to reduce the restrictions to universality to a minimum by (a) employing the power of model-to-model transformations on the UML/OCL level and (b) only excluding less relevant UML/OCL features that are hardly used in practice or conceptually infeasible to be tackled by verification engines at all. Note, however, that some restrictions are inevitable and have to be applied anyhow when considering validation and verification of UML/OCL models as, e.g. data types like Integer are unbounded in the standard UML semantics, while verification engines often only work on bounded, finite search spaces. These simplifications are mainly justified by the fact that actual implementations of the models will also have to run on finite resources.

For the foundation of the base model, we propose to use a reduced UML class diagram. This diagram type is well-suited as it natively supports structural definitions in form of classes and associations as well as model dynamics using OCL expressions for operation pre- and postconditions. Furthermore, transformations from other diagram types (such as sequence diagrams or activity diagrams) to class diagrams have already been investigated [19,20] and can be re-used here.

The feature sets of UML and OCL are reduced to a required minimum. This reduction has a few advantages to it: Flexibility and compatibility to verification engines is increased, because the feature set which needs to be supported by it is minimized. In addition, the reduction also enforces an early/high-level transformation of complex constructs into simpler ones which simplifies the analysis of the model and the determination of an appropriate verification engine. In the following, the elements of the reduced feature set of the base model are presented and described in more detail.

3.1   UML Elements in the Base Model

An overview on the different UML class diagram features and how they are included in the reduced feature set of the base model is given in Table 1. The core of the base model is formed of essential and atomic constructs – the so-called *core elements* which are marked with a "✓" and are natively supported in the base model. These have been chosen due to their fundamental importance for UML class diagrams and good compatibility with state-of-the-art verification approaches. Note that for a verification engine to support the base model, corresponding translations to the solver level need to be developed for these core elements only.

Further class diagram features that can be expressed within the base model, but do not appear in it as core elements, are marked with a "○". These can be transformed into semantically equivalent representations using only core elements. Details about these transformations will be presented in Sect. 4.

The last category of elements are marked with "×" and are neither part of the base model nor do we propose a corresponding transformation for them yet.

Table 1. UML Elements in the Base Model

Class features	Association features	Operation features
✓ Class	✓ Binary Association	✓ Operation (non query)
o Abstract Class	o N-ary Association	✓ Parameter
o Inheritance	o Aggregation	× Return Value
o Multiple Inheritance	o Composition	✓ Pre-/Postcondition
✓ Attribute	✓ Multiplicity	× Nested Operation Call
o Initial Value	o Association Class	o Query Operation
o Derived Value	o Qualified Association	✓ Parameter
✓ Enumeration	× Redefines, Subsets, Union	✓ Return Value
✓ Invariant		× Recursion

✓ core element; o transformed element (using only core elements); × unsupported element

These are either (1) hardly used in practice (like Redefines, Subsets, and Union), or (2) are conceptually infeasible for verification engines anyway (like recursive and nested operations)[2]. Consequently, the exclusion of these elements only has a minor impact on the universality of the base model.

3.2   OCL Elements in the Base Model

As for OCL, it is a lot harder to reduce the feature set without losing universality. This mostly results from the fact that OCL is a rich language with many diverse operations. Most operations can only be expressed by similar operations or their negated counterpart, e.g. the collection operations $C\rightarrow$isEmpty() and $C\rightarrow$notEmpty() can be represented using the operation $C\rightarrow$size(), and $C\rightarrow$reject(expr) can be represented using $C\rightarrow$select(not expr). A promising candidate to replace many of the standard OCL collection operations, the iterate operation, is, however, one of the least supported operations by verification engines – due to its high versatility. Thus, it also does not provide a satisfying solution regarding the reduction of OCL features in the base model.

Our solution is to accept the majority of standard OCL operations in the base model, keeping known alternatives at hand. Then, a verification engine is chosen based on the needs of the model, i.e. one that supports all employed operations or transformed alternatives, and the base model is prepared to be compatible before given to the verification engine.

Besides OCL operations, also data types have to be considered. We propose to use Integers and Sets as core data types. Integers are the mostly used primitive data type and often sufficient to emulate the functionality of other primitive data types like enumerations, Reals, and other numeric data types. Even Strings (on the word-level rather than on the character-level) may be emulated by Integers. Likewise, Sets are a well-suited representative for collection types. Besides that, other collection types like Sequence can also be emulated using UML classes as will be outlined later in Sect. 4 – although with considerable overhead.

---

[2] Note however that OCL provides the closure operation (which can solve some tasks that are typically formulated recursively) and which is supported by our approach.

Overall, data types are interpolated if necessary and a large set of OCL operations is accepted in the base model – even if the particular set of operations may possibly restrict the set of appropriate verification engines to be used for further processing. Verification engines used in combination with the base model are expected to support at least basic arithmetic on `Set` and `Integer` as well as the quantifiers `forAll` and `exist` (preferably also the `closure` operation).

4   Transformation to the Base Model

This section defines the transformation of class diagram features in UML/OCL source models into the target base model. The transformation consists of many smaller UML and OCL model transformations, some of which have already been sketched [18]. We focus on selected transformations (○ elements) from Table 1 that show the concepts of the base model best.

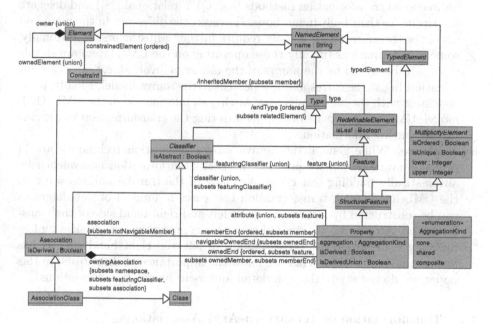

Fig. 3. Excerpt of relevant parts from the UML Metamodel

All transformations shown in this section operate on the UML and OCL layer. Where appropriate, we use instances of the UML metamodel to illustrate the transformation, showing system states before and after the transformation. Figure 3 shows the relevant parts of the UML metamodel used in the transformations. In the top left corner, the class `Element` is located, defining the base of every element in the model and on the right side you see the generalization hierarchy originating from it, defining different abstractions used by several elements throughout the metamodel. Finally, in the lower left part of the figure, the classes `Class`, `Association` and `AssociationClass` are defined extending the general class `Classifier`. These elements are connected via the class `Property` to define, e.g. roles and attributes. Note that transformations mostly concerning OCL expressions are not shown in the UML metamodel.

The transformation definitions on the UML metamodel are required to implement the transformations using tools like QVT [28] or ATL [22]. Along with the transformations, some further aspects have to be considered for the base model to work properly:

Tracability. As mentioned earlier, the base model is a "bridge" between the developer's source model and the verification engine, and results from the verification engine are presented in terms of the source model. Therefore, tracability is an important requirement for the base model. It has to be possible to transform models into the base model and solutions found by verification engines back into the source model. The easiest solution is to use bidirectional transformation methods (e.g. QVT relational [28]) and delegate the tracing to their built-in methods. However, the difference in the meta layers of the transformations usually require further adjustments. Additionally, some transformations (mainly those operating on the UML layer) are simple enough to be traced by the names of the elements involved, e.g. an invariant name hinting at the corresponding element in the source model. Finally, to be consistent with the base model idea, having all information in the UML/OCL model, UML comments can be applied during the transformation to provide further tracing information.

Equivalence. While general interactive model verification techniques are in principle available [3], we propose to check transformation equivalence by automatically building test cases. As many of the transformations work on the UML metamodel, transformation test cases in form of object diagrams can be constructed by instantiating the left and right hand side of the transformation. Afterwards the desired equivalence properties are checked by formulating OCL properties on the union of left and right hand side as has been studied in [15,16]. While we know the importance of these tests, in this paper, we do not study them in detail and focus on the transformations.

4.1   Transformation of Ternary (n-Ary) Associations

A rather simple model transformation is the replacement of ternary associations by a class and binary associations plus constraints. Figure 4 gives an overview of the transformation. The source model is on the left having a ternary association `ABC` connecting three classes. The model after the transformation is shown on the right side. Instead of the association, there is a new class named `ABC` connecting the three classes using three binary associations. The role names are carried over for the corresponding association ends and new ones are added where necessary. By this, ternary associations can be transformed into core elements.

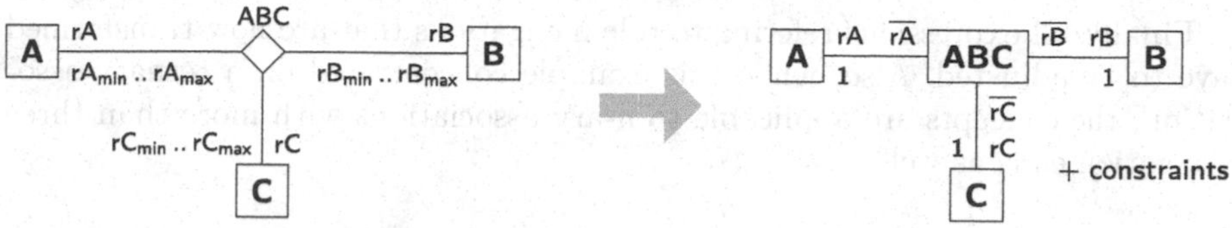

Fig. 4. Class diagram view of ternary to binary association transformation

Figure 5 shows the same models as instances of the UML metamodel[3]. The ternary association form the left-hand side is located in the top left area of the picture with the association object *abc* and its three connected classes. The role information is contained in the `Property` objects connected in between the classes and the association. The multiplicities shown by the attributes `/lower` and `/upper` for the roles are derived values from elements hidden in the figure. The links between the association and the properties define ownership and navigability as present in the metamodel. Dashed lines symbolize derived links, showing relations between objects that are indirectly related via other objects, i.e. `Property` objects. In the UML metamodel from Fig. 3, these links are instances of the association going from the class `Association` upwards and right to the class `Type` (role `/endType`), showing the `Type` objects linked with the association. For example, the derived link between the objects *a* and *abc* offers direct access to one of the end types of association *abc*.

In the lower right of Fig. 5, the right-hand side of the transformation is shown. The association object *abc* was transformed into a class and three new associations are created. The original properties are still present, however the multiplicities are changed and properties have been added to fill the missing roles. Furthermore, to ensure semantic equivalence between the models from the left and right hand side, two types of constraints, representing the properties of the ternary association, are added to the classes. First, three objects (*a*, *b*, *c*) can only be connected once by the association `ABC`. And second, multiplicities for the roles of the ternary association have to hold, i.e. the number of pairs of objects *b* and *c* that are connected to *a* objects must be within the specified multiplicity of role `rA`. If a multiplicity is specified as `0..*`, no constraint is required. The following two invariants exemplify these two properties:

```
context r, r' : ABC inv noDoubleLinks:        -- one link per tuple (A,B,C)
( r.rA = r'.rA and r.rB = r'.rB and r.rC = r'.rC ) implies r = r'
context b : B inv multiplicity-rA:            -- multiplicity for role rA
C.allInstances()→forAll( c | let linkCount =
    ABC.allInstances()→select( r | r.rB = b and r.rC = c )→size()
  in linkCount >= rA_min and linkCount <= rA_max )
```

---

[3] Many attributes, (derived) links and objects are not relevant for the transformation and, hence, are hidden for a better overview and understandability.

Finally, all expressions refering to role navigations that are now transformed have to be adjusted. Also, while this example concentrated on a ternary association, the concepts are applicable to *n*-ary associations with more than three association ends as well.

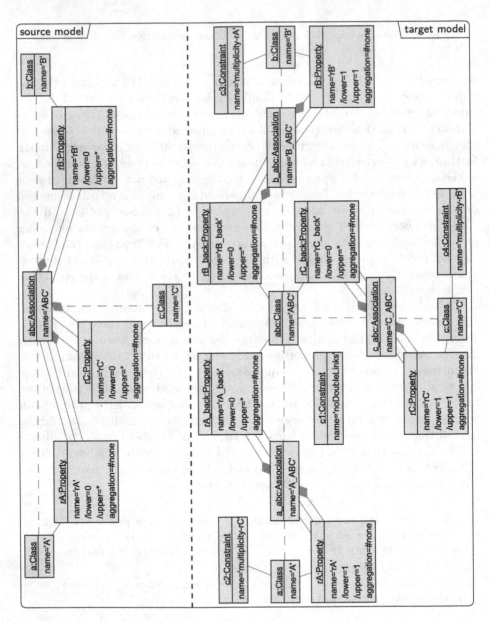

Fig. 5. Ternary association to class plus binary associations in UML metamodel

4.2   Transformation of Association Classes

Next the transformation of UML association classes into base model compatible description means is considered. Existing model transformations suggest the conversion into ternary associations plus OCL constraints, however only binary associations are allowed in the base model. To overcome this issue, the transformation rules for the base model can be combined together to sequentially transform the source model into a proper base model, i.e. after the transformation into the ternary association the transformation from the previous section is able to simplify it into binary associations.

The transformation from association classes into ternary associations is depicted in Fig. 6. The class and association information is split into a class and an association. Implicit definitions are made explicit, e.g. the implicit role name C in the source model for the association class has been made explicit on the right side. The semantic properties are expressed with OCL constraints. Figure 7 shows the transformation with instances of the UML metamodel. The separation of the association class into class and association is clearly visible.

Fig. 6. Association class to ternary association transformation

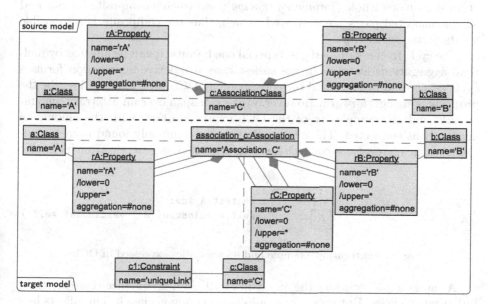

Fig. 7. Association Class to class plus ternary association in UML metamodel

Similar to the previous section, the association class has properties that this transformation has to adhere to. In particular, for every two objects *a* and *b* there may be at most one association class linking them. The following invariant is showing this property as an OCL invariant:

```
context c : C inv uniqueLink:                    -- one link per pair (A,B)
c.rA→size() = 1 and c.rB→size() = 1 and C.allInstances()→forAll( c' |
   (c.rA = c'.rA and c.rB = c'.rB) implies c = c' )
```

Finally, multiplicity constraints and adjustments to other OCL expressions relying on transformed navigations are similar to those of the transformation in the previous section.

4.3   Transformation of Aggregations and Compositions

Aggregations and compositions are special types of associations that specify a whole-part relationship. They have unique properties that distinctly define their semantics within the class diagram. However, these properties are not explicitly modeled in the UML metamodel, only the enumeration attribute `aggregation` of the class `Property` indicates whether an association is treated as an aggregation or composition. Thus, the transformation in the UML structure is trivial. The challenge is to express the inherent properties as OCL constraints. In the following, we will illustrate the generic transformation by means of examples.

The property of aggregations define that an aggregate cannot be part of itself (*cycle freeness*), i.e. navigating to a part results in "smaller" objects than the whole. Looking at compositions, a few more properties exist: Each part may at most have one whole (*forbidding sharing*); and when a composite is destroyed all its connected parts are destroyed as well, thus the composite is responsible for its parts (*ownership*).

The cycle freeness property is a special one because it can be affected by multiple aggregations at once. In the easiest case, a reflexive aggregation forms a cycle as pictured in Fig. 8 and the corresponding OCL expression to describe the property is straightforward. However, cycles can span over an arbitrary amount of links and the complexity of the OCL expression rises with the amount of aggregations connected. These constellations are commonly found in metamodels, when an aggregations connect elements related via a generalization hierarchy.

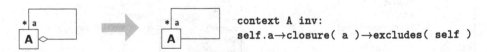

Fig. 8. Aggregation example and its semantics expressed in OCL

As an example, consider the model in Fig. 9. At a first glance there are three independent cycles. But these cycles all share a common class B. This affects how cycles can occur in a system state. For example, starting from class A, a cycle

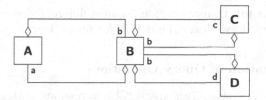

Fig. 9. Complex aggregation model

can be as simple as connecting to a B object and back to the original A object. However, since B is also connected to C and D, there can be an arbitrary amount of links in between. A single `closure` operation, as pictured in Fig. 8, does not cover all possible cases allowed by the class diagram. To consider all paths going from class B to itself, a second, *nested* `closure` operation is required. The full invariant ensuring cycle freeness for class A looks as follows:

```
context self : A inv:
self.b→closure( c.b→union( d.b ) ).a
   →closure( b→closure( c.b→union( d.b ) ).a )→excludes( self )
```

The repeating[4], highlighted expression in lines 2 and 3 is the essential part. Instead of only considering all navigations from class A to B and back, the nested `closure` operations (line 3) cover all intermediate navigations from class B to itself. Note that not all cycles of class B are inside the nested `closure` expression, since the one between classes A and B is already covered by the initial navigation.

The previous examples for cycle freeness shown with aggregations are also valid for compositions. Additionally, the other previously defined properties have to be considered. Figure 10 shows an example for the *forbidding sharing* property as an OCL invariant. The constraint ensures that none or exactly one of the possible composites is linked with every `Part`, thus preventing multiple links at the same time.

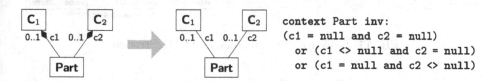

Fig. 10. Composition forbidding sharing property expressed in OCL

Finally, the *ownership* property is left. This property is different from the previous ones, since it defines behavior, e.g. during operation calls, instead of structure. Therefore, this property cannot be expressed as a structural invariant. To represent it in a class diagramm, we use operation pre- and postconditions.

---

[4] The lack of a non-reflexive transitive closure operation in OCL forces the repetition of the expression here.

However, since the full transformation requires different description means not discussed in this work, we leave the details for future work.

4.4 Transformation of Query Operations

Query operations are side-effect free OCL expressions assigned to classes as operations. The transformation of such operations in the base model is mainly operating on OCL expressions. In general, all calls to the query operation in any expression can be expanded into the expression associated with the operation. Parameter expressions are obtained from the respective operation call and the return value is simply the result of the expression.

In case of recursively defined query operations, the expansion never terminates. However, a general idea for these situations is to transform the expressions into closure expressions or expand the expression a fixed amount of times, depending on the estimated requirements, but this approximation is not always possible. Nevertheless, in terms of compatibility and performance, this transformation has next to no drawbacks.

4.5 Transformation of OCL Collection Types

In case that a verification engine cannot be used for a certain source model – due to incompatibilities on the OCL level, e.g. an unsupported collection type – a last resort can be the representation of such a type in the class diagram itself. Figure 11 shows a class with a `Sequence` typed attribute on the left side. The resulting model is extended by a (simplified) representation of such sequence as classes in the diagram. The sequence is connected to the class `IntegerValue`, which has an index and the actual integer value. Constraints are applied to ensure semantics, e.g. a well-defined order exists.

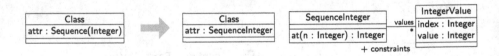

Fig. 11. Sequence transformation into UML Structure

The query operation `SequenceInteger::at(Integer)` shows an example for the transformation of the functionality of the modelled type. The OCL definition looks as follows:

```
context SequenceInteger::at( n : Integer ) : Integer =
  self.values→any( index = n ).value
```

Other common standard OCL operations can be defined accordingly. Also, the definition of a sequence is reusable for multiple occurrences of the same type in the source model.

This transformation is mostly interesting when no verification engine is able to handle a given model without this transformation. While the overhead is considerable, being able to apply validation and verification techinques to a previously incompatible model demonstrates the universality of the base model.

4.6 Combination of the Transformation Concepts

Using the transformations discussed above, source models can be transformed into base models by applying the transformations until no further matches can be found. That way, the resulting model consists of *core elements* ($\checkmark$) only, while the semantics of all *transformed elements* (o) is preserved (see Table 1). Along with the transformation of the respective model elements, all OCL expressions using these elements are transformed as well, to match the modifications.

5 Conclusion and Future Work

In this paper, we have proposed a transformation of UML/OCL models to base models. By this, we closed a significant gap for generic UML and OCL model validation and verification. The base model increases compatibility between source models and verification engines, by unifying various diagram types and expressing them using a reduced feature set, the so-called core elements. The result is a universal base model consisting of atomic elements only. We have also presented the corresponding transformation concepts for an important set of complex UML/OCL constructs like association classes, compositions, and OCL collection types. In order to transform a given source model into the corresponding base model representation, transformations are applied successively until the model only consists of core elements.

When in the future, verification engines support more complex features directly, it might be preferable to use those direct translations instead of performing the proposed transformations. However, an evaluation of the performance gain of direct translations by the verification engines versus the base model transformations is left for future work. If case studies reveal benefits for chosing different core elements, the base model can easily be adapted, due to the modular combination of transformations. Finally, transformations are required to be able to map verification results on the base model back to the source model.

Acknowledgement. Thanks to Lars Hamann for the constructive discussions about the model transformations, in particular the aggregation transformation. We also thank the reviewers for their useful feedback. This work was partially funded by the German Research Foundation (DFG) under grants GO 454/19-1 and WI 3401/5-1 as well as within the Reinhart Koselleck project DR 287/23-1.

References

1. Anastasakis, K., Bordbar, B., Georg, G., Ray, I.: UML2Alloy: a challenging model transformation. In: Engels, G., Opdyke, B., Schmidt, D.C., Weil, F. (eds.) MODELS 2007. LNCS, vol. 4735, pp. 436–450. Springer, Heidelberg (2007)

2. Banerjee, A., Ray, S., Dasgupta, P., Chakrabarti, P.P., Ramesh, S., Ganesan, P.V.V.: A Dynamic Assertion-Based Verification Platform for Validation of UML Designs. ACM SIGSOFT Software Engineering Notes **37**(1), 1–14 (2012)
3. Brucker, A.D., Wolff, B.: Semantics, calculi, and analysis for object-oriented specifications. Acta Inf. **46**(4), 255–284 (2009)
4. Cabot, J., Clarisó, R., Riera, D.: Verifying UML/OCL operation contracts. In: Leuschel, M., Wehrheim, H. (eds.) IFM 2009. LNCS, vol. 5423, pp. 40–55. Springer, Heidelberg (2009)
5. Cabot, J., Clarisó, R., Riera, D.: On the verification of UML/OCL class diagrams using constraint programming. J. Syst. Softw. **93**, 1–23 (2014)
6. Chen, Z., Zhenhua, D.: Specification and verification of UML2.0 sequence diagrams using event deterministic finite automata. In: SSIRI, IEEE (2011)
7. Chiorean, D., Pasca, M., Cârcu, A., Botiza, C., Moldovan, S.: Ensuring UML models consistency using the OCL environment. Electr. Notes Theor. Comput. Sci. **102**, 99–110 (2004)
8. Choppy, C., Klai, K., Zidani, H.: Formal verification of UML state diagrams: a petri net based approach. Softw. Eng. Notes **36**(1), 1–8 (2011)
9. Demuth, B., Wilke, C.: Model and object verification by using dresden OCL. In: IIT-TP, p. 81. Technical University (2009)
10. Dinh-Trong, T.T., Ghosh, S., France, R.B., Hamilton, M., Wilkins, B.: UMLAnT: An eclipse plugin for animating and testing UML Designs. In: Storey, M.D., Burke, M.G., Cheng, L., van der Hoek, A. (eds.) ETX. pp. 120–124. ACM (2005)
11. Duran, F., Gogolla, M., Roldan, M.: Tracing properties of UML and OCL models with maude. In: AMMSE, Electronic Proceedings in Theoretical Computer Science (2011)
12. Eshuis, R., Wieringa, R.: Tool support for verifying UML activity diagrams. IEEE Trans. Software Eng. **30**(7), 437–447 (2004)
13. Gogolla, M., Bohling, J., Richters, M.: Validating UML and OCL models in USE by automatic snapshot generation. J. Softw. Sys. Model. **4**(4), 386–398 (2005)
14. Gogolla, M., Büttner, F., Richters, M.: USE: A UML-based specification environment for validating UML and OCL. Sci. Comp. Prog. **69**(1–3), 27–34 (2007)
15. Gogolla, M., Hamann, L., Hilken, F.: Checking transformation model properties with a UML and OCL model validator. In: Amrani, M., Syriani, E., Wimmer, M. (eds.) VOLT@STAF, CEUR Proceedings. vol. 1325, pp. 16–25 (2014)
16. Gogolla, M., Hamann, L., Hilken, F.: On Static and dynamic analysis of UML and OCL transformation models. In: Dingel, J., de Lara, J., Lucio, L., Vangheluwe, H. (eds.) Analysis of Model Transformations (AMT). CEUR Proceedings, vol. 1277 (2014)
17. Gogolla, M., Kuhlmann, M., Hamann, L.: Consistency, independence and consequences in UML and OCL models. In: Dubois, C. (ed.) TAP 2009. LNCS, vol. 5668, pp. 90–104. Springer, Heidelberg (2009)
18. Gogolla, M., Richters, M.: Expressing UML class diagrams properties with OCL. In: Clark, A., Warmer, J. (eds.) Object Modeling with the OCL. LNCS, vol. 2263, p. 85. Springer, Heidelberg (2002)
19. Hilken, C., Seiter, J., Wille, R., Kühne, U., Drechsler, R.: Verifying consistency between activity diagrams and their corresponding OCL contracts. In: Forum on specification and Design Languages (FDL) (2014)
20. Hilken, C., Peleska, J., Wille, R.: A unified formulation of behavioral semantics for SysMLmodels. In: Modelsward (2015)

21. Hilken, F., Niemann, P., Wille, R., Gogolla, M.: Towards a base model for UML and OCL verification. In: Boulanger, F., Famelis, M., Ratiu, D. (eds.) MoDeVVa@MODELS. pp. 59–68 (2014)
22. Jouault, F., Allilaire, F., Bézivin, J., Kurtev, I.: ATL: A model transformation tool. Sci. Comput. Program. **72**(1–2), 31–39 (2008)
23. Kuhlmann, M., Hamann, L., Gogolla, M.: Extensive validation of OCL models by integrating SAT solving into USE. In: Bishop, J., Vallecillo, A. (eds.) TOOLS 2011. LNCS, vol. 6705, pp. 290–306. Springer, Heidelberg (2011)
24. Kurth, F., Schupp, S., Weißleder, S.: Generating test data from a UML activity using the AMPL interface for constraint solvers. In: Seidl, M., Tillmann, N. (eds.) TAP 2014. LNCS, vol. 8570, pp. 169–186. Springer, Heidelberg (2014)
25. Kuske, S., Gogolla, M., Kreowski, H.J., Ziemann, P.: Towards an integrated graph-based semantics for UML. Softw. Sys. Modeling **8**(3), 403–422 (2009)
26. Lam, V.S.W.: A formalism for reasoning about UML activity diagrams. Nord. J. Comp. **14**(1), 43–64 (2007)
27. Lima, V., Talhi, C., Mouheb, D., Debbabi, M., Wang, L., Pourzandi, M.: Formal verification and validation of UML 2.0 sequence diagrams using source and destination of messages. Electr. Notes Theor. Comput. Sci. **254**, 143–160 (2009)
28. OMG: Meta Object Facility (MOF) 2.0 Query/View/Transformation Specification. version 1.1 January 2011 edn. http://www.omg.org/spec/QVT/1.1/
29. Queralt, A., Teniente, E.: Reasoning on UML class diagrams with OCL constraints. In: Embley, D.W., Olivé, A., Ram, S. (eds.) ER 2006. LNCS, vol. 4215, pp. 497–512. Springer, Heidelberg (2006)
30. Rafe, V., Rafeh, R., Azizi, S., Miralvand, M.R.Z.: Verification and validation of activity diagrams using graph transformation. In: ICCTD, pp. 201–205. IEEE (2009)
31. Rodríguez, R.J., Fredlund, L.Å., Herranz, A., Mariño, J.: Execution and verification of UML state machines with erlang. In: Giannakopoulou, D., Salaün, G. (eds.) SEFM 2014. LNCS, vol. 8702, pp. 284–289. Springer, Heidelberg (2014)
32. Schwarzl, C., Peischl, B.: Static- and dynamic consistency analysis of UML state chart models. In: Petriu, D.C., Rouquette, N., Haugen, Ø. (eds.) MODELS 2010, Part I. LNCS, vol. 6394, pp. 151–165. Springer, Heidelberg (2010)
33. Soeken, M., Wille, R., Drechsler, R.: Verifying dynamic aspects of UML Models. In: DATE, pp. 1077–1082. IEEE (2011)
34. Soeken, M., Wille, R., Kuhlmann, M., Gogolla, M., Drechsler, R.: Verifying UML/OCL models using boolean satisfiability. In: DATE, pp. 1341–1344. IEEE (2010)
35. Wille, R., Gogolla, M., Soeken, M., Kuhlmann, M., Drechsler, R.: Towards a generic verification methodology for system models. In: DATE, pp. 1193–1196 (2013)

F-Alloy: An Alloy Based Model Transformation Language

Loïc Gammaitoni and Pierre Kelsen[✉]

University of Luxembourg, Luxembourg, Luxembourg
{loic.gammaitoni,pierre.kelsen}@uni.lu

Abstract. Model transformations are one of the core artifacts of a model-driven engineering approach. The relational logic language Alloy has been used in the past to verify properties of model transformations. In this paper we introduce the concept of functional Alloy modules. In essence a functional Alloy module can be viewed as an Alloy module representing a model transformation. We describe in this paper a sublanguage of Alloy called F-Alloy that allows the specification of functional Alloy modules. Transformations expressed in F-Alloy are analysable using the powerful automatic analysis features of Alloy but can also be interpreted efficiently without the use of backtracking.

1 Introduction

Alloy [13] is a formal language based on a first-order relational logic with transitive closure. It is based on a small set of core concepts, the main one being that of a mathematical relation. It was developed to support agile modeling of software designs. It does this by allowing fully automatic analysis of software design models using SAT solving. By providing immediate feedback to users, the use of Alloy is meant to facilitate identifying design errors early.

In the context of model-driven development the Alloy language has been used to verify properties of models and model transformations. The approach for verifying model transformations typically involves translating the model transformation language to Alloy. On the basis of this translation one can exercise the transformation on a suitably constrained set of input models. One can apply the Alloy Analyzer tool to generate the specified set of models as well as the corresponding target models.

Thus, one can execute a model transformation using the Alloy Analyzer as an execution engine. This approach has been implemented for the QVT-R language in [15]. It is impractical for two reasons:

- Despite many advances in the performance of SAT solvers the analysis of a model can become quite time consuming when it requires larger scopes to find a suitable instance.
- The problem of finding small upper bounds (scopes) for the number of entities of the different types is itself non-trivial (in fact it is undecidable). This is particularly problematic for complex models with many different entity types.

© Springer International Publishing Switzerland 2015
D. Kolovos and M. Wimmer (Eds.): ICMT 2015, LNCS 9152, pp. 166–180, 2015.
DOI: 10.1007/978-3-319-21155-8_13

In this paper, we introduce the notion of *functional Alloy modules* as specifications of model transformation from a source to a target metamodel (represented by Alloy modules). We show that under certain conditions such a functional Alloy module can be efficiently interpreted instead of being analyzed via SAT solving. More precisely we define a sublanguage of Alloy, named F-Alloy, that allows to express functional Alloy modules and that guarantees that these modules can be interpreted efficiently, that is, in polynomial time.

A central concept of F-Alloy are so-called *bridge mappings* which are essentially injective functions. The F-Alloy language can thus be viewed as a relational model transformation language (since functions are special cases of relations). Compared to existing relational model transformation languages (of which QVT Relational [16] is a prominent representative) our approach offers two notable features:

- rather than defining a new model transformation language from scratch we restrict an existing formal language in order to express model transformations. An important consequence of this approach is the possibility to reuse the formal semantics of the Alloy language, thus permitting verification of model transformations using Alloy's automatic analysis capabilities.
- execution (which we will refer to as interpretation) directly exploits the functional nature of model transformations. This allows efficient backtrack-free execution of model transformations. We demonstrate the effectiveness of this functional approach by applying it to a non-trivial example, namely, the CD to RDBMS model transformation that has been used as standard example for evaluating model transformation approaches.

The paper is structured as follows. In the next section we present the running example — namely a transformation from Class Diagrams to Relational Database Management Systems — that will be used to evaluate our approach. In Sect. 3 we give a formal presentation of central concepts of Alloy. In Sect. 4 we introduce the notion of functional Alloy module and illustrate its relation with model transformations. Sections 5 and 6 present the syntax and (translational) semantics of F-Alloy. In Sect. 7 we explain how F-Alloy modules can be efficiently interpreted. We provide an evaluation of our approach in Sect. 8 by comparing the performance of analysis and interpretation in the execution and verification of the CD2RDBMS transformation. We explain the context of our work and discuss related work in Sect. 9. The final section presents concluding remarks and future work.

2   Running Example: The CD2RDBMS Transformation

To evaluate our approach, we use the standard Class Diagram to Relational Database Management System transformation case study [6] — which we will call CD2RDBMS. The source and target metamodels of this transformation, CD and RDBMS, are shown as UML class diagrams in Fig. 1; further Alloy constraints have been left out for succinctness, nevertheless those constraints are present in the full solution (expressed in F-Alloy) available in [9]. We now give an informal specification of this transformation.

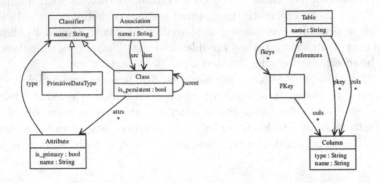

Fig. 1. CD and RDBMS metamodels (from [6])

For each persistent class c without a parent, a table is created. This table is populated with columns (1) corresponding to the primitive attributes of c, (2) referring to the class of class-typed attributes of c, (3) referring to the destination of the associations having as source c, (4) corresponding to attributes declared in children of class c.

In case (1) the column is typed after the primitive type of the attribute, and named after the attribute. In case (2), we create a column for each primary attribute of the type class. Those columns compose a foreign key which refers to the table representing the type class. Case (3) is similar to case (2). We create columns referring to the association's destination's primary attributes. Those columns compose a foreign key that refers to the table corresponding to the destination.

In case (4), each subclass's attribute is created in conformance to point (1) and (2) in the table corresponding to the topmost superclass.

Note that in cases (2), (3) and (4) the naming of the column depends both on the nature (referred class, association, super classes, respectively) and name of the attribute.

3   Background

3.1   Alloy Modules and Instances

A metamodel can be expressed in one or several Alloy modules, each module being associated to a single file. Modules are composed of signature and field declarations, and of constraints. A module may *import* other modules, in which case the importing module can use features of the imported modules.

Definition 1 (Alloy Module, Signature, Field). *An Alloy module is a tuple* (S, F, φ) *with S and F being the sets of signatures and fields declared in the module or any of its (recursively) imported modules, respectively. Signatures may be* *defined as subsignatures of other signatures (using the* extends *keyword). Fields of F have as type a sequence of signatures in S, the first one being the signature that contains it. φ is a first-order logic formula (plus transitive closure) representing the set of constraints expressed in the module.*

The RDBMS module is defined in Alloy as follows:

```
1  module RDBMS                  9      pkey : some Column,        17  sig FKey{
2                                 10     fkeys: set FKey            18     references: Table,
3  abstract sig RDBMSElem{        11  }{pkey in cols}               19     disj columns:set Column
4     disj label: seq String      12                               20  }{this in Table.fkeys}
5  }                              13  sig Column extends RDBMSElem{  21
6                                 14     type : Type                22  abstract sig Type{}
7  sig Table extends RDBMSElem{   15  }{this in Table.cols}         23  one sig Number,Text extends
8     disj cols : some Column,    16                                        Type{}
```

It can be written $m = (S, F, \varphi)$ with: vspace-3pt

- $S = \{\text{Table}, \text{Column}, \text{FKey}, \text{RDBMSElem}, \text{Type}, \text{Number}, \text{Text}\}$
- $F = \{\text{cols} : \text{Table} \times 2^{\text{Column}}, \text{pkey} : \text{Table} \times 2^{\text{Column}}, \text{fkeys} : \text{Table} \times 2^{\text{FKey}}, \text{type} : \text{Column} \times \text{Type}, \text{references} : \text{Fkey} \times \text{Table}, \text{columns} : \text{FKey} \times 2^{\text{Column}}, \text{label} : \text{RDBMSElem} \times \text{Int} \times \text{String}\}$
- $\varphi = (\forall t : \text{Table}, \text{pkey}(t) \in \text{cols}(t)) \wedge (\forall c : \text{Column}, \exists t : \text{Table}, c \in \text{cols}(t)) \wedge (\forall f : \text{FKey}, \exists t : \text{Table}, f \in \text{fkeys}(t)))$[1]

Considering now A, a set of indivisible entities called atoms, T, a set of atom tuples, and a module $m = (S, F, \varphi)$, we call *typed atoms* pairs (x, s) where $x \in A$ and $s \in S$. A typed atom (x, s) is also denoted x^s (read"atom x of type s"). A *typed tuple* is a pair (t, f) where $t \in T$ and $f \in F$. A typed tuple (t, f) is also denoted t^f (read"tuple t of type f"). Note that for a typed field t^f the following needs to hold: if the type of the field is $X_1, \ldots, X_n$, then the i-th component of the tuple needs to have as type X_i or a subsignature of X_i.

We call x^s an *s-atom* and t^f an *f-tuple*, and extend the superscript notation such that sets of s-atoms B and of f-tuples T, are denoted B^s and T^f, respectively.

Definition 2 (Alloy Instance). *An Alloy Instance of m is a triplet (X, Y, m) where $m = (S, F, \varphi)$, X is a set of atoms typed by signatures of m and Y is a set of tuples typed by fields of m and made up of atoms in X . We write $x \vDash \varphi$ if an instance x of m satisfies φ and call valid instances[2] of m the subset of instances of m which satisfy φ. We denote the set of valid instances of m by $I(m)$. Formally:*

$$I(m) = \{(X, Y, m) | \forall x^v \in X, v \in S \wedge \forall y^w \in Y, w \in F \wedge (X, Y, m) \vDash \varphi\}$$

Instance (X, Y, m) is a *subinstance* of (X', Y', m') if $X \subseteq X'$ and $Y \subseteq Y'$.

Note that the definition of the set of valid instances does not take into account bounds on the numbers of atoms typed by different signatures. These bounds

---

[1] We have omitted the constraints that express multiplicities and disjointedness.

[2] We relax here the Alloy terminology in which *instance* usually means *valid instance*.

are collectively known as the *scope* of a module (see [13]). Scopes need only to be taken into account when performing actual analyses with the Alloy Analyser, which is deferred until Sect. 8.

The projection of an instance x on a module m' is meant to extract an m'-instance out of atoms and tuples present in x. This operation will be used extensively later in the paper.

Definition 3 (Instance Projection). *A projection of an instance x : (X, Y, m) on a module m' : (S', F', φ') is the m'-instance composed of the atoms and tuples present in x and typed by signatures and fields of m', respectively. We denote projections using the evaluation symbol $\Downarrow$: $x \Downarrow m'$ reads" the projection of x on m'". Formally : $x \Downarrow m' = (X', Y', m')$ with $X' = \{a^s | a \in X \wedge s \in S'\}$ and $T' = \{t^f | t \in T \wedge f \in F'\}$.*

4   Functional Alloy Modules

Suppose an Alloy module m imports two modules m_1 and m_2. An instance of m will then contain an m_1- and m_2-subinstance. Furthermore, module m induces a binary relation R between $I(m_1)$ and $I(m_2)$ defined as follows:

$$\forall x_1 \in I(m_1), x_2 \in I(m_2) : R(x_1, x_2) \Leftrightarrow \exists x \in I(m) : x \Downarrow m_1 = x_1 \wedge x \Downarrow m_2 = x_2$$

In this paper we restrict ourselves to one-to-one model transformations, that is, one input model is mapped to exactly one output model. In other words the previously defined relation should be a mathematical function.

This motivates the following definition:

Definition 4 (Functional Alloy Module). *An Alloy module m importing two modules m_1 and m_2 is called a functional Alloy module from m_1 to m_2 if for any valid instances x and x' of m, if x and x' have the same projection on m_1, then they also have the same projection on m_2. Formally:*

$$\forall x, x' \in I(m), (x \Downarrow m_1 = x' \Downarrow m_1) \implies (x \Downarrow m_2 = x' \Downarrow m_2)$$

Caveat: This definition only makes sense if m_1 and m_2 are distinct, that is, for the case of exogenous transformations. Indeed if $m_1 = m_2$ the condition stated in the definition trivially holds. In the following we thus restrict our attention to *exogenous transformations*. Note, however, that the above definition could be applied to endogenous out-place transformations as well by duplicating the Alloy module representing the underlying metamodel.

To illustrate this definition, consider the CD2RDBMS transformation. An hypothetical Alloy module defining this transformation would import the modules defining the class diagram and the RDBMS metamodels and would define a set of "rules" that specify the transformation. Such a module would be a functional Alloy module if and only if any two valid instances of it having the same projection on the class diagram module would have the same projection on the RDBMS module. Of course we still have not explained how to write such a functional Alloy module. This will be explained in Sect. 5 when we define a sublanguage of Alloy for expressing functional Alloy modules.

5   Syntax of F-Alloy

In this section, we formally introduce the syntax of F-Alloy, a new language meant to ease the specification of functional Alloy modules.

We call *f-module m* from m_1 to m_2, a module m, written in F-Alloy, importing module m_1 and m_2 (in that order). An $< F - \text{Module} >$ is composed of:

- A $< \text{Bridge} >$ signature (of multiplicity one[3]) allowing to define and keep track of functions from m_1 to m_2. Those functions are called bridge $< \text{Mapping} >$.
- $< \text{Guard} >$ predicates, each associated to one bridge mapping. Their role is to define via the use of an Alloy Formula ($< \text{Formula} >$) under which condition an element of m_1 is part of the associated mapping.
- $< \text{Value} >$ predicates also associated to a bridge mapping. Their role is to provide additional details on how the output instance is constructed. It contains interpretable Alloy formulae called $< \text{Rules} >$.

We split the BNF definition of F-Alloy in two parts in order to ease its understanding. While the first part reveals the structure of F-modules, the second part focuses on those interpretable Alloy formulae called rules.

```
 1  <F-Module>::= module <qualName> <import> <Bridge><Guard>*<Value>*
 2  <import>::= import<qualName> import <qualName>
 3  <Bridge> ::= one sig Bridge {<Mapping>*}
 4  <Mapping> ::= <name> :   <qualName> (-><qualName>)+,
 5  <Guard> ::= pred guard_<name>   ( <paraDecl>* ){ <Formula>* }
 6  <Value> ::= pred value_<name>  (<paraDecl>*  ){ <Rule>* }
 7  <paraDecl>::= (<name> :<qualName> ,)*<name> :<qualName>
 8  <qualName>::= [ this/] (<name> /)* <name>
 9
10  <Rule>::= <Formula>  implies <Rule>|<Strict>|<Loose>|<Inductive>
11  <Strict> ::= <name>.<field>  = <val>
12  <Loose> ::= <name>  in Bridge.<field> .<field>
13  <Inductive> ::= <Strict><Step>
14  <Step> ::= all i:Int|<Formula> implies <name>.<field>[add[i,1]] = <val>
15  <val> ::= <Expr>| Bridge.<field>
16  <field> ::= <field> [[<Expr>]]
```

Listing 1.1. F-Alloy BNF

Additional static semantics constraints for the syntax are: (1) There is exactly one guard and one value predicate per bridge mapping, and the association is done by name; (2) the qualified names in the $< \text{Mapping} >$ except the last one correspond to signatures in m_1, while the last one refers to a signature of m_2; (3) there is one parameter in the guard predicate for each m_1-signature in the $< \text{Mapping} >$; (4) the same holds for the value predicate, with an additional parameter for the m_2-signature.

Here is an excerpt of the CD2RDBMS transformation expressed in F-Alloy:

---

[3] Valid instances of the f-Module will contain exactly one Bridge atom.

```
1  module UML2RDBMS                      15  }
2  open CD/AbstractSyntax/CD             16  pred value_primAttr2column(a:Attribute
3  open RDBMS/AbstractSyntax/RDBMS                           ,c:Column){
4  one sig Bridge{                       17    c.type=(a.type=STRING implies Text
5    class2table: Class -> Table,               else Number)
6    primAttr2column: Attribute -> Column, 18   c.label[0]= a.name
7    classAttr2column: Attribute ->      19    c.label[1]=((a.~attrs.parent)≠none implies
      Attribute -> Column,                      a.~attrs.name else none)
8    classAttr2Fkey: Attribute -> FKey,  20    all i:Int| i≥1 and i< #(a.~attrs.~parent)
9    association2column: Association ->         implies c.label[add[i,1]]=
      Attribute -> Column,                      c.label[i].~name.parent.name
10   association2FKey: Association -> FKey, 21   a.is_primary=True implies c in
11 }                                            Bridge.class2table[a.~attrs.*parent].pkey
12 pred guard_primAttr2column(a:Attribute){ 22  c in
13   a.type in PrimitiveDataType               Bridge.class2table[a.~attrs.*parent].cols
14   True in a.~attrs.*parent.is_persistent 23 }
```

This f-module UML2RDBMS (declared on l.1) from CD (imported on l.2) to RDBMS (imported on l.3) contains 6 bridge mappings (l.5-10) and the guard and value predicates of the primAttr2Column mapping only (others are omitted for lack of space). The bridge mapping primAttr2Column defines a partial function from Attribute to Column. The guard predicate of primAttr2Column defines that the domain of this function consists only of primitive-typed attributes (l.13) whose topmost class is persistent (l.14). The value predicate of primAttr2Column contains two strict rules (l.17-18), one inductive rule(l.19-20), and two loose rules(l.21-22).

We note that, from a syntactic point of view, any f-module is also an Alloy module since it is essentially composed of a signature and a collection of predicates. In that sense F-Alloy is a sublanguage of Alloy. The intended meaning of an f-module is however different from its Alloy semantics, as explained in the next section. Indeed additional constraints need to be added to ensure that the module is a functional Alloy module, i.e., it specifies a transformation.

6 Translational Semantics of F-Alloy

In this section we define the semantics of F-Alloy using the semantics of Alloy. For the purpose of this paper, we define the meaning of an Alloy module to be its set of valid instances. We map an f-module $m : (S, F, \varphi)$ expressed in F-Alloy to an Alloy module m_A - called *augmented module* - that is obtained by adding constraints to m. The meaning of f-module m is then equal to the meaning of the augmented Alloy module (defined above). Later we will show that the augmented module is in fact a functional Alloy module.

Five different types of Alloy constraints are added to m. We illustrate those using excerpts of our CD2RDBMS case study.

Map Disjunction. Bridge mappings of an f-module define partial functions which have disjoint ranges.

E.g., columns representing primitive and class attributes should be disjoint.

```
primAttr2column[Attribute] & classAttr2column[Attribute] = none
```

Map Injectiveness. Functions defined by Bridge mappings are injective. *E.g.*, distinct primitive attributes should be mapped to distinct columns.

```
forall disj a1,a2 : Attribute| primAttr2column[a1] ≠
    primAttr2column[a2]
```

Predicate Association. Guard and value predicates of an f-module associated with a bridge mapping restrict its valuation and the valuation of its output elements' field, respectively.

E.g., a column y is associated to an attribute x if and only if the guard predicate is satisfied for x. In that case, the value predicate has to hold for x and y as well.

```
all x : Attribute    |
  (guard_primAttr2column[x] and #primAttr2column[x]=1 and
      value_primAttr2column[x , primAttr2column[x] ]) or
  (not guard_primAttr2column[x] and primAttr2column[x]=none)
```

Minimum Output. In a valid instance of an f-module m from m_1 to m_2, atoms typed by a signature of m_2 are limited to the ones that are part of a bridge mapping of m.

E.g., RDBMS elements are limited to co-domains of declared mappings.

```
RDBMSElem = class2table[Class] + primAttr2column[Attribute] +
    classAttr2column[Attribute,Attribute] +
    association2column[Association,Attribute]
```

Minimal Assignment. Rules of an f-module follow the principle of minimal assignment. In other words, the valuation of a field is limited to the values explicitly assigned through the rules.

E.g., the label of a column being a sequence, its size is bounded by the number of elements explicitly assigned through rules (see the last of the following constraints).

```
c.label[0]= a2.name
c.label[1]= a1.name
c.label[2]= ((a1.~attrs.parent)≠none implies a1.~attrs.name
          else none)
    all i:Int| i≥1 and i≤ #(a1.~attrs.*parent) implies c.label[add
        [i,1]]= c.label[i].~name.parent.name//5
  #c.label.elems=add[#(a1.~attrs.*parent),1]
```

6.1   Rule Semantics

In order to prove in the next subsection that the augmented module m_A of m is a functional Alloy module, we need two properties of rules that are expressed in the two lemmas below.

The first lemma claims that each rule in a value predicate can be rewritten in the form:

$$F_r \text{ in } g$$

where g denotes a field in m_2, F_r is a set-valued expression typed by g and in denotes set inclusion (in Alloy). Since F_r depends in general on the instance x_A of m_A and on the parameters $\vec{x}$ and y of the value predicate containing r, we write F_r as $F_r(x_A, \vec{x}, y)$. We use the vector notation for $\vec{x}$ to represent a sequence of parameters typed by signatures of m_1.

Lemma 1 (Rules as Functions). *Any rule r of m_A can be written in the form $F_r(x_A, \vec{x}, y)$ in g for some field g in m_2.*

Proof Sketch. We only consider the case of loose rules. A loose rule of the form y in Bridge.f[expr1].g can be rewritten using the equivalent Alloy constraint: (Bridge.f[expr1] -> expr2 -> y) in g. If b and e denote the value of Bridge.f[expr1] and expr2 for a given instance x_A and arguments $\vec{x}$, then we can define $F_r(x_A, \vec{x}, y) = \{(b, e, y)^g\}$. F_r can be defined similarly for the other types of rules. $\square$

The second lemma (whose proof is omitted) states that function $F_r(x_A, \vec{x}, y)$ only depends on the projection of x_A on m_1.

Lemma 2 (F_r Is Independent of m_2). *For any rule r of an f-module m, considering the function F_r associated to r (see lemma 1), we have :*

$$\forall \vec{x}, y \; \forall x_A, x_A' \in I(m_A), F_r(x_A, \vec{x}, y) = F_r(x_A', \vec{x}, y) \text{ if } x_A \downarrow m_1 = x_A' \downarrow m_1$$

6.2 Augmented Modules and Functional Alloy Modules

Theorem 1 (m_A Is a Functional Alloy Module). *For any f-module m from m_1 to m_2 the corresponding augmented module m_A is a functional Alloy module from m_1 to m_2.*

Proof Sketch. By the minimum output constraints of m_A, the atoms in the projection of a valid instance x_A of m_A on m_2 are exactly those in the ranges of bridge mappings. The set of these atoms depends only on the projection of x_A on m_1.

From Lemmas 1 and 2, we know that each rule of each value predicate contributes to an instance x_A of m_A a set of tuples typed by a field of m_2 that only depends on the projection on m_1. By taking the union of these sets of tuples over all bridge mappings and rules, the resulting set of tuples still only depends on the projection of x_A on m_1. The construction rules for the augmented module guarantee that only those tuples explicitly added by rules will be in the projection of x_A on m_2. It follows that m_A is a functional Alloy module. $\square$

7   F-Alloy Interpretation

The following pseudocode shows how interpretation of an f-module works. Note that the output is an instance of the augmented module. If one is interested only in the m_2-subinstance, it can be obtained by projecting the m_A-instance on m_2.

For an instance $x = (X, Y, m)$, a set of atoms A and a set of tuples T, we use the notation $x \cup A$ and $x \cup T$ to denote the instances $(X \cup A, Y, m)$ and $(X, Y \cup T, m)$, respectively. We use the vector notation $\vec{X}$ to denote the sequence of m_1-signatures in the definition of a bridge mapping.

```
1  Input:  -f-module m from m₁ : (S₁, F₁, φ₁) to m₂ : (S₂, F₂, φ₂)
2          -Instance x₁ of m₁
3  Output: -Instance x_A = (X_A, Y_A, m_A) s.t.  x_A ↓ m₁ = x₁
4
5  BEGIN
6      x_A := x₁ ∪ {b^Bridge}
7      FOR EACH mapping f : X⃗ → Y IN m DO:
8          LET  X⃗_f denote the set of X⃗ tuples (of atoms present in x₁) that satisfy
                    the guard of mapping f
9          LET  Y_f be a set of Y-atoms s.t. |Y_f| = |X⃗_f| and Y_f ∩ x_A = ∅
10         LET  T_f ⊆ X⃗_f × Y_f be a set of tuples (x⃗, y) that maps X⃗_f bijectively to Y_f
11         x_A := x_A ∪ Y_f ∪ T_f
12     DONE
13     FOR EACH mapping f : X⃗ → Y IN m DO:
14         FOR EACH rule r IN pred value_f DO:
15             FOR EACH  tuple (x⃗, y) IN T_f DO: // T_f defined on line 10
16                 x_A := x_A ∪ F_r(x_A, x⃗, y) //F_r defined in lemma 1
17             DONE
18         DONE
19     DONE
20     IF x_A ⊨ φ₁ ∧ φ₂ THEN
21         RETURN x_A
22     ELSE
23         invalid transformation
24 END
```

Listing 1.2. F-Alloy Interpretation pseudo code

Let us analyse the time complexity of interpretation. Let n denote the number of atoms in x_1. Both in the first and the second loop we need to evaluate an Alloy constraint or expression on a number of tuples that is at most polynomial in n. If we assume that the evaluation of Alloy expressions and constraints can be done in time polynomial in n - which can be shown by structural induction - then the overall time will be at most polynomial in n. Thus we expect interpretation to be more efficient than analysis. This will be shown in the next section.

The following theorem states that the interpretation of f-modules implemented by the pseudo code of Listing 1.2 conforms to the translational semantics given to F-Alloy.

Theorem 2. *Given an f-module m from m_1 to m_2 and a valid instance x_1 of m_1, the instance x_A returned by interpretation (in line 21) on inputs m and x_1 is a valid instance of m_A. Moreover interpretation returns no instance only when there is no valid instance for m_A whose projection on m_1 is x_1.*

Proof Sketch. From lines 9 and 10 we see that map disjunction and map injectiveness constraints are satisfied. From lines 13 — 19 it follows that the predicate association constraints are satisfied in x_A. From lines 7—12 it follows that the atoms in the projection of x_A on m_2 are exactly those in the ranges of bridge mappings, implying that the minimum output constraints are satisfied. Finally the minimal assignment constraints follow from the fact that only those tuples are added on lines 13 — 19 which are explicitly required by the rules.

In the case the interpretation of an f-module m fails to produce an instance satisfying constraints of m_1 and m_2, then so will analysis. Indeed, because of the constraints of m_A, any valid instance of m_A will have the same atoms and the same tuples in the projection of x_A on m_2 (up to atom renaming) than the interpreted instance since those tuples are exactly the tuples explicitly required by the rules.   □

8 Evaluation

In this section, we evaluate the benefits of using F-Alloy to specify model transformations. This evaluation is based on comparing the performance of the analysis carried by the Alloy Analyzer and of the interpretation of F-Alloy performed by the Lightning tool [1] in two cases:

1. The computation of a transformation (for a given input instance)
2. The verification of a transformation (no input given)

The manipulation needed to obtain the results presented in this section were performed on models of the CD2RDBMS case study.

8.1 Transformation Computation

We start by comparing the performance of analysis and interpretation in the computation of the CD2RDBMS transformation.

This manipulation consists, given a CD-instance x_1 and the CD2RDBMS transformation expressed as an f-module m from m_1 (CD) to m_2 (RDBMS):

– **In the Case of Analysis:** (1) in deriving the augmented module m_A from m; (2) in"over-constraining" m_1 such that $\forall x_A \in I(m_A), x_A \downarrow m_1 = x_1$; (3) in computing appropriate scopes (which will depend on the size of x_1) for the signatures in the augmented module; (4) in launching the actual analysis based on these scopes.
– **In the Case of Interpretation:** In interpreting the f-module m given instance x_1.

The result of those manipulations for CD-instances of three different sizes are given in Table 1.

The complexity of analysis grows very quickly with the size of the input instance while interpretation exhibits a nearly linear behavior. This can be viewed as a first confirmation of the theoretical complexity analysis done in Sect. 7.

Table 1. Transformation Computation : Time performance comparison table

Number of UMLElem atoms	CD2RDBMS analysis (ms)	CD2RDBMS interpretation (ms)
10	2324	71
20	8052	162
25	20006	188

8.2   Transformation Verification

We now compare the performance of analysis and interpretation in the verification of a transformation. While different types of verification may be done, we consider here only the generation of examples of the transformation, which would help in establishing consistency and also point to abnormal behavior.

The manipulation consists:

– **In the Case of Analysis:** in analysing the augmented module m_A for the given exact scope associated with the UMLElem signature.
– **In the Case of Interpretation:** In analysing m_1 for the given scope and for each m_1-instance x_1 thus obtained, in interpreting the f-module m. Note that from Theorems 1 and 2 it follows that the set of instances thus produced is equivalent — i.e., its instances have the same projections on m_2 — to the set of instances obtained by analysis.

The result of those manipulations are given in Table 2.

Table 2. Transformation Verification : Time performance comparison table

UMLElem scope (number of atoms)	Analysis	Interpretation		
	CD2RDBMS analysis (ms)	CD analysis (ms)	CD2RDBMS interpretation (ms)	Total Time (ms)
10	5448	448	68	516
20	83759	974	159	1133
25	∞	1256	192	1448

The *Total Time* column gives the average amount of time needed in the case of verification with interpretation to obtain the first instance. The other instances are obtained seamlessly when browsing the instances.

We notice from those results that the complexity of analysing the transformation module can be roughly reduced, with the use of interpretation, to the complexity of analysing its input module.

9 Discussion and Related Work

Context. The present work is carried out in the context of investigating the use of Alloy for designing a language workbench [1,10]. In an earlier publication [8], we already showed that the concrete syntax of a language can be defined as a transformation using Alloy. The current work opens up the possibility to integrate the specification of general model transformations (e.g., for specifying operational semantics of languages) into the Alloy based language workbench.

F-Alloy vs. Alloy. Analyzing Alloy models is generally an undecidable problem. That is why actual analyses with the Alloy analyser are always done for a finite scope using SAT-solving, itself an NP-complete problem. In practice Alloy's analysis, although having a high worst case complexity, works surprisingly well, as documented in numerous publications. No guarantees can be given, though, on the time needed for analysing Alloy modules. Contrary to this we show that F-Alloy identifies a subset of Alloy modules for which analysis via interpretation can be done in polynomial time (see Sect. 7). Furthermore interpretation of modules written in F-Alloy relieves the analyst of having to determine proper scopes for the signatures, itself a non-trivial problem.

Related Work on Model Transformation Languages. We can consider the F-Alloy language as a simple relational model transformation language. Relational model transformation languages (such as those given in [2,11,16]) are those where the main concept is that of a mathematical relation [7]. Note that in F-Alloy the mathematical relations, represented by the bridge mappings, are in fact injective functions. In their pure form (e.g., [2]) relational specifications are not executable. In other cases (e.g., [16]) they are executable in principle but still lack proper tool support. In the case of QVT there are some tools that execute QVT specifications but none of them take into account all the features of the QVT language. This is an indication that providing execution semantics for a relational language is a non-trivial task, especially if some semantic inconsistencies exist as is the case for QVT ([15]). In this paper we have shown that F-Alloy specifications are efficiently executable.

One distinguishing feature of F-Alloy is that it inherits a formal semantics from the host language Alloy. Not all model transformation languages are formal. For instance a popular model transformation language called ATL [14] was defined semi-formally. A formal semantics in terms of rewriting logics was later given by [19]. Even if a formal semantics is given there is in general no guarantee that the implementation does indeed conform to the semantics. A good illustration of this is the case of the triple graph grammar approach [17,18], for which the authors of [12] describe an approach to show conformance of an existing implementation to the formal semantics.

Related Work on Verifying Model Transformation Languages. As mentioned in the introduction Alloy has been used in the past to verify model transformations. Anastasakis et al. [4] use Alloy to analyze the correctness of model transformations. They resort to their tool UML2Alloy [3] to transform the source and target metamodels into Alloy and translate the transformation rules into mapping relations and predicates at the Alloy level. The goal of their work is to check that the target instances are conforming to the target metamodel of the transformation. This is done by checking an Alloy assertion using the Alloy analyzer. In a similar line of work Baresi et al. [5] use Alloy to represent graph transformations represented in the AGG formalism. They use the Alloy analyzer to verify the correctness of the transformation by generating possible traces. We can similarly use Alloy's analysis features to verify model transformations represented in F-Alloy. Furthermore, as we show in the evaluation section, in certain cases we can speed up the analysis using interpretation.

10   Conclusion and Future Work

In this paper we have introduced the notion of functional Alloy module which corresponds to an Alloy module representing a transformation. We have defined a sublanguage of Alloy, named F-Alloy, which can be used to express functional Alloy modules and allows efficient interpretation of these modules. We have given first evidence of this for the CD2RDBMS model transformation. A more thorough evaluation will be needed for further confirmation.

F-Alloy inherits the formal semantics of Alloy, thus making the transformations analyzable. This contrasts with other approaches where a separate formal semantics has to be defined.

Our current approach has one important restriction: it only applies to out-place transformations. Further work will investigate how to extend the approach to in-place (endogenous) model transformations.

Another area of investigation concerns bidirectional transformations. These are transformations that allow forward and backward transformations to be generated from a unique transformation specification. Bidirectional transformations are useful in the context of synchronisation between models. Future work will examine whether we can make our approach bidirectional. This has already been achieved by existing relational model transformation languages such as QVT but also graph based approaches such as triple graph grammars.

References

1. Lightning tool website. http://lightning.gforge.uni.lu
2. Akehurst, D.H., Kent, S., Patrascoiu, O.: A relational approach to defining and implementing transformations between metamodels. Softw. Sys. Model. **2**(4), 215–239 (2003)
3. Anastasakis, K., Bordbar, B., Georg, G., Ray, I.: UML2Alloy: a challenging model transformation. In: Engels, G., Opdyke, B., Schmidt, D.C., Weil, F. (eds.) MODELS 2007. LNCS, vol. 4735, pp. 436–450. Springer, Heidelberg (2007)
4. Anastasakis, K., Bordbar, B., Küster, J.M.: Analysis of model transformations via Alloy. In: Proceedings of the 4th MoDeVVa workshop: Model-Driven Engineering, Verification, and Validation, pp. 47–56 (2007)

5. Baresi, L., Spoletini, P.: On the use of alloy to analyze graph transformation systems. In: Corradini, A., Ehrig, H., Montanari, U., Ribeiro, L., Rozenberg, G. (eds.) ICGT 2006. LNCS, vol. 4178, pp. 306–320. Springer, Heidelberg (2006)

6. Bézivin, J., Schürr, A., Tratt, L.: Model transformations in practice workshop. In: Bruel, J.-M. (ed.) MoDELS 2005. LNCS, vol. 3844, pp. 120–127. Springer, Heidelberg (2006)

7. Czarnecki, K., Helsen, S.: Classification of model transformation approaches. In: Proceedings of the 2nd OOPSLA Workshop on Generative Techniques in the Context of the Model Driven Architecture, vol. 45, pp. 1–17 (2003)

8. Gammaitoni, L., Kelsen, P.: Domain-specific visualization of alloy instances. In: Ait Ameur, Y., Schewe, K.-D. (eds.) ABZ 2014. LNCS, vol. 8477, pp. 324–327. Springer, Heidelberg (2014)

9. Gammaitoni, L., Kelsen, P.: An F-Alloy specification for the CD2RDBMS case study (2015). http://lightning.gforge.uni.lu/doc/TR-LASSY-15-01.pdf

10. Gammaitoni, L., Kelsen, P., Mathey, F.: Verifying modelling languages using Lightning: a case study. In: Proceedings of the 11th MoDeVVa Workshop: Model-Driven Engineering, Verification and Validation, pp. 19–28 (2014)

11. Gerber, A., Lawley, M., Raymond, K., Steel, J., Wood, A.: Transformation: the missing link of MDA. In: Corradini, A., Ehrig, H., Kreowski, H.-J., Rozenberg, G. (eds.) ICGT 2002. LNCS, vol. 2505, pp. 90–105. Springer, Heidelberg (2002)

12. Giese, H., Hildebrandt, S., Lambers, L.: Toward bridging the gap between formal semantics and implementation of triple graph grammars. In: Proceedings of the 7th MoDeVVa Workshop: Model-Driven Engineering, Verification, and Validation, pp. 19–24 (2010)

13. Jackson, D.: Software Abstractions. MIT press, Cambridge (2012)

14. Jouault, F., Allilaire, F., Bézivin, J., Kurtev, I.: ATL: A model transformation tool. Sci. Comput. Pogram. **72**(1), 31–39 (2008)

15. Macedo, N., Cunha, A.: Implementing QVT-R bidirectional model transformations using alloy. In: Cortellessa, V., Varró, D. (eds.) FASE 2013 (ETAPS 2013). LNCS, vol. 7793, pp. 297–311. Springer, Heidelberg (2013)

16. OMG. Meta Object Facility (MOF) 2.0 Query/View/Transformation Specification, Version 1.1, January 2011

17. Schürr, A.: Specification of graph translators with triple graph grammars. In: Mayr, E.W., Schmidt, G., Tinhofer, G. (eds.) Graph-Theoretic Concepts in Computer Science. LNCS, pp. 151–163. Springer, Heidelberg (1995)

18. Schürr, A., Klar, F.: 15 Years of Triple Graph Grammars. In: Ehrig, H., Heckel, R., Rozenberg, G., Taentzer, G. (eds.) ICGT 2008. LNCS, vol. 5214, pp. 411–425. Springer, Heidelberg (2008)

19. Troya, J., Vallecillo, A.: A rewriting logic semantics for ATL. J. Object Technol. **10**(5), 1–29 (2011)

Foundations of Model Transformation

Translating ATL Model Transformations to Algebraic Graph Transformations

Elie Richa[1,2]([✉]), Etienne Borde[1], and Laurent Pautet[1]

[1] Institut Telecom, TELECOM ParisTech, LTCI - UMR 5141,
46 Rue Barrault, 75013 Paris, France
{elie.richa,etienne.borde,laurent.pautet}@telecom-paristech.fr
[2] AdaCore, 46 Rue D'Amsterdam, 75009 Paris, France
richa@adacore.com

Abstract. Analyzing and reasoning on model transformations has become very relevant for various applications such as ensuring the correctness of transformations. ATL is a model transformation language with rich semantics and a focus on usability, making its analysis not straightforward. Conversely, Algebraic Graph Transformation (AGT) is an approach with strong theoretical foundations allowing for formal analyses that would be valuable in the context of ATL. In this paper we propose a translation of ATL to the AGT framework in the objective of bringing theoretical analyses of AGT to ATL transformations. We validate our proposal by translating a set of feature-rich ATL transformations to the Henshin AGT framework. We execute the ATL and AGT versions on the same set of models and verify that the result is the same.

Keywords: ATL · Henshin · Algebraic graph transformation · OCL · Nested graph conditions · Analysis of model transformations

1 Introduction

Model transformations play a central role in Model Driven Engineering (MDE) processes. They formalize and automate design decisions (*e.g.* optimisations), implementation strategies (*e.g.* code generation) or translations/synchronization between different model representations. Analyzing model transformations and reasoning about them has therefore become increasingly interesting for various concerns such as demonstrating the correctness of transformations via testing or static formal analysis. Many transformation approaches have been proposed with varying languages and semantics targeting different concerns.

ATL [11] is a widely used model transformation language, both in academia and in the industry. It features a hybrid rule-based language with a rich execution semantics allowing for a mostly declarative and user-friendly specification. *Algebraic Graph Transformation* (AGT) [8] is a formal framework that provides mathematical definitions to express graph manipulation. Its strong theoretical foundations allow for powerful analyses such as state space reachability analysis

© Springer International Publishing Switzerland 2015
D. Kolovos and M. Wimmer (Eds.): ICMT 2015, LNCS 9152, pp. 183–198, 2015.
DOI: 10.1007/978-3-319-21155-8_14

and formal proof of termination, confluence and correctness. Given the graph-like structure of models in the sense of MDE, the theoretical results of AGT are increasingly being used to reason on model transformations.

Various analyses have already been proposed for ATL without relying on AGT. This includes test generation [9] and verification of correctness properties [6,16] through translations of ATL to other analyzable specifications. However we are interested in an analysis that is not possible with existing formalisations of ATL: the construction of *Weakest Precondition* (WP) [10]. This analysis operates on *constraints* and transforms a *postcondition* into an equivalent *precondition* of a transformation. It is defined in AGT and used in several scenarios such as synthesizing transformation preconditions that ensure the preservation of validity constraints [7], and formally proving the correctness of transformations [13]. Moreover in a previous publication [15], we have proposed a new use of this analysis to support the testing of model transformation chains. In that context we use WP construction as a way to propagate unit test requirements of intermediate steps of a chain into equivalent integration test requirements over the input of the chain which are easier to satisfy and maintain. We believe that WP-based analyses would be valuable for ATL transformations (and chains) and therefore propose to make them possible via a translation to AGT.

In this paper we propose a translation of ATL transformations to equivalent AGT analysable transformations and provide an implementation in our tool *ATLAnalyser*[1]. The first challenge in this work is handling ATL's *default* and *non-default resolve mechanisms* which do not have an equivalent in the AGT semantics. The second challenge is the translation of OCL constraints and queries of ATL rules into application conditions in the form of *Nested Graph Conditions* (NGC) in AGT. While translations of OCL to NGC have been proposed in the literature [3,4], they do not support ordered collections which we found to be an important limitation for ATL transformations. Our work extends the existing translations with support for ordered sets. Finally, we validate our proposal by considering a set of representative ATL transformations taken from the ATL Zoo [1] and other sources. We translate each transformation to the Henshin AGT framework [2] and verify that the execution of both the ATL and AGT versions over the same set of input models gives the same results.

The remainder of the paper is organised as follows. We start by recalling the semantics of ATL and AGT in Sect. 2. Then we present in Sect. 3 the main contribution of this paper: the translation of ATL to AGT. Section 4 reports on the experimental validation and the limitations of our proposal. Related work is discussed in Sect. 5 before concluding with future work in Sect. 6.

2   Semantics of ATL and AGT

2.1   ATL and OCL

ATL [11] is a model-to-model transformation language combining declarative and imperative approaches in a hybrid semantics. ATL transformations are primarily

---

[1] *ATLAnalyser*, https://github.com/eliericha/atlanalyser.

out-place, *i.e.* they produce an output model different from the input model (though both may be in the same language), and a so-called *refining mode* allows for *in-place* model refinement transformations. In the scope of this paper, we focus only on the declarative features of ATL in the standard *out-place* mode.

A transformation consists of a set of declarative *matched rules*, each specifying a *source pattern* (the **from** section) and a *target pattern* (the **to** section). The source pattern is a set of objects of the input metamodel and an optional OCL [12] constraint acting as a *guard*. The target pattern is a set of objects of the output metamodel and a set of *bindings* that assign values to the attributes and references of the output objects. For example in Fig. 1, **R1** has one source pattern element **s** and two target pattern elements: **t1** with 3 bindings and **t2** with 1 binding.

```
1   rule R1 {
2   from s  : IN!A
3       (s.refB->exists(b | b.name = 'Hodor'))
4   to t1 : OUT!D
5       (name <- s.name + '1',
6        refD <- t2,
7        refE <- s.refB),
8      t2 : OUT!D
9       (name <- s.name + '2') }
10  rule R2 {
11  from s : IN!B
12  to t : OUT!E
13      (refD <- thisModule.resolveTemp(s.refA, 't2') ) }
```

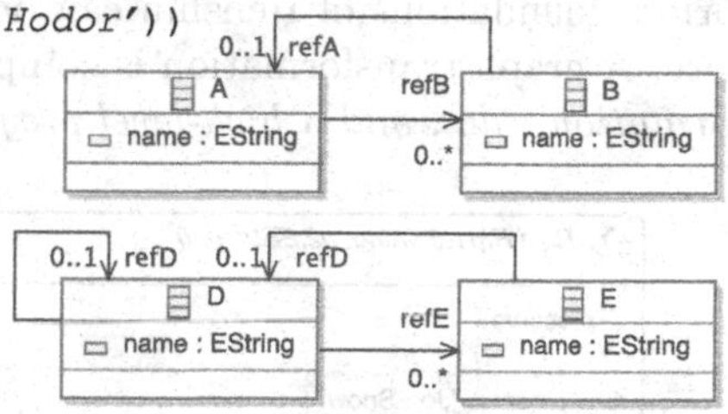

Fig. 1. Example of ATL rules

An ATL transformation is executed in two phases. First, the matching phase searches in the input model for objects matching the source patterns of rules (*i.e.* satisfying their filtering guards). For each match of a rule's source pattern, the objects specified in the target pattern are instantiated. Second, the target elements' initialization phase executes the bindings for each triggered rule.

A *binding* defines a *target property* which is an attribute or a reference on the left side of the **<-** symbol, and an OCL query on the right side of the symbol. A binding maps a scalar value to a target attribute (line 5), target objects (instantiated by the same rule) to a target reference (line 6), or source objects to a target reference (line 7). In the latter case, a *resolve* operation is automatically performed to find the rule that matched the source objects, and the *first* output pattern object created by that rule is used for the assignment to the target reference. This is referred to as the *default resolve mechanism*. For example in Fig. 1, the binding at line 7 resolves the objects in **s.refB** into the output objects of type **E** created by **R2**, and assigns them to **t1.refE**.

Another *non-default resolve mechanism* allows resolving a (set of) source object(s) to an arbitrary target pattern object instead of the first one as in the default mechanism. It is invoked via the following ATL standard operations:

```
thisModule.resolveTemp(obj, tgtPatternName)
thisModule.resolveTemp(Sequence{obj1, ...}, tgtPatternName)
```

The former is used to resolve with rules having one source pattern element while the latter is used to resolve with rules having multiple source pattern elements. For example, the execution of the binding on line 13 in rule **R2** will retrieve the target object **t2** (instead of **t1** as with the default resolve) that was created by **R1** when it matched **s.refA**.

2.2 AGT and Nested Graph Conditions

Algebraic Graph Transformation (AGT) [8] is a formal framework that provides mathematical definitions to model graph transformations. We will be using the *Henshin* [2] graph transformation framework which applies the theoretical semantics to standard EMF models in the Eclipse platform. The details of the formal foundations of Henshin can be found in [5] and are only briefly recalled here. A graph transformation is composed of two main elements: a set of *transformation rules*, and a *high-level program* defining the sequencing of rules.

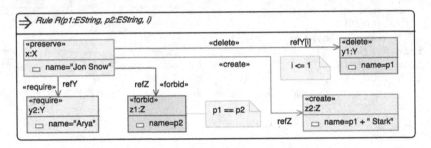

Fig. 2. Henshin graphical representation of an AGT rule

An AGT rule consists of a Left-Hand Side (LHS) graph and a Right-Hand Side (RHS) graph both depicted on the same diagram as in Fig. 2. LHS elements are annotated with «*preserve*» or «*delete*» while RHS elements are annotated with «*preserve*» or «*create*». Roughly, a rule is executed by finding a match of LHS in the transformed graph, deleting the elements of $LHS - RHS$ («*delete*»), and creating the elements of $RHS - LHS$ («*create*»). Elements of $LHS \cap RHS$ are preserved («*preserve*»). A rule transforms elements matched by the LHS into the RHS, therefore an AGT is an *in-place* rewriting of the input model. For example, rule R in Fig. 2 matches nodes x of type X and $y1$ of type Y and edge $refY$ in the transformed graph, deletes the node matched by $y1$ and the edge matched by $refY$, and creates node $z2$ of type Z and the edge $refZ$.

Matches of a rule may be restricted with additional constraints by assigning *attribute values* to nodes. For example the rule in Fig. 2 can only match an object x when $x.name = $ "Jon Snow". Moreover, attribute values may be stored in *rule parameters* such as in $y1.name = p1$ where the *name* attribute of the object matched by $y1$ is stored in the rule parameter $p1$. Finally, a rule may assign new values to attributes such as in $z2$ where $z2.name$ is initialized to $p1$ concatenated to the string *"Stark"*.

In Henshin, edges typed by a *multi-valued ordered reference* (*i.e.* with upper bound higher than 1) can be labeled with an *index*. This feature will play an important role in the handling of the ATL resolve mechanisms and the support of ordered sets in Sect. 3. A literal integer index such as $ref[2]$ represents a matching constraint: only the object at index 2 may be matched by the rule. A rule parameter index such as $ref[i]$ allows to read an object's index in the ordered reference and store it in the parameter. For example in Fig. 2, $refY[i]$ indicates that the index of $y1$ is stored in i. Edge indexes are zero-based.

An AGT rule can have an *application condition* (AC) which constrains its possible matches. An AC is a *Nested Graph Condition* (NGC) over the *LHS*. Formally, a NGC over a graph P is of the form *true* or $\exists(a \,|\, \gamma, c)$ where $a : P \hookrightarrow C$ is an injective morphism, γ is a boolean expression over rule parameters and c is a NGC over C. A match $p : P \hookrightarrow G$ of P in a graph G satisfies an AC $\exists(a \,|\, \gamma, c)$ if there exists a match $q : C \hookrightarrow G$ of C in G such that $p = q \circ a$ and γ evaluates to *true* under the parameter assignment defined by p and q satisfies c. Boolean formulas can be constructed such as the negation $\neg c$, the conjunction $\bigwedge_i c_i$ and the disjunction $\bigvee_i c_i$ of NGCs c_i over P. We use short notations $\forall(a, c)$ and $c_1 \implies c_2$ for $\neg \exists(a, \neg c)$ and $\neg c_1 \lor c_2$ respectively. For example the AC in Fig. 3 defined for rule R requires the existence of a node $y2$ whose *name* attribute is *"Arya"* and forbids the existence of a node $z1$ with the same *name* as $y1$. The boolean expression $i <= 1$ constrains the rule to match only for the first two objects in the ordered reference $x.refY$. Note that P is omitted from the notation when it can be inferred from the context, and so are γ and c when they are *true*. The AC is graphically represented in Fig. 2 using the annotations «*require*» and «*forbid*», however this is only possible for one level of nesting in the AC. For complete NGCs the full notation of Fig. 3 is necessary. In Sect. 3 we will translate OCL guards and bindings into suitable ACs of AGT rules.

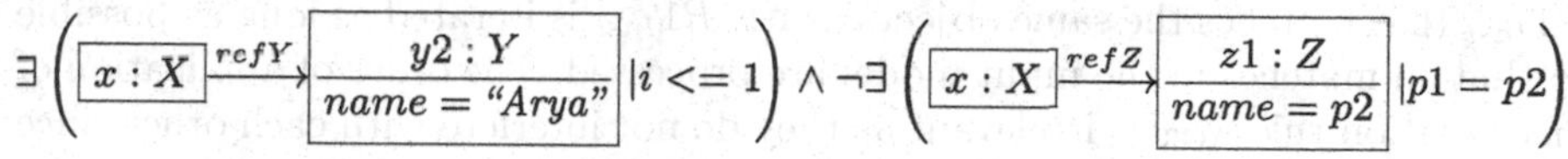

$$\exists \left(\boxed{x : X} \xrightarrow{refY} \boxed{\begin{array}{c} y2 : Y \\ \hline name = \text{``Arya''} \end{array}} \Big| i <= 1 \right) \land \neg \exists \left(\boxed{x : X} \xrightarrow{refZ} \boxed{\begin{array}{c} z1 : Z \\ \hline name = p2 \end{array}} \Big| p1 = p2 \right)$$

Fig. 3. Example of a Nested Graph Condition

Finally we define a so-called *high-level program* which specifies in which order AGT rules are applied. A program can be (1) elementary, consisting of a rule r, (2) the sequencing of two programs P and Q denoted by $(P; Q)$, or (3) the iteration of a program P as long as possible, denoted by $P{\downarrow}$, which is equivalent to a sequencing $(P; (P; (P \cdots)$ until the program P can no longer be applied.

3 Translating ATL to AGT

Having presented the semantics of ATL and AGT, we now tackle the main contribution of this paper: the translation of ATL transformations to AGT transformations. Section 3.1 focuses on the first challenge, the emulation of the ATL resolve mechanisms in AGT, and Sect. 3.2 addresses the second challenge, the translation of OCL constraints and queries embedded in ATL transformation with support for ordered sets. To avoid confusion between ATL and AGT transformation rules, we will denote them respectively by $rule_{ATL}$ and $rule_{AGT}$.

3.1   Translating the ATL Resolve Mechanism

Given the *out-place* nature of the ATL transformations we consider and *in-place* nature of AGT we propose to model the ATL transformation in AGT as a refinement of the input model which only adds the elements of the output model without modifying the input elements.

Challenges. A first challenge is dealing with the ATL resolve mechanisms. In AGT no such mechanisms exist, and any objects that a $rule_{AGT}$ needs to use must already exist in the transformed graph and must be matched by the $rule_{AGT}$'s LHS. If a $rule_{AGT}$ $R1$ needs to use an object created by $rule_{AGT}$ $R2$, then $R2$ must be executed before $R1$. This becomes a problem if $R1$ and $R2$ mutually require objects created by each other which is a perfectly valid scenario in ATL that cannot be solved with simple $rule_{AGT}$ sequencing. Moreover, the non-default resolve mechanism requires to relate output objects to output pattern identifiers so that we can retrieve the object corresponding to a specific output pattern identifier given as argument to the **resolveTemp** operation.

General Solution. We propose to construct the AGT transformation similarly to the ATL execution semantics, as two sequential phases: an *instantiation* phase followed by a *resolving* phase. Moreover, we introduce *trace nodes* that maintain the relationship between input and output elements. The first phase applies a sequence of *instantiation rules*$_{AGT}$ that create output objects without initializing their attributes and references, and relate them to input objects through *trace nodes*. Each $rule_{ATL}$, *e.g.* **R1** from Fig. 1, yields one instantiation $rule_{AGT}$ $R1_{Inst}$ that matches the same objects as **R1**. $R1_{Inst}$ is iterated as long as possible so that all matches in the input model are processed. The order of application of instantiation rules$_{AGT}$ is irrelevant as they do not interfere with each other since objects are allowed to match for only one $rule_{ATL}$, as per the ATL semantics.

The second phase of the transformation applies a set of *resolving rules*$_{AGT}$ which initialize references and attributes of output objects. Each binding in a $rule_{ATL}$ is translated to one or more resolving rules$_{AGT}$ as will be discussed shortly. For example, **R1** yields 4 resolving rules$_{AGT}$ $R1_{Res}^{t1,name}$, $R1_{Res}^{t1,refD}$, $R1_{Res}^{t1,refE}$ and $R1_{Res}^{t2,name}$. Resolving rules$_{AGT}$ navigate the input model and rely on the trace nodes created in the instantiation phase to perform the resolving and retrieve the corresponding output objects if needed. Like instantiation rules$_{AGT}$, resolving rules$_{AGT}$ are also iterated as long as possible so that bindings are applied to all output objects. The resulting AGT transformation is the following:

$$R1_{Inst} \downarrow; \ R2_{Inst} \downarrow; \ R1_{Res}^{t1,name} \downarrow; \ R1_{Res}^{t1,refD} \downarrow; \ R1_{Res}^{t1,refE} \downarrow; \ R1_{Res}^{t2,name} \downarrow; \ R2_{Res}^{t,refD} \downarrow$$

This scheme addresses the highlighted concerns regarding the resolve mechanism. Separating the creation of output objects from their use allows resolving rules$_{AGT}$ to use any output object even in the case of mutual resolve dependencies. Moreover, the trace nodes maintain the information required to perform the resolving as explained next.

Trace Nodes. The *trace nodes* we introduce are typed by a set of metaclasses produced by our translation. We assume that both the input and output meta-models define a root abstract metaclass from which all other metaclasses inherit directly or transitively[2] and refer to them respectively as *RootIn* and *RootOut*. The trace metaclasses are produced as follows. First, an *abstract* metaclass *Trace* is defined with a *from* reference to *RootIn* and a *to* reference to *RootOut* (Fig. 4a). For each rule$_{ATL}$, *e.g.* **R1**, a so-called *typed trace* metaclass named *R1_Trace* inheriting the abstract *Trace* metaclass is created. For each input and output pattern element of the rule$_{ATL}$, a reference with the same name is created from the typed trace to the type of the pattern element. For **R1** this yields references *s*, *t1* and *t2* in Fig. 4a.

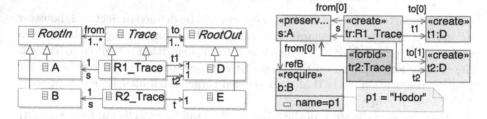

Fig. 4. a. Trace metamodel, b. Instantiation rule$_{AGT}$ R1$_{Inst}$

Instantiation Rules$_{AGT}$. Each rule$_{ATL}$, **R1** for example, yields one instantiation rule$_{AGT}$, R1$_{Inst}$, which matches the same objects as **R1** and creates the output objects as well as a typed trace node. As can be seen in Fig. 4b, the instantiation rule$_{AGT}$ is constructed by creating a «*preserve*» node for each input pattern element (node *s : A*). Then the OCL rule$_{ATL}$ guard is translated to an AC as per Sect. 3.2. This yields the «*require*» navigation to node *b : B* with *name = p1* and *p1 = "Hodor"*. Then, a «*create*» node is created for each output pattern element (nodes *t1 : D*, *t2 : D*) as well as a typed trace node (*tr : R1_Trace*). The trace node is connected to input nodes with generic *from* references and typed references (*s*) and to output node with generic *to* references and typed references (*t1* and *t2*). The order of input and output pattern elements is preserved in *from* and *to* references by indexing the created edges accordingly (*from*[0], *to*[0] and *to*[1]). This will allow resolve rules$_{AGT}$ to retrieve the first output object (*to*[0]) for the default resolve mechanism or any arbitrary output object (*t1* or *t2*) for the non-default resolve mechanism. Finally, since a rule$_{ATL}$ only applies once per match, we add a negative AC preventing the application of the rule$_{AGT}$ if *another* trace node *tr*$_2$ with the exact same *from* elements already exists. That AC is as follows:

---

[2] if it is not the case, such a root abstract metaclass can be added automatically.

$$\neg\exists \left(\boxed{s : A} \xleftarrow{from[0]} \boxed{tr_2 : Trace} , \underbrace{\neg\exists \left(\boxed{: RootIn} \xleftarrow{from} \boxed{tr_2 : Trace} \right)}_{exactFrom(tr_2)} \right)$$

The NGC $exactFrom(tr_2)$ (not visible on Fig. 4.b) is needed to express the fact that the object s is allowed to participate in another rule$_{ATL}$ if there are other objects in the source pattern (*i.e.* the set of *from* elements is not exactly the same). *exactFrom* is reused for resolving rules$_{AGT}$ in the following sections.

Resolving Rules$_{AGT}$ with Default Resolving. Each binding in a rule$_{ATL}$ is translated to one resolving rule$_{AGT}$. Let us first consider the case of bindings with default resolving or no resolving at all. Each such binding results in one rule$_{AGT}$ that matches the same elements as the OCL query in the binding, performs the default resolving if needed, and initializes the target attribute/reference of the binding. Let us consider a binding of the following general shape:

$$tgtObj : tgtType \ (\ tgtProp \leftarrow oclQuery \ )$$

The supported subset of OCL in *oclQuery* will be defined in Sect. 3.2, however the general translation remains the same. Such a binding is translated to a resolving rule$_{AGT}$ $R_{Res}^{tgtObj,tgtProp}$ according to the algorithm presented in Table 1. The translation depends on the type of the target property *tgtProp* hence the tabular presentation. Note that multi-valued target attributes are not supported at the current stage.

Figure 5 shows the steps of the translation of binding **t1:D (refE <- s.refB)** in **R1** (Fig. 1) to rule$_{AGT}$ $R1_{Res}^{t1,refE}$. Note that $to[0]$ in *Step 3* allows to retrieve the first target pattern element as per the default resolve semantics. Moreover, for multivalued target references such as **t1.refE**, the translation is a sort of a *flattening* whereby the result elements of the OCL query **s.refB** are not handled all at once but one by one. Each application of $R1_{Res}^{t1,refE}$ matches one element in **s.refB** and appends the corresponding output object to the target reference **t1.refE**. However, since there are no guarantees in AGT on the order in which elements are matched, $R1_{Res}^{t1,refE}$ as presented in Fig. 5 is only correct if **refB** is a non-ordered reference. This will be detailed and addressed in Sect. 3.2.

Resolving Rules$_{AGT}$ with Non-default Resolving. Let us now consider bindings involving non-default resolving which have the following shape:

$tgtObj : tgtType \ (\ tgtRef \leftarrow$
    thisModule.resolveTemp(Sequence{$navExp_1, \ldots, navExp_N$ **},** $tgtPat$**))**

The construction of the resolving rule$_{AGT}$ $R_{Res}^{tgtObj,tgtRef}$ operates in the same steps as Table 1 except for steps 2 and 3 which are presented in Table 2. The case where the first parameter of **resolveTemp** is an object is treated in the same way as a **Sequence** containing only that object.

In this section we have presented the general ATL to AGT translation scheme focusing on the emulation of the resolve mechanisms by introducing trace nodes. The next section will focus on the translation of OCL guards and queries.

Table 1. Translation of an ATL binding with default resolving

Binding	$tgtObj$: $tgtType$ ($tgtProp$ **<-** $oclQuery$)	
Single-valued Attribute $tgtAtt \equiv tgtProp$	**Single-valued Reference** $tgtRef \equiv tgtProp$	**Multi-valued Reference** $tgtRef \equiv tgtProp$

Step 1 — Initialize LHS with $: \text{<ruleName>}\_ Trace \xrightarrow{tgtObj} tgtObj : tgtType$

Step 2 — Translate $oclQuery$ as per Sec. 3.2. This will complement the LHS with the required navigations and ACs and return a result.

Result is an expression $expr$ over rule$_{\text{AGT}}$ parameters	Result is a node $qNode$ representing the query result	Result is a node $qNode$ representing one element of the result set

Step 3

Not Applicable. Step 3 is specific to reference target properties.	If the node is a source model element, perform a *default resolve* by matching a trace node with the exact *from* object using the following in the LHS: $qNode \xleftarrow{from[0]} tr : Trace \xrightarrow{to[0]} rNode : type(tgtRef)$ and the AC $exactFrom(tr)$. If not, let $\boxed{rNode} \equiv \boxed{qNode}$	

Step 4

Create the following attribute in the RHS $\dfrac{tgtObj}{tgtAtt = expr}$	Create $tgtObj \xrightarrow{tgtRef} rNode$ in the RHS	

Step 5 — Add a negative AC to force the application of the rule *once* per match

$\neg\exists \left(\begin{array}{c} \dfrac{tgtObj}{tgtAtt = p1} \\ \\ p1 = expr \end{array} \middle| \right)$	$\neg\exists \left(\left(tgtObj \xrightarrow{tgtRef} rNode \right) \right)$	

3.2 Translating OCL Guards and Binding Expressions

As explained previously, rule$_{\text{ATL}}$ guards and binding expressions are translated to ACs of respectively *instantiation* and *resolving* rules$_{\text{AGT}}$. Despite the considerable difference between NGC and OCL, NGC has been shown to be expressively equivalent to first order logic [13] which is the core of OCL. Translations of subsets of OCL to NGC have been proposed in [3] with a highly theoretical approach and in [4] with a wider supported OCL subset and an experimental approach. We have taken inspiration from both works and have found that none of them supports ordered sets, leading us to tackle this problem in particular. In the

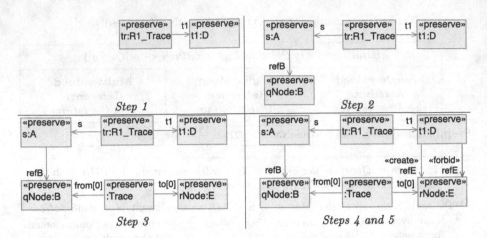

Fig. 5. Construction of resolving rule$_{\text{AGT}}$ $R1_{Res}^{t1,refE}$

following we will only recall the general principles of the existing translations and detail the problem at hand and our proposal.

The main idea is to translate OCL object queries into graphs that match the objects in the query's result set, and OCL constraints into NGCs that are satisfied under the same conditions. For example, the navigation of a reference **s.refB** is translated by creating the graph $\boxed{s}\xrightarrow{refB}\boxed{r}$ where r represents one object in the result set of the query and is returned as a result of the translation (see Step 2 in Table 1). As for the navigation of an object attribute such as in **s.name + '1'**, it is translated by creating a rule parameter p and assigning the attribute value to it "$name = p$" in the node s, and returning the expression $p + "1"$ as a result of the translation (Step 2 in Table 1). The supported subset of OCL is similar to the one in [4] which is limited to basic navigation, first order logic constructs and **Set** as the only collection type with basic set operations such as **select()**, **collect()**, **union()**. We extend this support to **OrderedSet** with support for indexing **at(i)** and the preservation of order in output collections.

Challenge 1. A first challenge is the handling of bindings that aggregate results of several queries. This is the case of the following binding shapes where in (1) resolved objects in *tgtRef* should be in the same order as the source objects in the **OrderedSet**, and in (2) *oclQuery$_1$* should be resolved before *oclQuery$_2$*.

$$tgtRef \texttt{<- OrderedSet\{} oclQuery_1, oclQuery_2 \ldots oclQuery_N\texttt{\}} \tag{1}$$

$$tgtRef \texttt{<-} oclQuery_1 \texttt{->union(} oclQuery_2 \texttt{)} \tag{2}$$

Solution 1. To preserve the ordering of elements, we propose to translate such bindings as separate successive bindings: *tgtRef* **<-** *oclQuery$_1$*, *tgtRef* **<-** *oclQuery$_2$*, ... Each such binding results in a separate resolving rule$_{\text{AGT}}$ and the

Table 2. Translation of an ATL binding with non-default resolving

resolveTemp(Sequence{$navExp_1$, ..., $navExp_N$}, $tgtPat$)
Step 2 Translate each $navExp_i$ as per Sec. 3.2. This will complement the LHS with the required navigations and ACs and return as a result a set of nodes $qNode_i$ representing the navigated objects
Step 3.a Perform a *non-default resolve* by matching a trace node with the exact *from* tuple. Differently than for the default resolve, *to* is not indexed. and add the AC $exactFrom(tr)$
Step 3.b Compute *CRules* as the set of all candidate rules$_{ATL}$ that have N source pattern elements and $tgtPat$ as one of their target pattern elements.
Step 3.c Add to the rule$_{AGT}$'s AC the following disjunction: $$\bigvee_{cRule\ \in\ CRules} \exists \left(\boxed{tr : <cRule>\_Trace} \xrightarrow{tgtPat} \boxed{rNode} \right)$$

rules$_{AGT}$ are sequenced in the same order as the queries in the original binding. Consequently objects are appended to *tgtRef* in the right order at run-time. Therefore (1) is translated to N sequential resolving rules$_{AGT}$ and (2) is translated to 2 sequential resolving rules$_{AGT}$.

Challenge 2. The second challenge is the navigation of ordered multi-valued references. Let us illustrate this problem with the following binding from **R1** in Fig. 1:

$$t1\ :\ OUT!D\ (\ refE\ <-\ s.refB\ )$$

refB is a multivalued reference (*i.e.* upper bound larger than 1). We have previously shown the translation of this binding in Fig. 5 under the assumption that **refB** is a *non-ordered* reference. The navigation **s.refB** is *flattened*, meaning that the elements of the collection are not handled all at once, but rather one by one thanks to the iteration of $R1_{Res}^{t1,refE}$. According to AGT graph matching, objects in **s.refB** may be matched in any order. Therefore objects in **t1.refE** may end up in a different order than their counterparts in **s.refB** which is a problem if **refB** and **refE** are ordered. That constitutes a divergence from the ATL semantics which honours the order of objects in collections. Therefore we need a way to force the matching of objects in **s.refB** in an orderly fashion.

Solution 2. We propose to complement the regular translation of navigation expressions [3,4] with an additional NGC forcing objects to be matched in the correct order. Intuitively, this NGC should express the fact that an object in **s.refB** should be matched only if all preceding objects in **s.refB** have already been handled by the resolving rule$_{AGT}$. This corresponds to the following NGC:

$$orderingAC = \exists \left(\boxed{s:A} \xrightarrow{refB[i]} \boxed{qNode:B} \,, \right.$$
$$\left. \forall \left(\boxed{s:A} \xrightarrow{refB[j]} \boxed{qNode_1:B} \,\Big|\, j < i,\ wasResolved_{R1}^{t1,refE}(qNode_1) \right) \right)$$

Where:

- i : index of the object $qNode$ currently being handled.
- j : index of the object $qNode_1$ which iterates over objects preceding $qNode$.
- $wasResolved_{R1}^{t1,refE}(n)$: A NGC which evaluates to *true* if node n has already been handled by the resolving rule$_{AGT}$.

Now we need to define $wasResolved_{R1}^{t1,refE}(n)$. We can determine that a node n has been already handled by checking if the node to which it resolves exists in the target reference $t1.refE$. Therefore the following definition is suitable:
$$wasResolved_{R1}^{t1,refE}(n) =$$

$$\exists \left(\boxed{n} \xleftarrow{from[0]} \boxed{tr:Trace} \xrightarrow{to[0]} \boxed{:E} \xleftarrow{refE} \boxed{t1:D} \,,\ exactFrom(tr) \right)$$

With the above definitions, adding $orderingAC$ as an application condition of $R1_{Res}^{t1,refE}$ ensures that objects in **s.refB** are processed in the correct order, thus honoring the ATL semantics. Let us now generalize this reasoning to the case where the navigation is filtered with a **select** operation:

```
t1 : OUT!D ( refE <- s.refB->select(e |body(e))
```

Now an object in **s.refB** should be matched only if it satisfies the **select** condition, and if all preceding objects in **s.refB** which also satisfy the **select** condition have been handled by the resolving rule$_{AGT}$. Therefore the AC that would ensure the orderly processing of objects is the following:

$$orderingAC = \exists \left(\boxed{s:A} \xrightarrow{refB[i]} \boxed{qNode:B} \,,\ tr_{body}(qNode) \bigwedge \right.$$
$$\left. \forall \left(\boxed{s:A} \xrightarrow{refB[j]} \boxed{qNode_1:B} \,\Big|\, j < i, \right. \right.$$
$$\left. \left. tr_{body}(qNode_1) \implies wasResolved_{R1}^{t1,refE}(qNode_1) \right) \right)$$

Where $tr_{body}(n)$ is the NGC resulting from the translation of the OCL constraint $body(\mathbf{e})$, applied to a node n. The generalization can be extended to all supported OCL expressions but will not be detailed here for lack of space.

4   Experiments and Validation

4.1   Validation Protocol

We have used the *Henshin* Eclipse framework as the target of the translation as it is well integrated with EMF and allows the execution of AGT transformations on standard EMF models. The ATL to AGT translation is implemented in our

Java-based tool *ATLAnalyser* and validated by considering a set of ATL transformations from the ATL Zoo [1] and from other sources. Each transformation is translated to AGT using our implementation and the resulting AGT transformation is validated manually by review. Then both the ATL and AGT versions are executed over a set of input models and in each case the output models of the two versions are checked to be identical using EMFCompare. Except for the manual review, this experimental validation protocol is fully automated (using JUnit) which allows to easily expand our test base with new transformations and models, and monitor the non-regression of existing tests as the prototype evolves. We have also identified the ATL features that each transformation contains to make sure we exercise all aspects of the translation.

Our prototype was successfully validated with the transformations listed in Table 3. *Simulink CodeGen* is a simplified version of an industrial Simulink to C code generator[3]. Note that in *Families2Persons*, the high number of resolving rules (relative to only 2 bindings) is due to the translation scheme of nested **if-then-else** binding queries which has not been developed in this paper.

Table 3. List of test transformations and tested features

	Families2-Persons [1]	Class2-Relational [1]	ER2REL [6]	SimulinkCodeGen[4]
Metrics				
ATL rules	2	6	6	6
ATL bindings	2	22	13	30
Instantiation rules	2	6	6	6
Resolving rules	8	23	15	32
ATL Features				
Default Resolve	X	X	X	X
resolveTemp				X
Helpers	X	X		X
Attribute binding	X	X	X	X
Reference binding		X	X	X
OrderedSet{}		X		X
union()		X	X	X
select()		X		X
collect(), at()				X

4.2   Limitations and Threats to Validity

A first limitation of our proposal is the lack of formal evidence of its validity. Though part of our translation is based on the one in [3] which is formally proven to be correct, our OCL subset is significantly wider preventing any direct claim of correctness of the complete translation. Second, while the addressed scope was found sufficient to translate a wide range of ATL transformations, features like

---

[3] Project P, http://www.open-do.org/projects/p.

non-unique collections (**Bag, Sequence**), collections of collections, and special values (**null, invalid**) are not supported because they cannot be represented in the AGT framework used in this paper. Finally, with the validation scheme presented in Sect. 4.1, we are faced with the challenge of any test-based validation which is the coverage and relevance of the test transformations and test models. We have tried to address this issue by identifying the ATL features used by each transformation to make sure that all aspects of the translation are tested (see Table 3). However we acknowledge that our tool is essentially a language compiler, and the verification of such tools is known to be a difficult problem.

5 Related Work

Though translations of OCL to NGC have been conducted [3,4], no previous work has proposed a translation of ATL to AGT to the best of our knowledge. In [14] the authors propose to translate model transformations from the Epsilon language family (arguably similar to ATL and OCL) to AGT to show through formal proof that a given pair of unidirectional transformations forms a bidirectional transformation. However this work is still at an early stage and an automatic translation is not yet proposed.

In the broader context of the analysis of model transformations several works have translated ATL to other formalisms. ATL transformations are translated in [6] to a transformation model with suitable constraints expressing the ATL semantics and in [16] to a Maude specification with a rewriting logic arguably similar to our graph rewriting transformation. The analyses made possible by these and other formalisations include Hoare-style correctness analyses, *i.e.* verifying that an ATL model transformation ensures a postcondition under the assumption of a precondition [6], and reachability analysis [16] to find errors in the ATL transformation. Despite these existing results, we have targeted AGT in our work to benefit from the construction of *weakest precondition* (WP) in AGT [10] which is the translation of a postcondition NGC on the output of a transformation into an equivalent precondition NGC on its input. This analysis which is not possible in the existing formalisations of ATL is used for the synthesis of validity-preserving preconditions [7] and for the formal proof of Hoare-style correctness [13]. Applying it to ATL using our translation is one of our main future prospects in a novel approach for testing model transformation chains [15].

6 Conclusion

This paper has presented a translation of ATL transformations to the formal framework of Algebraic Graph Transformation (AGT). The main challenges of this work were the translation of the ATL resolve mechanisms which do not have a direct equivalent in AGT, and the translation of OCL guards and queries to suitable Nested Graph Conditions (NGC). In the latter translation, we have complemented existing OCL to NGC translations with support for ordered sets, allowing to faithfully translate a wider range of ATL transformations. We have implemented our translation targeting the Henshin AGT framework and have validated it by translating a set of representative ATL transformations from various sources, and comparing the execution of both ATL and AGT versions.

In future work, we plan to extend the translation to support more ATL and OCL features such as arbitrary sorting with **sortedBy** as well as multi-valued attributes. A more challenging task will be to support imperative features of ATL such as lazy rules and **do** blocks. As a first intuition we believe this would require enriching trace nodes with more information and using more imperative features of AGT. Finally, we plan to use the proposed translation to apply AGT formal analyses to ATL transformation, starting with the construction of weakest preconditions as a way to generate tests for ATL transformation chains [15].

References

1. ATL Transformation Zoo. http://www.eclipse.org/atl/atlTransformations/
2. The Henshin project. http://www.eclipse.org/henshin
3. Arendt, T., Habel, A., Radke, H., Taentzer, G.: From core OCL invariants to nested graph constraints. In: Giese, H., König, B. (eds.) ICGT 2014. LNCS, vol. 8571, pp. 97–112. Springer, Heidelberg (2014)
4. Bergmann, G.: Translating OCL to Graph Patterns. In: Dingel, J., Schulte, W., Ramos, I., Abrahão, S., Insfran, E. (eds.) MODELS 2014. LNCS, vol. 8767, pp. 670–686. Springer, Heidelberg (2014)
5. Biermann, E., Ermel, C., Taentzer, G.: Formal foundation of consistent EMF model transformations by algebraic graph transformation. Softw. Syst. Model. **11**(2), 227–250 (2012)
6. Büttner, F., Egea, M., Cabot, J., Gogolla, M.: Verification of ATL transformations using transformation models and model finders. In: Aoki, T., Taguchi, K. (eds.) ICFEM 2012. LNCS, vol. 7635, pp. 198–213. Springer, Heidelberg (2012)
7. Deckwerth, F., Varró, G.: Attribute handling for generating preconditions from graph constraints. In: Giese, H., König, B. (eds.) ICGT 2014. LNCS, vol. 8571, pp. 81–96. Springer, Heidelberg (2014)
8. Ehrig, H., Ehrig, K., Prange, U., Taentzer, G.: Fundamentals of algebraic graph transformation, vol. 373. Springer, Heidelberg (2006)
9. González, C.A., Cabot, J.: ATLTest: A white-box test generation approach for ATL transformations. In: France, R.B., Kazmeier, J., Breu, R., Atkinson, C. (eds.) MODELS 2012. LNCS, vol. 7590, pp. 449–464. Springer, Heidelberg (2012)
10. Habel, A., Pennemann, K.-H., Rensink, A.: Weakest preconditions for high-level programs. In: Corradini, A., Ehrig, H., Montanari, U., Ribeiro, L., Rozenberg, G. (eds.) ICGT 2006. LNCS, vol. 4178, pp. 445–460. Springer, Heidelberg (2006)
11. Jouault, F., Kurtev, I.: Transforming models with ATL. In: Bruel, J.-M. (ed.) MoDELS 2005. LNCS, vol. 3844, pp. 128–138. Springer, Heidelberg (2006)
12. Object Management Group (OMG). Object Constraint Language (OCL) 2.4 (2012). http://www.omg.org/spec/OCL/2.4
13. Poskitt, C.M.: Verification of graph programs. Ph.D. thesis, University of York (2013)
14. Poskitt, C.M., Dodds, M., Paige, R.F., Rensink, A.: Towards rigorously faking bidirectional model transformations. In: AMT 2014 Workshop Proceedings, pp. 70–75 (2014)

15. Richa, E., Borde, E., Pautet, L., Bordin, M., Ruiz, J.F.: Towards testing model transformation chains using precondition construction in algebraic graph transformation. In: AMT 2014 Workshop Proceedings, pp. 34–43 (2014)
16. Troya, J., Vallecillo, A.: A rewriting logic semantics for ATL. J. Object Technol. **10**(5), 1–29 (2011)

A Methodology for Designing Dynamic Topology Control Algorithms via Graph Transformation

Roland Kluge$^{(\boxtimes)}$, Gergely Varró, and Andy Schürr

Real-Time Systems Lab, TU Darmstadt, Darmstadt, Germany
{roland.kluge,gergely.varro,andy.schuerr}@es.tu-darmstadt.de

Abstract. This paper presents a constructive, model-driven methodology for designing dynamic topology control algorithms. The proposed methodology characterizes valid and high quality topologies with declarative graph constraints and formulates topology control algorithms as graph transformation systems. Afterwards, a well-known static analysis technique is used to enrich graph transformation rules with application conditions derived from the graph constraints to ensure that this improved approach always produces topologies that (i) are optimized wrt. to a domain-specific criterion, and (ii) additionally fulfill all the graph constraints.

Keywords: Topology control · Graph constraints · Static analysis

1 Introduction

In the telecommunication engineering domain, wireless sensor networks (WSNs) [14] are a highly active research area. For instance, WSNs are applied to monitor physical or environmental conditions with distributed, autonomous, battery-powered measurement devices that cooperatively transmit their collected data to a central location. To extend the battery lifetime of these measurement devices, topology control (TC) [14] is carried out on WSNs to inactivate redundant communication links by reducing their transmission power. The most significant requirements on TC algorithms include the ability to (i) handle continuously changing network topologies, (ii) operate in a highly distributed environment, in which each node can only observe and modify its local neighborhood, and (iii) still guarantee important local and global formal properties for their neighborhood and the whole network, respectively.

The design and implementation of TC algorithms are, therefore, challenging and elaborate tasks, especially if a high quality of service is a non-functional requirement of the overall WSN. In a typical development setup, several variants of different TC approaches have to be prepared and quantitatively assessed in an iterative process. In each iteration, (i) a new variant must be individually designed and implemented for a distributed environment, (ii) the preservation of required formal properties (e.g., connectivity) must be proved, and (iii) performance measurements must be carried out in a corresponding runtime environment (testbed or simulator).

© Springer International Publishing Switzerland 2015
D. Kolovos and M. Wimmer (Eds.): ICMT 2015, LNCS 9152, pp. 199–213, 2015.
DOI: 10.1007/978-3-319-21155-8_15

This last point also assumes an interaction between the TC algorithm and the runtime environment. More specifically, the runtime environment alters the topology, which has to be repaired by the TC algorithm in an *incremental* manner, namely, by retaining unaltered parts of the topology as much as possible.

The main challenge with the individual design of each new algorithm variant is that it strongly relies on the experience of highly qualified experts. To enable a more systematic and well-engineered approach, model-driven principles [1] can be applied to the development of TC algorithms, as in the case of many other success stories [17]. More specifically, topologies can be described by graph-based models, and possible local modifications in the topology can be specified declaratively with graph transformation (GT) rules [13]. Although this approach provides a well-defined procedure for repairing the topology even in a distributed environment, it cannot ensure that all required formal properties hold for the repaired topology.

A well-known, constructive, static analysis technique [7] has been established in the GT community to formulate structural invariants and to guarantee that these invariants hold. In this setup, graph constraints specify positive or negative patterns, which must be present in or missing from a valid graph, respectively. An automated process then derives additional rule application conditions from graph transformation rules and graph constraints to ensure that the application of the enriched new rules never produces invalid graphs. Although this technique has already been employed in scenarios where graph constraints represent invariants that must hold permanently [10], its applicability in the TC domain is hindered by the fact that topology modifications performed by the runtime environment may temporarily (and unavoidably) violate graph constraints.

In this paper, we propose a new, constructive, model-driven methodology for designing TC algorithms by graph transformation. We demonstrate the approach on the kTC algorithm [15]. More specifically, we define graph constraints from algorithm-specific formal and quality requirements to characterize valid and high quality topologies. Such desirable topologies are to be produced by a TC algorithm, which is formulated as a graph transformation system. We iteratively refine this transformation by applying the constructive approach of [7], which enriches the rules at compile-time with additional application conditions, derived from the graph constraints. Finally, we prove that our improved GT-based TC algorithm terminates and always produces connected topologies that fulfill all the graph constraints.

Section 2 introduces modeling and TC concepts. Section 3 describes graph constraints and their application to describe invariants of TC algorithms. Section 4 illustrates GT concepts on a basic TC algorithm. Section 5 delineates the construction methodology that enriches the generic TC algorithm with graph constraints. Section 6 summarizes related work, and Sect. 7 concludes our paper with a summary and an outlook.

2 Modeling Concepts and Topology Control

This section introduces fundamental modeling and topology control concepts.

2.1   Basic Modeling Concepts

A *metamodel* describes the basic concepts of a domain as a graph. In this paper, network topologies are used as a running example, whose metamodel is shown in Fig. 1a. *Classes* represent the nodes of the metamodel, and *associations* represent the edges between classes. An association end is labeled with a *multiplicity*, which restricts the number of target objects that can be reached by navigating along an association in the given direction. *Attributes* (depicted in the lower part of the classes) store values of primitive or enumerated types.

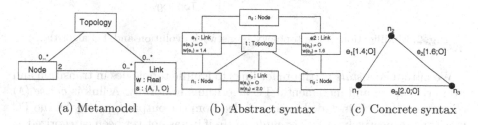

(a) Metamodel   (b) Abstract syntax   (c) Concrete syntax

Fig. 1. Topology metamodel and a sample topology in abstract/concrete syntax

A *topology* is a graph that consists of *nodes* and *(communication) links* between nodes. As specified in Fig. 1a, a link connects exactly 2 nodes, and a node can be an endpoint of zero or more incident links. A link e has an algorithm-specific *weight* $w(e)$ and *state* $s(e)$ attribute, whose role will be explained together with the corresponding topology control concepts, shortly.

Example. Figure 1b and c depict a sample topology with three nodes (n_1, n_2, n_3) and three links (e_1, e_2, e_3) forming a triangle in abstract and concrete syntax, respectively. In the rest of the paper, the concrete syntax notation is used, which denotes nodes and links by black circles and solid lines, respectively. Each link is labeled with its name, followed by its weight and state in brackets.

2.2   Topology Control

Topology control (TC) is the discipline of adapting WSN topologies to optimize network metrics such as network lifetime [14]. The nodes in a WSN topology are often battery-powered sensors, which limits the lifetime of the network. For each node, TC selects a logical neighborhood, which is a subset of the nodes within its transmission range. Afterwards, each node may reduce its transmission power to reach its farthest logical neighbor. The weight attribute $w(e)$ of a link e describes the cost of communicating across this link. In this paper, we use the distance of the end nodes of a link as a weight metric.

Figure 2 shows the interaction of an evolving network, represented as a stream of topology change events (e.g., link weight change, addition or removal of nodes or links[1]), and a topology control algorithm, which takes an input topology and produces

---
[1] Such events occur, e.g., when nodes move and join or leave the network.

an output topology, which is a subgraph of the input topology. In this setup, a *batch TC algorithm* reconsiders every link in the topology in each execution, irrespective of the actual topology change events, while an *incremental TC algorithm* only reevaluates the modified parts of the topology. In this paper, we assume that no topology change events occur while the TC algorithm is running.

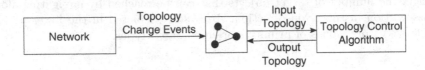

Fig. 2. Modification of the topology by network evolution and TC algorithm

We introduce a *state* attribute for links to handle topologies in transition and to describe batch and incremental TC algorithms uniformly. A link is *active* (A) or *inactive* (I) if it is included in or excluded from the output topology by the TC algorithm, respectively. A link is *outdated* (O) if it has not yet been categorized as active or inactive by the TC algorithm. A `topology control algorithm` tries to activate or inactivate outdated links, while `topology change events` may outdate links. Note that the set of active links represents the `output topology`, which is always a subgraph of the whole input topology.

Important Properties of Topologies and TC. Every TC algorithm must (i) terminate without outdated links and (ii) preserve topology connectivity. The first property ensures that each link in the input topology is definitely part or not part of the output topology. A topology is *connected* if the subgraph induced by its active and outdated links is connected. This entails that the output topology is connected if and only if its subgraph induced by the active links is connected.

Example. Figure 3 illustrates an incremental variant of the kTC algorithm [15], which inactivates exactly those links in the sample topology that are the longest link in a triangle and that are at least k-times longer than the shortest link in the same triangle. We always assume $k > 1$.

Initially, all links are outdated ①. The first execution of kTC ($k = 1.5$) activates or inactivates all links ②. A move of node n_4 might trigger a weight change on link e_4, which outdates this link ③. As link e_4 is no longer the longest link in the triangle (n_2,n_3,n_4), the next (incremental) iteration of kTC activates e_2, inactivates e_4, and retains the state of links e_1, e_3, and e_5 ④.

3   Characterizing Topologies with Graph Constraints

As a first step in our constructive TC design methodology, formal properties and quality requirements of the TC algorithm are analyzed, and graph constraints are defined as invariants to characterize valid and high quality topologies.

A *pattern* is a graph consisting of node and link variables together with a set of attribute constraints. A *node (link) variable* serves as a placeholder for

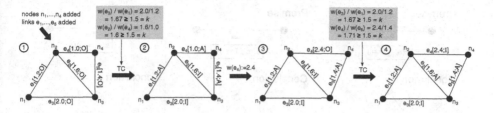

Fig. 3. Incremental topology control with kTC

a node (link) in a topology. An *attribute constraint* is a predicate over attributes of node and link variables. A *match of a pattern P in a topology G* maps the node and link variables of P to the nodes and links of G, respectively, such that this mapping preserves the end nodes of the link variables and all attribute constraints are fulfilled.

A *graph constraint* consists of a *premise* pattern and a *conclusion* pattern such that (i) the premise is a subgraph of the conclusion, and (ii) the attribute constraints of the conclusion imply the attribute constraints of the premise. A *positive (negative) graph constraint $\mathcal{P}$ ($\mathcal{N}$) is fulfilled on a topology G* if each match of the premise in the topology G can (cannot) be extended to a match of the conclusion in the same topology G.

Demonstration on kTC. For our running example, we specify three constraints: two algorithm-specific constraints of kTC and a third constraint that forbids outdated links in the output topology.

kTC inactivates a link *if and only if* this link is the longest link in a triangle and if it is additionally at least k-times longer than the shortest link in the same triangle. This equivalence yields the following two constraints:

$\Rightarrow$ The *inactive-link constraint* $\mathcal{P}_{inact}$, depicted in Fig. 4a, states that *each* inactive link e_{max} must be part of a triangle in which (i) e_{max} is the longest link, (ii) e_{max} is at least k-times longer than the shortest link, and (iii) e_{s1} and e_{s2} are either active or inactive.

$\Leftarrow$ The *active-link constraint* $\mathcal{N}_{act}$, depicted in Fig. 4b, states that *no* active link e_{max} may be part of a triangle in which (i) e_{max} is the longest link, (ii) e_{max} is at least k-times longer than the shortest link, and (iii) e_{s1} and e_{s2} are either active or inactive.

Due to the attribute constraints that require e_{s1} and e_{s2} to be active or inactive, the active-link constraint may only be violated and the inactive-link constraint may only be fulfilled if all links in the triangle are either active or inactive. Therefore, topology change events never violate the active-link constraint $\mathcal{N}_{act}$ because no new match of its conclusion may arise. In contrast, the inactive-link constraint $\mathcal{P}_{inact}$ may be violated by a topology change event, for instance, if an inactive link belongs to exactly one match of the conclusion of $\mathcal{P}_{inact}$ and if any of the links e_{s1} or e_{s2} gets outdated.

Finally, the *outdated-link constraint* $\mathcal{N}_{out}$, depicted in Fig. 4c, describes the general requirement that the (output) topology shall not contain any outdated

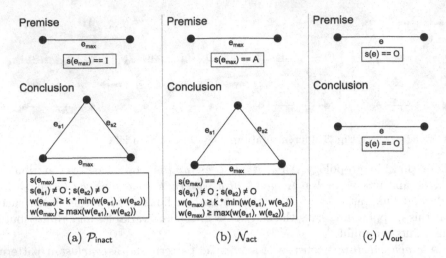

Fig. 4. Two algorithm-specific constraints and one general graph constraint

links. Any outdated link causes a violation of $\mathcal{N}_{out}$ because its premise and conclusion are identical.

4   Specifying Topology Control with Programmed Graph Transformation

In the second step of our design methodology, topology change events and TC operations are described by graph transformation (GT) rules. The dynamic behavior of TC algorithms is specified by programmed graph transformation [4], which carries out basic topology modifications by applying graph transformation rules whose execution order is defined by an explicit control flow.

Programmed Graph Transformation Concepts. A *mapping from pattern P to pattern P'* maps a subset of node and link variables of pattern P to a subset of node and link variables of pattern P', respectively, such that this mapping preserves the end nodes of the link variables. A *graph transformation rule* consists of a *left-hand side (LHS)* pattern, a *right-hand side (RHS)* pattern, *negative application condition (NAC)* patterns, and mappings from the LHS pattern to the RHS and NAC patterns. To enable meaningful attribute assignments, the predicate in the attribute constraints of the RHS pattern can only be an equation with an attribute of a single node or link variable on its left side.

A *GT rule is applicable to a topology G* if a match of the LHS pattern exists in the topology that cannot be extended to a match of any NAC pattern. The *application of a GT rule at a match of its LHS pattern to a topology G produces a topology G'* by (1) preserving all nodes (links) of the topology that are assigned to a node (link) variable of the LHS pattern, which *has* a corresponding node (link) variable in the RHS pattern (black elements without additional markup); (2) removing those nodes (links) of the topology that are assigned to a node (link) variable of the LHS pattern, which has *no* corresponding node (link) variable in the RHS pattern (red elements with a '−−' markup); (3) adding a new node (link) to the topology for each node (link) variable of the RHS pattern, which has no corresponding node (link) variable in the LHS pattern (green elements with a '++' markup); and (4) assigning node (link) attributes (operator ':=') in such a manner that the attribute constraints of the RHS pattern are fulfilled.

Control flow is specified in our approach with an activity diagram based notation in which each activity node contains a graph transformation rule. A *regular activity node* (denoted by a single framed, rounded rectangle) with one unlabeled outgoing edge applies the contained GT rule *once* to *one* arbitrary match. A regular activity node with an outgoing [Success] and [Failure] edge applies the contained GT rule and follows the [Success] edge if the rule is applicable at an arbitrary match, and it follows the [Failure] edge if the rule is inapplicable. A *foreach activity node* (denoted by a double framed rounded rectangle) applies the contained GT rule to *all* matches and traverses along the optional outgoing edge labeled with [EachTime] for each match. When all the matches have been completely processed, the control flow continues along the [End] outgoing edge. Black and green node and link variables are *bound* by a successful rule application. Subsequent activity nodes can reuse nodes and links that have been bound by an earlier rule application.

Example. Figure 5 depicts GT rules for each of the five possible topology change events – link weight change (R_{chg}), link addition ($R_{addLink}$), link removal ($R_{remLink}$), node addition ($R_{addNode}$), and node removal ($R_{remNode}$) – and the two TC rules, link activation (R_{act}) and link inactivation (R_{inact}). In Fig. 5, x_1 denotes the new weight $w(e)$ of link e. Modified and new links are marked as outdated.

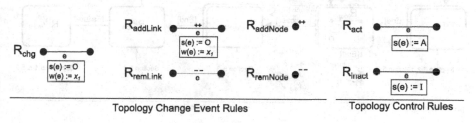

Topology Change Event Rules   Topology Control Rules

Fig. 5. GT rules describing topology change events and TC rules

Figure 6 shows a basic TC algorithm that activates all outdated links.[2] Link variable e_O is bound by R_{loop} and reused in R_{act} and R_{inact}. Check marks inside the gray boxes indicate which constraints must be fulfilled in the input topology (precondition[3]) and which constraints will be fulfilled in the output topology (postcondition).

---

[2] The inactivation rule R_{inact} is deliberately unreachable and only shown for completeness.

[3] The example in Sect. 3 contains a discussion why certain preconditions may be violated.

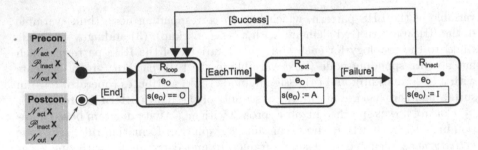

Fig. 6. Basic TC algorithm

5   Enriching the Graph Transformation with Constraints

The third step of our design methodology is to enrich graph transformation rules step-by-step with additional application conditions that are derived from the graph constraints. The resulting topology control algorithm always produces output topologies that fulfill all the graph constraints.

Our approach is demonstrated again on an incremental variant of kTC. Figure 7 serves as an overview, particularly during the subsequent sections. The final transformation is produced by iteratively refining the generic TC algorithm of Fig. 6 according to the following procedure.

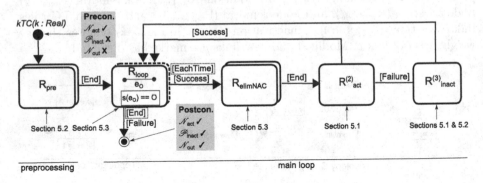

Fig. 7. kTC algorithm after performing steps of Sects. 5.1 – 5.3

Section 5.1. To ensure that the active-link constraint $\mathcal{N}_{act}$ is still fulfilled in the output topology, a NAC derived from the active-link constraint $\mathcal{N}_{act}$ is attached to the activation rule R_{act} and the inactivation rule R_{inact}. This step produces the refined rules $R_{act}^{(2)}$ and $R_{inact}^{(2)}$.

Section 5.2. To ensure that the inactive-link constraint $\mathcal{P}_{inact}$ is fulfilled in the output topology, two steps are necessary: (i) The LHS pattern of the inactivation rule $R_{inact}^{(2)}$ is extended by the inactive-link constraint $\mathcal{P}_{inact}$, resulting in the refined rule $R_{inact}^{(3)}$. (ii) A NAC derived from the inactive-link constraint $\mathcal{P}_{inact}$ is attached to a new (preprocessing) rule R_{pre}.

Section 5.3. To ensure that the outdated-link constraint $\mathcal{N}_{out}$ is fulfilled in the output topology, the LHS pattern of a new (NAC match eliminating) rule $R_{elimNAC}$ is constructed from the common NACs of the activation and inactivation rules $R_{act}^{(2)}$ and $R_{inact}^{(3)}$.

Section 5.4. The connectivity of the output topology and the termination of the final version of kTC algorithm are proved.

5.1 Fulfilling the Active-Link Constraint

This first step ensures that the active-link constraint $\mathcal{N}_{act}$ is fulfilled in the output topology. Since the input topology fulfills the constraint, it is enough to ensure that applying the activation and inactivation rules does not violate the active-link constraint $\mathcal{N}_{act}$.

Methodology. The methodology to ensure that a GT rule fulfills a negative constraint is well-known in literature [7]: The negative constraint is translated into a number of NACs of the GT rules. Each overlap of the conclusion of the negative constraint with the RHS of the rule yields one NAC.

Demonstration on kTC. First, we consider the activation rule R_{act}: The conclusion of the active-link constraint $\mathcal{N}_{act}$ and the RHS of the activation rule R_{act} can be glued in three different ways such that the link e_O overlaps with the link variables e_{max}, e_{s1}, or e_{s2}, respectively. This yields the three NACs N_{max}, N_{s1}, and N_{s2}. Note that the latter two NACs are *equivalent* in the sense that any match of N_{s1} is also a match of N_{s2}, and vice versa. Figure 8 depicts the refined activation rule $R_{act}^{(2)}$.

Next, we consider the inactivation rule R_{inact}: The conclusion of the inactive-link constraint $\mathcal{P}_{inact}$ and the RHS of the inactivation rule R_{inact} can be glued in two ways such that the link e_O overlaps the link variables e_{s1} or e_{s2}, respectively. This yields two equivalent NACs, N_{s1} and N_{s2}, which are isomorphic to the NACs of $R_{act}^{(2)}$ with the same name. Figure 9 depicts the refined inactivation rule $R_{inact}^{(2)}$.

Due to the added NACs, applying the refined activation rule $R_{act}^{(2)}$ and the refined inactivation rule $R_{inact}^{(2)}$ never violates the active-link constraint $\mathcal{N}_{act}$.

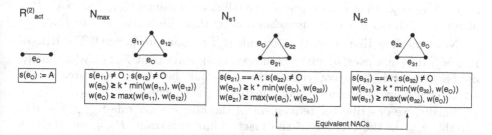

Fig. 8. Activation rule $R_{act}^{(2)}$ preserving active-link constraint $\mathcal{N}_{act}$

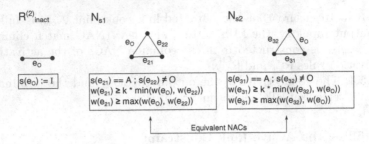

Fig. 9. Inactivation rule $R^{(2)}_{\text{inact}}$ preserving active-link constraint $\mathcal{N}_{\text{act}}$

5.2   Fulfilling the Inactive-Link Constraint

To ensure that the positive inactive-link constraint $\mathcal{P}_{\text{inact}}$ is fulfilled in the output topology, two modifications are necessary: First, an additional preprocessing rule R_{pre} ensures that any violation of $\mathcal{P}_{\text{inact}}$ in the input topology is repaired. Second, a refinement of the inactivation rule $R^{(2)}_{\text{inact}}$ ensures that the constraint is never violated in the main loop.

Methodology. Due to the page limitation, we present an adaptation of the methodology described in [7], which is tailored to our scenario: We consider GT rules without deletion that modify an attribute of a single link.

If a topology fulfills a positive graph constraint before applying a rule, two steps are necessary to ensure that the topology still fulfills the constraint after the rule application: (i) If applying the rule produces a new match of the premise of the constraint, then the RHS of the rule needs to ensure that the conclusion of the constraint holds. (ii) Applying the rule may not violate the constraint by destroying any match of the conclusion of the constraint that existed prior to the rule application.

This means that, first, the LHS pattern of each rule is extended with the conclusion of the constraint if its RHS overlaps the premise of the constraint. Second, it is analyzed whether the modified rule may destroy any existing match of the conclusion of the constraint.

Demonstration on kTC. The input topology may violate the inactive-link constraint $\mathcal{P}_{\text{inact}}$, which necessitates a new preprocessing rule R_{pre}, which outdates all inactive links that violate the inactive-link constraint $\mathcal{P}_{\text{inact}}$. The NAC N_{pre} of rule R_{pre}, shown in Fig. 10, matches exactly those links that violate $\mathcal{P}_{\text{inact}}$.

Next, we show that the activation rule $R^{(2)}_{\text{act}}$ remains unchanged: The RHS of rule $R^{(2)}_{\text{act}}$ does not overlap with the inactive-link constraint $\mathcal{P}_{\text{inact}}$. Additionally, applying the rule does not violate the constraint because it activates a link, which obviously cannot destroy any match of the conclusion of $\mathcal{P}_{\text{inact}}$.

Finally, we describe the refinement of the inactivation rule $R^{(2)}_{\text{inact}}$: The link variable e_{max} in the premise of the inactive-link constraint $\mathcal{P}_{\text{inact}}$ and the link e_O in the RHS of $R^{(2)}_{\text{inact}}$ overlap. Therefore, the LHS of $R^{(2)}_{\text{inact}}$ is extended by an image of the conclusion of the constraint. The refined inactivation rule $R^{(3)}_{\text{inact}}$ is depicted in Fig. 11.

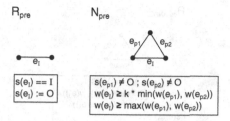

Fig. 10. Preprocessing rule R_{pre}, which outdates all inactive links violating $\mathcal{P}_{inact}$

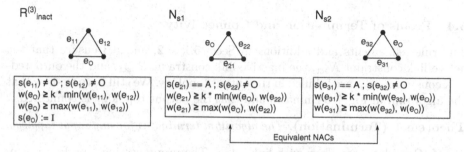

Fig. 11. Inactivation rule $R_{inact}^{(3)}$ preserving $\mathcal{N}_{act}$ and $\mathcal{P}_{inact}$

Due to the additional preprocessing rule R_{pre}, which ensures that the topology fulfills the inactive-link constraint $\mathcal{P}_{inact}$ at the beginning of the main loop, and the refined inactivation rule $R_{inact}^{(3)}$, the inactive-link constraint $\mathcal{P}_{inact}$ is fulfilled in the output topology as well.

5.3 Fulfilling the Outdated-Link Constraint

To ensure that the outdated-link constraint $\mathcal{N}_{out}$ is fulfilled in the output topology, a new GT rule is added in this section because the activation rule $R_{act}^{(2)}$ and inactivation rule $R_{inact}^{(3)}$ share the NACs N_{s1} and N_{s2}, which may block the activation *and* inactivation of outdated links in some topologies. Due to the equivalence of the NACs N_{s1} and N_{s2}, we only consider N_{s1} in the following.

NAC-Elimination Rule. We propose to insert a new rule $R_{elimNAC}$, depicted in Fig. 12, prior to the activation rule $R_{act}^{(2)}$, which removes all matches of NAC N_{s1}. The LHS of rule $R_{elimNAC}$ is an image of N_{s1}, and the RHS outdates the longest link e_{max}. Note that the outdated state propagates only toward longer links.

Loop Rule. The new NAC elimination rule $R_{elimNAC}$ results in additional outdated links that are not considered when R_{loop} is first applied. Consequently, the foreach activity node around loop rule R_{loop} changes to a regular activity node in this step, as shown earlier in Fig. 7. For this reason the algorithm terminates if and only if the topology contains no more outdated links. Consequently, the output topology fulfills the outdated-link constraint $\mathcal{N}_{out}$.

$R_{elimNAC}$

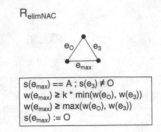

$$s(e_{max}) == A\ ;\ s(e_3) \neq O$$
$$w(e_{max}) \geq k * min(w(e_0),\ w(e_3))$$
$$w(e_{max}) \geq max(w(e_0),\ w(e_3))$$
$$s(e_{max}) := O$$

Fig. 12. NAC elimination rule $R_{elimNAC}$

5.4 Proofs of Termination and Connectivity

The rule refinements and additions in Sects. 5.1, 5.2, and 5.3 ensure that the active-link constraint $\mathcal{N}_{act}$, the inactive-link constraint $\mathcal{P}_{inact}$, and the outdated-link constraint $\mathcal{N}_{out}$ are fulfilled in the output topology. We still have to show that the algorithm in Fig. 7 terminates and that the output topology is connected.

Theorem 1 (Termination). *The algorithm terminates for any input topology.*

Proof. Consider a topology with link set E. The preprocessing loop R_{pre} is executed at most once for each link, so it suffices to show that the main loop terminates.

We consider the sequence of all link states $s_i(e_1), \ldots, s_i(e_m)$ with $m := |E|$ after the i-th execution of R_{loop}, where the links e_k are ordered according to their weight. We compare two sequences of link states, s_i and s_j, as follows: $s_i \prec s_j$ if and only if (i) some link e_k is outdated in s_i and active or inactive in s_j, and (ii) the states of all links shorter than e_k are identical in s_i and s_j, formally:

$$s_i \prec s_j :\Leftrightarrow \exists k, 1 < k \leq m : s_i(e_k) = O \wedge s_j(e_k) \in \{A, I\}$$
$$\wedge\ \forall \ell, 1 \leq \ell \leq k-1 : s_i(e_\ell) = s_j(e_\ell)$$

Note that any sequence of active and inactive links is an upper bound for $\prec$.

We now show that $s_{i-1} \prec s_i$ for $i > 1$. Let e_k be the link that is bound by applying the loop rule R_{loop}. The NAC elimination rule $R_{elimNAC}$ outdates links e_j with $w(e_j) > w(e_k)$ and thus $j > k$. The activation rule $R_{act}^{(2)}$ or the inactivation rule $R_{inact}^{(3)}$ activate or inactivate e_k, respectively.

Therefore, $s_{i-1} \prec s_i$ because (i) the first $k-1$ elements of s_{i-1} and s_i are identical, and (ii) $s_{i-1}(e_k) = O$ and $s_i(e_k) \in \{A, I\}$. The termination follows because any ordered sequence $s_1 \prec s_2 \prec \ldots$ has finite length. $\qquad\square$

Theorem 2 (Connectivity). *The output topology of the algorithm is connected if its input topology is connected.*

Sketch of Proof. The output topology only contains active and inactive links because the outdated-link constraint $\mathcal{N}_{out}$ is fulfilled. It is thus enough to show the claim that the end nodes of each link are connected by a path of active links in the output topology. This trivially holds for the end nodes of active links.

By induction, we show that the claim also holds for all inactive links: We consider the inactive links $e_{i_1}, \ldots, e_{i_k}$ of the topology ordered by weight.

Induction Start: The shortest inactive link, e_{i_1}, is part of a triangle with two shorter, active links that connect the end nodes of link e_{i_1}. Thus, the claim holds for link e_{i_1}.

Induction Step: We now consider an inactive link $e_{i_{\ell+1}}$ with $1 \leq \ell \leq k-1$, which is part of a triangle with two links, e_1 and e_2. We assume that only e_1 is inactive.[4] Thus, there is some $s \leq \ell$ such that $e_1 := e_{i_s}$. Since the claim has been proved for all inactive links shorter than $e_{i_{\ell+1}}$, there is a path of active links between the end nodes of e_{i_s}. A path of active links between the end nodes of link $e_{\ell+1}$ can be constructed by joining the two paths between the end nodes of e_1 and e_2.

6 Related Work

We briefly present related work on verification and model-based development.

Verification. Model checking [12] is an analysis technique used to verify particular properties of a system. If a symbolic problem description is missing, model checking tools are often limited to a finite model size. The approach in this paper constructively integrates constraints at design time so that it can be shown that constraints are fulfilled on arbitrary topologies.

In [7], graphical consistency constraints, which express that particular combinations of nodes and edges should be present in or absent from a graph, are translated into application conditions of GT rules. This technique has been generalized later [3] and extended to cope with attributes [2]. The basic idea is to translate consistency conditions, characterizing "valid" graphs, into application conditions of GT rules. This paper applies and extends this generic methodology for a practical and complex application scenario. We represent positive application conditions in [7] as extensions of the LHS of GT rules, which is equivalently expressive [5]. This representation is unsuitable to express global constraints such as connectivity, which requires, e.g., second-order monadic logic [7]. This paper ensures connectivity of topologies by an additional proof.

In [6], the authors distinguish four situations in which a model transformation considers consistency conditions, including the preservation and enforcement of consistency constraints. The algorithm in this paper preserves the active-link constraint, and it enforces and preserves the inactive-link constraint.

Model-Based Development. Model-based techniques have shown to be suitable to describe [16] and construct [8] adaptive systems. Formal analysis of supposed properties of complex topology adaptation algorithms has already revealed special cases in which the implemented algorithms violate crucial topology constraints [18]. In [9], model checking is applied to detect bugs and to point at

---

[4] If both links are active, the claim follows trivially. If both links are inactive, the argument applies for each link individually.

their causes in the TC algorithm LMST, leading to an improved implementation thereof. This paper, in contrast, applies a constructive methodology [7] for GT to develop correct algorithms in the first place.

In [11], variants of the TC algorithm kTC [15] are developed using GT, integrating the GT tool eMoflon[5] with a network simulator. While [11] focuses on improving a concrete algorithm, this paper aims at devising a generic methodology to develop TC algorithms that fulfill the given constraints by design.

7   Conclusion

In this paper, we proposed a new, model-driven methodology for designing topology control algorithms by graph transformation, and demonstrated the approach on an incremental variant of the kTC algorithm. The presented procedure characterizes valid topologies with graph constraints, specifies topology control algorithms as graph transformation system, and applies a well-known static analysis technique to enrich graph transformation rules with application conditions derived from the graph constraints. The new algorithm always terminates and produces connected, valid topologies.

Future research includes interleaving the network evolution with topology control and evaluating the methodology on further topology control algorithms.

Acknowledgment. This work has been funded by the German Research Foundation (DFG) within the Collaborative Research Center (CRC) 1053 – MAKI. The authors would like to thank Matthias Hollick (subprojects A03 and C01) for his valuable input.

References

1. Beydeda, S., Book, M., Gruhn, V.: Model-Driven Software Development, 15th edn. Springer, Heidelberg (2005)
2. Deckwerth, F., Varró, G.: Generating preconditions from graph constraints by higher order graph transformation. ECEASST **67**, 1–14 (2014)
3. Ehrig, H., Ehrig, K., Prange, U., Taentzer, G.: Fundamentals of Algebraic Graph Transformation. Springer, Heidelberg (2006)
4. Fischer, T., Niere, J., Torunski, L., Zündorf, A.: Story diagrams: a new graph rewrite language based on the unified modeling language and java. In: Ehrig, H., Engels, G., Kreowski, H.-J., Rozenberg, G. (eds.) TAGT 1998. LNCS, vol. 1764, pp. 296–309. Springer, Heidelberg (2000)
5. Habel, A., Heckel, R., Taentzer, G.: Graph grammars with negative application conditions. Fundamenta Informaticae **26**(3/4), 287–313 (1996)
6. Hausmann, J.H., Heckel, R., Sauer, S.: Extended model relations with graphical consistency conditions. In: Proceedings of the UML 2002 Workshop on Consistency Problems in UML-based Software Development, pp. 61–74 (2002)
7. Heckel, R., Wagner, A.: Ensuring consistency of conditional graph rewriting - a constructive approach. In: Proceedings of the Joint COMPUGRAPH/SEMAGRAPH Workshop. ENTCS, vol. 2, pp. 118–126. Elsevier (1995)

---

[5] www.emoflon.org.

8. Jacob, R., Richa, A., Scheideler, C., Schmid, S., Täubig, H.: A distributed polyloga-rithmic time algorithm for self-stabilizing skip graphs. In: Proceedings of the ACM Symposium on Principles of Distributed Computing, pp. 131–140. ACM (2009)
9. Katelman, M., Meseguer, J., Hou, J.: Redesign of the LMST wireless sensor pro-tocol through formal modeling and statistical model checking. In: Barthe, G., de Boer, F.S. (eds.) FMOODS 2008. LNCS, vol. 5051, pp. 150–169. Springer, Heidel-berg (2008)
10. Koch, M., Mancini, L.V., Parisi-Presicce, F.: A graph-based formalism for RBAC. ACM Trans. Inf. Syst. Secur. **5**(3), 332–365 (2002)
11. Kulcsár, G., Stein, M., Schweizer, I., Varró, G., Mühlhäuser, M., Schürr, A.: Rapid prototyping of topology control algorithms by graph transformation. In: Proceed-ings of the 8th International Workshop on Graph-Based Tools. ECEASST, vol. 68 (2014)
12. Rensink, A., Schmidt, A., Varró, D.: Model checking graph transformations: a com-parison of two approaches. In: Ehrig, H., Engels, G., Parisi-Presicce, F., Rozenberg, G. (eds.) ICGT 2004. LNCS, vol. 3256, pp. 226–241. Springer, Heidelberg (2004)
13. Rozenberg, G.: Handbook of Graph Grammars and Computing by Graph Trans-formation. Foundations, vol. 1. World Scientific, River Edge (1997)
14. Santi, P.: Topology control in wireless ad hoc and sensor networks. ACM Comput. Surv. (CSUR) **37**(2), 164–194 (2005)
15. Schweizer, I., Wagner, M., Bradler, D., Mühlhäuser, M., Strufe, T.: kTC - Robust and adaptive wireless ad-hoc topology control. In: Proceedings of the 21st Inter-national Conference on Computer Communications and Networks (2012)
16. Taentzer, G., Goedicke, M., Meyer, T.: Dynamic change management by distrib-uted graph transformation: towards configurable distributed systems. In: Ehrig, H., Engels, G., Kreowski, H.-J., Rozenberg, G. (eds.) TAGT 1998. LNCS, vol. 1764, pp. 179–193. Springer, Heidelberg (2000)
17. Völter, M., Stahl, T., Bettin, J., Haase, A., Helsen, S.: Model-Driven Software Development: Technology, Engineering, Management. John Wiley & Sons, Hobo-ken (2013)
18. Zave, P.: Using lightweight modeling to understand chord. SIGCOMM Comput. Commun. Rev. **42**(2), 49–57 (2012)

Extending Model to Model Transformation Results from Triple Graph Grammars to Multiple Models

Frank Trollmann[✉] and Sahin Albayrak

Faculty of Electrical Engineering and Computer Science,
DAI-Labor, TU-Berlin, Berlin, Germany
{Frank.Trollmann,Sahin.Albayrak}@dai-labor.de

Abstract. Triple graph grammars are a formally well-founded and widely used technique for model transformation. Due to their formal foundation several transformation approaches and analysis methods exists. However, triple graphs are restricted to represent two models at a time. In this paper we describe how the formalism of triple graphs can be generalised to enable a representation of multiple models and relations. We show that basic results from triple graph grammars can also be extended. The results in this paper provide a foundation for the generalisation of other results in model transformation, integration and synchronisation to multiple models.

Keywords: Model transformation · Triple graphs · Model driven engineering

1 Introduction

Model transformation is one of the central concepts in model driven engineering. Generally speaking, a model transformation is a process that transforms a set of source models into a set of target models [14]. Triple graph grammars (TGG) [16] have been used as formal basis for model to model transformation in a variety of approaches [17]. However, triple graphs are restricted to represent two models.

A modelling framework can contain more than two models. For example, Model Driven Architecture (MDA) proposes three layers of models. These models are edited and transformed into each other to develop the final application code. To be applied in such frameworks a generalisation of TGGs to more than two models is required. The language of graph diagrams [18] is a suitable candidate for this generalisation. Although it was originally used for the purpose of representing model consistency it can also be used as a foundation for model transformation.

Match consistency is one of the main results in model transformation with TGGs. In this paper we show that this result can be transferred to graph diagrams. TGGs and match consistency are described in Sect. 2. Section 3 reviews related work. Graph diagram grammars are defined in Sect. 4, followed by a generalisation of match consistency in Sect. 5. We give proof for the main theorems in Sect. 6. Section 7 concludes the paper and hints to future work.

© Springer International Publishing Switzerland 2015
D. Kolovos and M. Wimmer (Eds.): ICMT 2015, LNCS 9152, pp. 214–229, 2015.
DOI: 10.1007/978-3-319-21155-8_16

2 Triple Graph Grammars

This section describes TGGs and the results we generalise in this paper. The definitions are based on definitions in category theory from [4].

TGGs have been defined by A. Schürr as triples of graphs that represent two related models [16]. The models are represented by two graphs, called source and target. The relation is represented by a third graph, called connection, and two morphisms. These morphisms relate each element in the connection to one element in source and target. Transformation rules in TGGs are triple graph morphisms. These morphisms consist of three graph morphisms, one for the source, target and connection component. The formal definition of triple graphs and triple graph morphisms is as follows:

Definition 1 (Triple Graph and Triple Graph Morphism (Based on [4])). Three graphs S_G, C_G and T_G, called source, connection, and target graph, together with two graph morphisms $s_G : C_G \to S_G$ and $t_G : C_G \to T_G$ form a **triple graph** $G = (S_G \overset{s_G}{\leftarrow} C_G \overset{t_G}{\to} T_G)$. G is called empty if S_G, C_G, and T_G are empty graphs.

A **triple graph morphism** $m = (s, c, t) : G \to H$ between two triple graphs $G = (S_G \overset{s_G}{\leftarrow} C_G \overset{t_G}{\to} T_G)$ and $H = (S_H \overset{s_H}{\leftarrow} C_H \overset{t_H}{\to} T_H)$ consists of three graph morphisms $s : S_G \to S_H, c : C_G \to C_H$ and $t : T_G \to T_H$ such that $s \circ s_G = s_H \circ c$ and $t \circ t_G = t_H \circ c$. It is injective, if morphisms s, c and t are injective.

An example for a triple graph is given in Fig. 1. As running example we use models from UsiXML [19], a framework for model-based user interface development. The example contains a task model and an abstract user interface (AUI) model. It represents a login form. The task model describes the general task structure supported by the user interface. The abstract task *Login* requires the user to perform *Input Information*, then *Commit Information*, after which the system performs *Check Password*. Tasks that require user input are marked as interaction tasks while tasks that require computation are called system tasks. Child tasks of the same parent are ordered via edges of type *next*. These edges are annotated with temporal relations that denote whether two tasks can be executed in parallel (‖) or sequential (≫) order. The AUI model is a modality-independent description of user interaction. The connection describes a relation between these models by mapping interaction tasks to AUI elements. In the

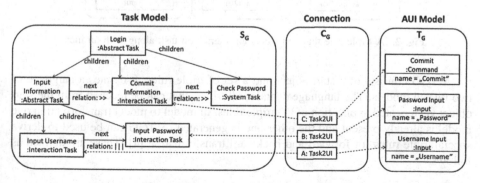

Fig. 1. The task and AUI model represented as triple graph

example the relations A and B relate the tasks for inserting username and password with the corresponding *Input* elements. The element C relates the task for submitting the information with an element of type *Command*.

Although triple graphs are defined based on graphs in Definition 1, the running example uses attributes and types. According to Ehrig et al. triple graphs can also be constructed as diagram category over other categories [4]. Attributes and types can be included by using the category of attributed typed graphs [2]. Triple graphs grammars also work with this category, although there is ongoing research on the transformation of attributes [20]. However, that is of no consequence to the running example.

Triple graph grammars specify how the source and target model can be jointly constructed by applying triple rules. These rules can add elements to source, target and connection. Triple rules and TGGs are formally defined as follows:

Definition 2 (Triple Rule, Triple Graph Grammar (Based on [4])). A **triple rule** *tr* consists of triple graphs L and R, called left-hand and right-hand side, and an injective triple graph morphism $tr = (s, c, t) : L \rightarrow R$.

A **triple graph grammar** $TGG = (S, TR)$ consists of a triple graph S and a set TR of triple rules.

A triple rule is an injective triple graph morphism that can be seen as a before (L) after (R) description of a transformation. Figure 2 shows a triple rule for the running example. The top row is the triple graph L and the bottom row the triple graph R. The rule adds an interaction task as child of an existing abstract task. The interaction task is added together with a related input element. L specifies that an abstract task in the task model is needed to execute the rule. R adds the interaction task, input element and relation of type *Task2UI*.

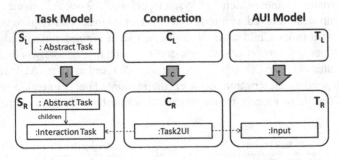

Fig. 2. A triple rule that constructs an interaction task along with an input

A TGG consists of a start object and a set of triple rules. It defines a language of two related models. The language contains all triples that can be reached from the start object via repeated application of the triple rules. In model to model transformation one model is already present and the other one is generated. A TGG can be used to derive special triple rules for forward and backward transformation [4]. These are defined as follows:

Definition 3 (Derived Triple Rules (Based on [4])). Given a triple rule $tr = (S_L \overset{s_L}{\leftarrow} C_L \overset{t_L}{\rightarrow} T_L) \rightarrow (S_R \overset{s_R}{\leftarrow} C_R \overset{t_R}{\rightarrow} T_R)$, we have the following **derived triple rules**:

$$
\begin{array}{cccc}
\begin{array}{ccc}
S_L & \leftarrow \varnothing \rightarrow & \varnothing \\
{\scriptstyle s}\downarrow & \downarrow \quad\quad \downarrow & \\
S_R & \leftarrow \varnothing \rightarrow & \varnothing
\end{array}
&
\begin{array}{ccc}
\varnothing & \leftarrow \varnothing \rightarrow & T_L \\
\downarrow & \downarrow \quad\quad \downarrow{\scriptstyle t} & \\
\varnothing & \leftarrow \varnothing \rightarrow & T_R
\end{array}
&
\begin{array}{ccc}
S_R & \overset{s \circ s_L}{\longleftarrow} C_L \overset{t_L}{\longrightarrow} & T_L \\
{\scriptstyle id_{S_R}}\downarrow & \downarrow{\scriptstyle c} \quad \downarrow{\scriptstyle t} & \\
S_R & \overset{s_R}{\leftarrow} C_R \overset{t_R}{\rightarrow} & T_R
\end{array}
&
\begin{array}{ccc}
S_L & \overset{s_L}{\leftarrow} C_L \overset{t \circ t_L}{\longrightarrow} & T_R \\
{\scriptstyle s}\downarrow & \downarrow{\scriptstyle c} \quad \downarrow{\scriptstyle id_{T_R}} & \\
S_R & \overset{s_R}{\leftarrow} C_R \overset{t_R}{\rightarrow} & T_R
\end{array}
\\[2mm]
\text{source rule } tr_S & \text{target rule } tr_T & \text{forward rule } tr_{S \rightarrow T} & \text{backward rule } tr_{T \rightarrow S}
\end{array}
$$

Given a triple rule tr, the source and target rules tr_S and tr_T can be used to create the source and target model individually. These rules are constructed by forgetting all parts of tr that do not concern the respective model. The source rule for the example production is shown in Fig. 3. It creates the interaction task in the task model but not the corresponding elements in the AUI model and the connection.

Source Rule   **Forward Rule**

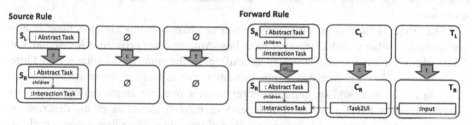

Fig. 3. Source and Forward rule for the triple rule in Fig. 2

Forward and backward rules can be used to derive one of the models from the other one. The corresponding rules are derived from a triple rule by using an identical (non-altering) morphism for the existing model and the original transformation for the other model and the relation. Figure 3 shows a forward rule for the running example. This rule does not add a new interaction task. It assumes an existing interaction task and adds a related input element to the AUI model.

Given a source model, the transformation into a target model requires finding a sequence of triple rules such that applying the source rules of this sequence leads to the source model. The target model can be derived by applying the forward rule for each source rule in this sequence as prescribed by the source rule. If this application is possible such a sequence is called match consistent. The main theorems for this sequence are [4]:

- **Theorem 1- Decomposition and Composition:** The original transformation and the match consistent sequence with source and forward rules are equivalent.
- **Theorem 2 - Equivalence of Directions:** The match consistent sequence with target and backward rules is equivalent to the match consistent rule with source and forward rules.

According to these theorems the match consistent sequences for forward and backward transformation yield the same result as the original joint creation of the models. In this paper we generalise the creation of derived rules, the notion of match consistent transformation sequences and these two theorems to multiple models via graph diagrams.

3   Related Work

Several existing modelling frameworks can profit from the extension of TGGs to more than two models. The example used in this paper is UsiXML [19]. In addition to the task and AUI model this framework contains two more models: a concrete user interface (CUI) model and a domain model. These models can be developed in any order [12]. UsiXML is also conform to model driven architecture (MDA) [15], which specifies three model layers connected via model transformation. Multiple one-to-one transformations can be represented using multiple TGGs [10]. However, they are still restricted to one source and one target model per transformation. An extension to multiple models allows more general transformations that use or produce more than one model.

The need to have transformations for more than two models at a time is also recognised in other transformation approaches. Among other properties Mens and Van Gorp classify model transformations according to the number of source and target models [14]. They observe that a transformation can contain multiple source models (e.g., in model merging) or multiple target models (e.g., to create multiple platform specific models from a platform independent model). Macedo et al. describe an extension of QVT-R to enable better handling of transformations that concern multiple models [13]. Diskin et al. formalise relations between models for transformations involving multiple models and illustrate them on a model-merging use case [1]. This formalism is able to represent relations between model elements and their attributes by making use of queries for derived attributes. Multiple relations can be represented. However, each relation is restricted to two models.

Distributed graphs [3] are also able to represent multiple models and could be an alternative to graph diagrams for a generalisation of triple graph grammars. However, distributed graphs have not been shown to be an M-adhesive category and several results derived from M-adhesive categories are required for proofs of our main theorems. In addition, the distribution capabilities of this formalism can lead to complications, e.g., the creation of elements without application of graph transformation rules to stay consistent to a remote model. For these reasons we selected the formalism of graph diagrams for our generalisation. Nevertheless, distributed graphs may be a viable alternative to graph diagrams, provided the theoretical results required for extending results from triple graph grammars hold.

The concept of using derived rules for triple graph grammars has been proposed by Königs and Schürr [10, 11] in the scope of tool integration and has been applied for model transformation, model integration and model synchronisation [9]. Several model transformation approaches are based on the above described decomposition into source and forward rules, e.g., an on the fly construction of transformation sequences [6]. Other derived rules are used to integrate existing models by establishing the connection [5]. Model synchronisation requires both the (partial) transformation of models and the integration of the existing elements and thus is based on both types of derived rules. Several approaches in triple graphs deal with this problem, e.g., the bidirectional update propagation by Hermann et al. [8] or the incremental approach by Giese and Wagner [7]. The generalisation of the basic results in model transformation in this paper forms a basis for generalising these results to multiple models and relations.

4   Graph Diagram Grammars

In this section we define graph diagrams and extend the notion of triple graph grammars to graph diagram grammars. Triple graphs can be constructed as diagram category [4]. In this construction a diagram is built over objects and morphisms from another category. In triple graphs the objects are graphs and the morphisms are graph morphisms. The structure of the diagram is the fixed structure described above.

Graph diagrams are also defined via diagram category construction but with a less restrictive structure. They can contain any number of nodes and edges. For the generalisation we require the structure to represent relations similar to how triple graphs do. Such a structure is called a diagram base:

Definition 4 (Diagram Base). A **diagram base** $B = (C, Models, Relations)$ consists of a small category $C = (O_C, M_C)$ with objects O_C and morphisms M_C and two dedicated sets of objects, called *Models* and *Relations*, with $Models \cap Relations = \emptyset$ and $Models \cup Relations = O_C$. For all non-identical morphisms $o_1 o_2 \in M_C$ the following statement has to hold: $o_1 \in Relations \wedge o_2 \in Models$.

A set of models and relations $M \subseteq O_C$ is called closed if for all relations ($r \in M$ and $r \in Relations$) and all morphisms $e : r \rightarrow m \in M_C$ the model m is also in M.

The diagram base consists of a category whose objects can be divided into *Models* and *Relations*. Morphisms are restricted to map relations into models. The structure of a triple graph fulfils these properties. It contains two models (source and target), and one relation (connection) and both morphisms map the relation into one model.

To illustrate the capabilities of graph diagrams the running example is extended. The diagram base is shown in Fig. 4. It contains two more models: a CUI model, which contains modality-specific user interface elements, and a domain model, which serves as information storage. An additional relation *Task 2 Domain* connects tasks in the task model to elements in the domain model. The relation *Task 2 UI* is extended to the CUI model. This relation now relates interaction tasks to their abstract interaction elements and their implementation via concrete UI elements in the CUI model.

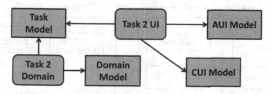

Fig. 4. The diagram base of the running example

The structure of a graph diagram is given by the diagram base. As with triple graphs, it is possible to base graph diagrams on different modelling languages. In this paper we formulate graph diagrams over an arbitrary M-adhesive category. M-adhesive categories (called weak adhesive HLR categories in [2]) are a framework in category theory that allows for the application of graph transformation and several existing formal results. The proofs of our main theorems in Sect. 6 make use of these results. The diagram can be constructed over any category that has been shown to be M-adhesive. This has for example been shown for graphs and attributed graphs [2]. Graph diagrams and graph diagram morphisms are defined as follows:

Definition 5 (Graph Diagrams, Graph Diagram Morphisms). Given a diagram base $B = (C, Models, Relations)$ with category $C = (O_C, M_C)$ and an M-adhesive category $Cat = (O_{Cat}, M_{Cat})$ with initial object $\varnothing$, the category of graph diagrams **GraphDiagrams$_B$** is a diagram category of Cat over C. B is called the scheme of the graph diagram.

A **Graph Diagram** with scheme B is a functor $(o, m) : C \to Cat$ where $o : O_C \to O_{Cat}$ and $m : M_C \to M_{Cat}$.

A **Graph Diagram Morphism** f between two graph diagrams $D_1 = (o_1, m_1)$ and $D_2 = (o_2, m_2)$ over the same scheme B is a natural transformation consisting of a family of morphisms in Cat. For each object $o \in O_C$ there is a morphism $f(o) : o_1(o) \to o_2(o)$. For each morphism $e : a \to b \in M_C$ the following statement holds: $f(b)^\circ m_1(e) = m_2(e)^\circ f(a)$.

Formally a Graph Diagram is a functor, consisting of two components. These components specify which of the objects (o) and morphisms (m) of the diagram base are represented by which attributed graphs and attributed graph morphisms. Similar to triple graphs, graph diagram morphisms match the models and relations component-wise and have to commute with the morphisms in the diagram.

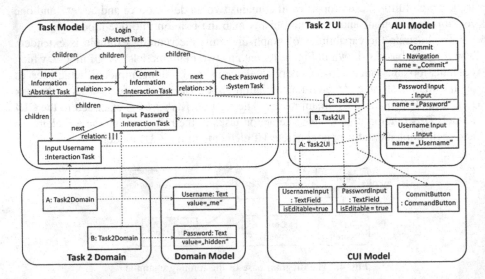

Fig. 5. The graph diagram of the running example

A graph diagram for the running example is shown in Fig. 5. The task model, AUI model and their relation *Task 2 UI* remain the same as in the running example for triple graphs. The relation *Task 2 UI* is mapped into the CUI model by a third morphism. The interaction tasks for entering username and password are each related to a text field for entering the respective information. The interaction task *Commit Information* is related to a command button that triggers this task. The additional relation *Task 2 Domain* relates the tasks for entering username and password to text elements in the domain model that reflect the entered information.

The definitions of graph diagram rule and graph diagram grammar are analogous to the respective definitions in triple graphs. A graph diagram rule is defined as injective graph diagram morphism and a graph diagram grammar contains a start object and a set of graph diagram rules. The formal definition is given in Definition 6.

Definition 6 (Graph Diagram Rule, Graph Diagram Grammar). A graph diagram rule $tr = L \to^{tr} R$ for a diagram base B consists of graph diagrams L and R with scheme B and an injective graph diagram morphisms tr.

A **graph diagram grammar** $GDG = (S, TR)$ for a diagram base B consists of a graph diagram S with scheme B and a set of graph diagram rules TR for B.

An example for a graph diagram rule is shown in Fig. 6. The example is analogous to the triple graph example. An interaction task is added to the task model together with an input element in the AUI model and related text field in the CUI model. In addition, a text element to store the interaction result is added in the domain model and related via the relation *Task 2 Domain*.

The next section describes how the results from model transformation described in Sect. 2 can be transferred to graph diagram grammars.

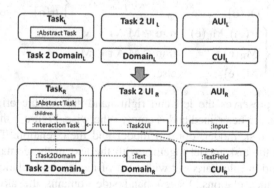

Fig. 6. A graph diagram rule from the running example

5 Derived Rules and Match Consistency

This section describes the generalisation of the derived rules and match consistency. In general, a model transformation can start with multiple models and create the remaining models in multiple transformation steps. The derived rules described in this section enable one transformation step. At the end of the section we discuss how they can be used to implement multiple transformation steps.

The generalisation of source and target rules is called model rule. A model rule only manipulates a restricted set of models and relations. The generalisation of backward and forward rules is called transformation rule. This rule is based on a set of existing models and relations and generates the remaining ones. The definitions of these two types of rules are as follows:

Definition 7 (Model Rule). Given a graph diagram rule $tr = (O_L, M_L)(O_R, M_R)$ for a diagram base $B = (C, Models, Relations)$ with category $C = (O_C, M_C)$, the **model rule** for a closed set of models and relations $M \subseteq O_C$ is a rule $tr_{Mod}^M : (O'_L, M'_L) \to (O'_R, M'_R)$ such that for all $o \in O_C$ and all $e : r \to m M_C$ the following holds:

$$O'_L(o) = \begin{cases} O'_L(o) & if\ o \in M \\ \emptyset & else \end{cases} \qquad O'_R(o) = \begin{cases} O_R(o) & if\ o \in M \\ \emptyset & else \end{cases}$$

$$M'_L(e) = \begin{cases} M_L(e) & if\ r \in M \\ \emptyset & else \end{cases} \qquad M'_R(e) = \begin{cases} M_R(e) & if\ r \in M \\ \emptyset & else \end{cases}$$

$$tr_{Mod}^M(o) = \begin{cases} tr(o) & if\ o \in M \\ \emptyset & else \end{cases}$$

Definition 8 (Transformation Rule). Given a graph diagram rule $tr = (O_L, M_L) \to (O_R, M_R)$ for a diagram base $B = (C, Models, Relations)$ with category $C = (O_C, M_C)$, **the transformation rule** for a closed set of models and relations $M \subseteq O_C$ is a rule $tr_{Trans}^M : (O'_L, M'_L) \to (O_R, M_R)$ such that for all $o \in O_C$ and all $e : r \to m \in M_C$ the following holds:

$$O'_L(o) = \begin{cases} O_R(o) & if\ o \in M \\ O_L(o) & else \end{cases} \qquad tr_{Trans}^m(o) = \begin{cases} id_{O_R}(o) & if\ o \in M \\ tr(o) & else \end{cases}$$

$$M'_L(e) = \begin{cases} tr(m)°M_L(e) & if\ m \in M \wedge r \notin M \\ M_R(e) & if\ m \in M \wedge r \in M \\ M_L(e) & else \end{cases}$$

A model rule preserves the left and right hand side of the original rule for all models and relations to be created and is empty otherwise. Figure 7 shows a model rule that constructs the task model, domain model and their relation. The rule adds the interaction task in the task model together with the text in the domain model.

The transformation rule starts out with a set of models and relations M and creates all other models and relations. Its left hand side contains the already transformed version for models and relations in M and the untransformed version for all others. Morphisms in the left hand side are constructed based on their source and target. If both are in M the transformed version is used, if none are in M the original version is used and if only the target is in M the original version is combined with transformation itself. The resulting rule does not change any models or relations in M and is identical to the original rule for all others. Figure 7 shows a transformation rule for the running example. Starting from the related task and domain model all other models are generated.

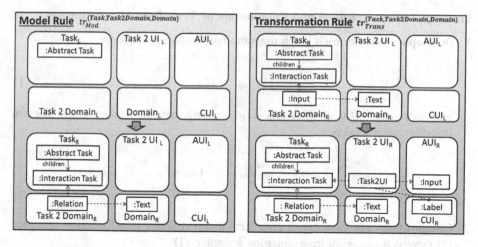

Fig. 7. The model and transformation rule of the running example

Model and transformation rules can be considered generalisations of the derived triple rules. Source and forward rule are the model and transformation rule with the set M containing only the source model. Target and backward rule are model and transformation rule for the target model.

In triple graphs a (forward) transformation requires a sequence of source rules that builds up the already existing model. If this sequence exists then the respective forward rules can be applied with the matches implied by the source rules to derive the other model. This sequence of source and forward rules is called match consistent. A match consistent sequence implies that the result of the transformation is correct with respect to the original triple rules, i.e. the result of the transformation could also have been reached by applying the original triple rules to the initial model. This notion of match consistency can be elevated to graph diagrams as follows:

Definition 9 (Match Consistency). Given a diagram base $B = (C, Models, Relations)$ with category $C = (O_C, M_C)$ and a closed set $M \subseteq O_C$, a graph diagram transformation sequence $G_{00} \overset{tr1^M_{Mod}}{\Rightarrow} G_{10} \Rightarrow \ldots \overset{trn^M_{Mod}}{\Rightarrow} G_{n0} \overset{tr1^M_{Trans}}{\Rightarrow} G_{n1} \ldots \overset{trn^M_{Trans}}{\Rightarrow} G_{nn}$ is called **match consistent** if the match $m1^M_{Trans}$ of $G_{n0} \overset{tr1^M_{Trans}}{\Rightarrow} G_{n1}$ for all components for elements of M is completely determined by the co-match $n1^M_{Mod}$ of $G_{00} \overset{tr1^M_{Mod}}{\Rightarrow} G_{10}$ and the transformation morphism $d1: G_{10} \to Gn0$, i.e., $m1^M_{Trans}(m) = d1(m)°n1^M_{Mod}(m)$ for all $m \in M$, and similar for all matches of the transformation tri^M_{Trans} for $i > 1$. For $n = 1$ this means $m1^M_{Trans}(m) = n1^M_{Mod}(m)$.

In graph diagrams the match consistent sequence consists of a sequence of model rules that create the already existing models followed by the application of the respective transformation rules for these model rules in the same sequence. The two main theorems from TGGs described in Sect. 2 can also be generalised. Similarly to TGGs it can be shown that the match consistent sequence leads to the same result as the original transformation sequence. This is formulated in the following Theorem:

Theorem 1 (Decomposition and Composition of Transformation Sequences)

1. **Decomposition:** For each graph diagram transformation sequence

$$G_0 \overset{tr1}{\Rightarrow} G_1 \Rightarrow \ldots \overset{trn}{\Rightarrow} G_n \tag{1}$$

and each closed $M \subseteq O_C$ there is a corresponding match consistent graph diagram transformation sequence

$$G_0 = G_{00} \overset{tr1_{Mod}^M}{\Rightarrow} G_{10} \Rightarrow \ldots \overset{trn_{Mod}^M}{\Rightarrow} G_{n0} \overset{tr1_{Trans}^M}{\Rightarrow} G_{n1} \Rightarrow \ldots \overset{trn_{Trans}^M}{\Rightarrow} G_{nn} = G_n \tag{2}$$

2. **Composition:** For each match consistent graph diagram transformation sequence (2) there is a canonical transformation sequence (1)
3. **Bijective Correspondence:** Composition and Decomposition are inverse to each other

In addition, the match consistent transformation sequences for any set of models are equivalent. This is formulated in the following theorem:

Theorem 2 (Equivalence of Graph Diagram Transformation -Sequences).

For any two closed $M, M' \subseteq O_C$ the following two match consistent graph diagram transformation sequences imply each other:

1. $G_0 = G_{00} \overset{tr1_{Mod}^M}{\Rightarrow} G_{10} \Rightarrow \ldots \overset{trn_{Mod}^M}{\Rightarrow} G_{n0} \overset{tr1_{Trans}^M}{\Rightarrow} G_{n1} \Rightarrow \ldots \overset{trn_{Trans}^M}{\Rightarrow} G_{nn} = G_n$

2. $G_0 = G_{00} \overset{tr1_{Mod}^{M'}}{\Rightarrow} G'_{10} \Rightarrow \ldots \overset{trn_{Mod}^{M'}}{\Rightarrow} G'_{n0} \overset{tr1_{Trans}^{M'}}{\Rightarrow} G'_{n1} \Rightarrow \ldots \overset{trn_{Trans}^{M'}}{\Rightarrow} G'_{nn} = G_n$

According to this theorem the match consistent sequences for any subset of models lead to the same result. The original transformation sequence can be seen as a special case in which the set of models and relations is empty. In this case the model rule is empty and the transformation rule is equal to the original graph diagram rule. In the next section we provide proof for these theorems.

The results described in this section assume that all missing models are created from the existing ones in one transformation step. Thus, they are not directly applicable to situations where the missing models are to be created via multiple transformation steps. E.g., it is not possible to start with a UsiXML domain model and derive the task model in the first step and the two UI models in a separate second step. However, each individual step can be represented by our theory. This can be done by reducing the graph diagram to the models relevant to the current step, e.g., the task and domain model in the first step of our example. The scheme of this diagram is a sub-graph of the original scheme. This way, new models can be added in each step with a bigger scheme until all models are present. If the subset of models and relations is closed in each step it can be guaranteed that the end-result of such a sequence of match consistent transformation sequences could have been derived from the original triple graph grammar. We will further formalise this treatment of multiple transformation steps and formulate the formal results in future work.

6 Proofs

In this section we discuss M-adhesiveness of the category of graph diagrams, followed by proofs for Theorems 1 and 2. The proofs in this section are based on the proofs in [4]. A major structural difference is in the proof for decomposition in Theorem 1 where we substituted the direct argument over all transformation sequences with a structural induction over the length of the sequence to make the arbitrary diagram structure of graph diagrams easier to handle.

6.1 *M*-Adhesiveness of Graph Diagrams

Since graph diagrams are constructed as diagram categories over an M-adhesive category and this construction preserves M-adhesiveness [2] graph diagrams themselves are an M-adhesive category. This enables the application of the Local Church-Rosser and Concurrency Theorem [2].

According to the Local Church Rosser Theorem two sequentially independent transformations can be applied in any order leading to the same result. Two rules are sequential independent if a morphism d with $m_2 = g_1^\circ d$ exists as illustrated on the left hand side of Fig. 8.

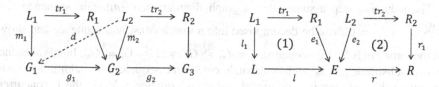

Fig. 8. Illustrations for the local church rosser theorem (left) and the concurrency theorem (right)

According to the Concurrency Theorem two graph transformation rules tr_1 and tr_2 can be merged into an E-concurrent rule that encompasses the effects of both rules. An E-concurrent rule $r^\circ l$ is illustrated on the right hand side of Fig. 8. Given morphisms e_1 and e_2 and object E the objects L and R and the according morphisms are constructed via pushouts (1) and (2) from rules tr_1 and tr_2.

For a given graph diagram rule tr and a closed set of models and relations M the E-concurrent rule for model and transformation rule can be constructed using the left hand side of the transformation rule as object E. Figure 9 shows an example for

$M = \{Task, Task2Domain, Domain\}$. The morphisms into E are n, which maps all objects from M as identity and all other objects with empty morphisms, and the identity id. By pushouts (1) and (2) the left and right hand side of tr are derived. Accordingly, this E-concurrent rule is the same as the original rule tr.

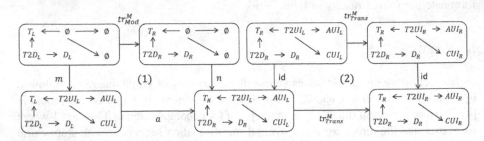

Fig. 9. Example for the E-Concurrent rule of a model and transformation rule for the running example

6.2   Proof for Theorem 1

Proof. Each statement of the theorem is proven separately assuming an arbitrary but fixed set of models and relations $M \subseteq M_C$ □

Decomposition: This statement is proven via induction over the length of the canonical transformation sequence. The inductive beginning is the sequence with length one (the statement also holds for empty sequences of length 0). This sequence consists of one rule. As shown in the previous section this rule is the same as the E-concurrent rule of its model and transformation rule. Since the matches of all models in M for both rules are identities and thus coincide this sequence is match consistent.

The inductive step assumes that a graph diagram transformation sequence $s_n = G_0 \overset{tr1}{\Rightarrow} G_1 \Rightarrow \ldots \overset{trn}{\Rightarrow} G_n$ can be decomposed into a match consistent sequence and shows that the same holds for the sequence $s_m = G_0 \overset{tr1}{\Rightarrow} G_1 \Rightarrow \ldots \overset{trn}{\Rightarrow} G_n \overset{trm}{\Rightarrow} G_m$. In this sequence we can substitute the s_n with its match consistent sequence. In addition we can decompose the last step into its model and transformation rule via the E-concurrent rule. This decomposition leads to the following sequence: $G_0 = G_{00} \overset{tr1^M_{Mod}}{\Rightarrow} G_{10} \Rightarrow \ldots \overset{trm^M_{Mod}}{\Rightarrow} G_{n0} \overset{tr1^M_{Trans}}{\Rightarrow} G_{n1} \Rightarrow \ldots \overset{trm^M_{Trans}}{\Rightarrow} G_{nn} \overset{trm^M_{Mod}}{\Rightarrow} G_{mn} \overset{trm^M_{Trans}}{\Rightarrow} G_{mm}$.

We can arrive at the match consistent sequence for s_m by shifting trm^M_{Mod} after the last model rule by stepwise switching it with the previous transformation rule. This can be done according to the Local Church Rosser Theorem if both are sequentially independent. For this the morphism d as illustrated on the left hand side of Fig. 8 is required. The rule trm^M_{Mod} is a model rule, which is defined as $\emptyset$ for all models that are not in M. Since $\emptyset$ is initial these objects can be mapped into d such that they commute with m_2 and g_1 The transformation rule, is defined to be an identity for all models in M. Accordingly, the morphism $g_1$is an identity for these models and d can be defined the same as m_2. Thus, by construction we have $m_2 = g_1^{\circ}d$ for all objects in and outside of M. Thus, a model rule is sequentially independent with any previous transformation rule and the shift as described above can be made.

Since the decomposition can be made for sequences of length 0 and 1 and can be extended stepwise to longer sequences it holds for all sequences.

Composition: The previous proof can be made analogously for the composition of match consistent transformation sequences. This is due to the fact that the Concurrency Theorem, which has been used to decompose transformations into their model and transformation rule, holds in both directions and the parallel independence described above allows the shift of the model rule back to the end of the transformation sequence.

Bijective Correspondence: The bijective correspondence of composition and decomposition is a consequence of the bijective correspondence of composition and decomposition in the Concurrency Theorem [2] and the bijective correspondence of the Local Church Rosser Theorem (as noted in [4]).

6.3   Proof for Theorem 2

Proof. This theorem is a direct consequence of Theorem 1, since any match consistent sequence can be composed into the canonical sequence (Theorem 1-1) and further decomposed into any other match consistent sequence (Theorem 1-2).   □

7   Conclusion and Future Work

This paper proposes graph diagram grammars as a generalisation of TGGs that is able to represent multiple models and relations. Based on a graph diagram grammar we show how derived rules and match consistency can be generalised such that existing results in triple graph grammars can be considered a special case of our generalised results for exactly two models and one relation. This generalisation forms the basis for extending other results in model transformation, integration and synchronisation to multiple models and relations in future work.

Furthermore, we plan on extending the formalism of graph diagrams with other extensions that have applied required in the scope of TGGs. Among them are the integration of conditions for further restricting the grammar and the integration of a typing system on the level of the graph structure that allows for specifying relations between elements on the type level.

As described in Sect. 6 our results strictly only represents model transformations in which all missing models are created in one transformation step but can be applied for multiple transformation steps by considering a smaller diagram. This can be formalised by a graph diagram whose scheme is a sub-category of the original scheme. In future work we intend to formalise this process.

Acknowledgements. Das diesem Bericht zugrundeliegende Vorhaben wurde mit Mitteln des Bundesministeriums für Bildung, und Forschung unter dem Förderkennzeichen 16SBB011B gefördert. Die Verantwortung für den Inhalt dieser Veröffentlichung liegt beim Autor.

References

1. Diskin, Z., Maibaum, T., Czarnecki, K.: Intermodeling, queries, and kleisli categories. In: de Lara, J., Zisman, A. (eds.) Fundamental Approaches to Software Engineering. LNCS, vol. 7212, pp. 163–177. Springer, Heidelberg (2012)
2. Ehrig, H., Ehrig, K., Prange, U., Taentzer, G.: Fundamentals of Algebraic Graph Transformation. Springer, Heidelberg (2006)
3. Ehrig, H., Orejas, F., Prange, U.: Categorical foundations of distributed graph transformation. In: Corradini, A., Ehrig, H., Montanari, U., Ribeiro, L., Rozenberg, G. (eds.) ICGT 2006. LNCS, vol. 4178, pp. 215–229. Springer, Heidelberg (2006)
4. Ehrig, H., Ehrig, K., Ermel, C., Hermann, F., Taentzer, G.: Information preserving bidirectional model transformations. In: Dwyer, M.B., Lopes, A. (eds.) FASE 2007. LNCS, vol. 4422, pp. 72–86. Springer, Heidelberg (2007)
5. Ehrig, H., Ehrig, K., Hermann, F.: From Model Transformation to Model Integration based on the Algebraic Approach to Triple Graph Grammars. In: Electronic Communications of the EASST 10 (2008)
6. Ehrig, H., Ermel, C., Hermann, F., Prange, U.: On-the-fly construction, correctness and completeness of model transformations based on triple graph grammars. In: Schürr, A., Selic, B. (eds.) MODELS 2009. LNCS, vol. 5795, pp. 241–255. Springer, Heidelberg (2009)
7. Giese, H., Wagner, R.: Incremental model synchronization with triple graph grammars. In: Wang, J., Whittle, J., Harel, D., Reggio, G. (eds.) MoDELS 2006. LNCS, vol. 4199, pp. 543–557. Springer, Heidelberg (2006)
8. Hermann, F., Ehrig, H., Orejas, F., Czarnecki, K., Diskin, Z., Xiong, Y.: Correctness of model synchronization based on triple graph grammars. In: Whittle, J., Clark, T., Kühne, T. (eds.) MODELS 2011. LNCS, vol. 6981, pp. 668–682. Springer, Heidelberg (2011)
9. Kindler, E., Wagner, R.: Triple graph grammars: concepts, extensions, implementations, and application scenarios. In: Technical report, no. tr-ri-07-284. Software Engineering Group, Department of Computer Science, University of Paderborn (2007)
10. Königs, A., Schürr, A.: MDI a rule-based multi-document and tool integration approach. Softw. Syst. Model. 5(4), 349–368 (2006)
11. Königs, A., Schürr, A.: Tool integration with triple graph grammars - a survey. Electric Notes in Theoret. Comput Sci. 148(1), 113–150 (2006)
12. Limbourg, Q., Vanderdonckt, J., Michotte, B., Bouillon, L., López-Jaquero, V.: USIXML: a language supporting multi-path development of user interfaces. In: Feige, U., Roth, J. (eds.) DSV-IS 2004 and EHCI 2004. LNCS, vol. 3425, pp. 200–220. Springer, Heidelberg (2005)
13. Macedo, N., Cunha A., Pacheco H.: Towards a framework for multi-directional model transformations. In: 3rd International Workshop on Bidirectional Transformations - BX. 1133 (2014)
14. Mens, T.: A taxonomy of model transformation and its application to graph transformation technology. In: International Workshop on Graph and Model Trans-formation (GraMoT 2005) (2005)
15. Miller, J., Mukerji, J.: Model driven architecture (MDA). Draft Technical report ormsc/2001-07-01, Architecture Board ORMSC (2001)
16. Schürr, A.: Specification of graph translators with triple graph grammars. In: Mayr, E.W., Schmidt, G., Tinhofer, G. (eds.) International Workshop on Graph-Theoretic Concepts in Computer Science, LNCS, vol. 903, pp. 151–163. Springer, Heidelberg (1994)
17. Schürr, A., Klar, F.: 15 years of triple graph grammars. In: Ehrig, H., Heckel, R., Rozenberg, G., Taentzer, G. (eds.) Graph Transformations, vol. 5214, pp. 411–425. Springer, Heidelberg (2008)

18. Trollmann, F., Albayrak, S.: Expressing model relations as basis for structural consistency analysis in models@run.time. In: Proceedings of the 7th Workshop on Models@run.time, pp. 74–75. ACM (2012)
19. Vanderdonckt, J.: A MDA-compliant environment for developing user interfaces of information systems. In: Pastor, Ó., Falcão e Cunha, J. (eds.) CAiSE 2005. LNCS, vol. 3520, pp. 16–31. Springer, Heidelberg (2005)
20. Lambers, L., Hildebrandt, S., Giese, H., Orejas, F.: Attribute handling for bidirectional model transformations: the triple graph grammar case. In: Electron. Commun. EASST 49 (2012)

Author Index

Printed in the United States
By Bookmasters